0061453

DATE DUE

JAN. 6 1994	
MAY 25 1994	
NOV. 2 8 1994	
FEB 1 2 1996	
OCT 0 8 1996	

E
169.12
G63
1991

Goldfarb, Jeffrey C.

The cynical society.

$22.50

THE CYNICAL SOCIETY

THE CYNICAL
SOCIETY

THE CULTURE OF POLITICS
AND THE
POLITICS OF CULTURE IN
AMERICAN LIFE

Jeffrey C. Goldfarb

The University of Chicago Press
Chicago & London

Jeffrey C. Goldfarb is professor of sociology at the New School for Social Research. He is the author of *The Persistence of Freedom: The Sociological Implications of Polish Student Theater; On Cultural Freedom: An Exploraion of Public Life in Poland and America*; and *Beyond Glasnost: The Post-Totalitarian Mind,* the latter two of which are also published by the University of Chicago Press.

The University of Chicago Press, Chicago 60637
The University of Chicago Press, Ltd., London
© 1991 by The University of Chicago
All rights reserved. Published 1991
Printed in the United States of America
00 99 98 97 96 95 94 93 92 91 5 4 3 2 1

Library of Congress Cataloging-in-Publication Data

Goldfarb, Jeffrey C.
    The cynical society : the culture of politics and the politics of
culture in American life / Jeffrey C. Goldfarb.
        p.   cm.
    Includes bibliographical references (p.) and index.
    ISBN 0-226-30106-0 (cloth : alk. paper). — ISBN 0-226-30107-9
(pbk. : alk. paper)
    1. United States—Civilization—1970– 2. United States—Social
conditions—1980– 3. Cynicism—Social aspects—United States.
4. Politics and culture—United States—History—20th century.
I. Title
E169.12.G63   1991
973.92—dc20
                                                                90-11187
                                                                CIP

∞ The paper used in this publication meets the minimum requirements of the American National Standard for Information Sciences—Permanence of Paper for Printed Library Materials, ANSI Z39.48—1984.

In memory of my grandparents
Victor and Brana Frimet
and
Israel and Razel Goldfarb

CONTENTS

PREFACE

A refined and open democratic culture, in my judgment, is an ongoing part of American life. This judgment has guided my inquiry into cynicism. It has suggested both the subject matter and the form of the study. I want to show that the ideals of democracy, as self-governance, and culture, as the arts and sciences, can be made compatible and mutually supportive, and that these ideals stand as alternatives to the easy cynicism which has overwhelmed American politics, journalism, and social science. With this in mind, my study has two goals: to demonstrate how the confusion of cynicism with political judgment and wisdom significantly enervates American political culture; and to highlight ways of thinking and acting which work against cynicism's confusions.

Mine is not, as a matter of conviction, a "pure" academic exercise in the social sciences, nor is it an abstract consideration of major issues in political and cultural theory. Although I have a great deal of respect for the fruits of academic labors and the insights of abstract theory, I think that they have real meaning only when they help to inform a public philosophy and improve common sense. For this reason, the major theoretical issues I raise in this essay are considered as they emerge from our historical and daily experiences and struggles. The debates about our electoral politics, the criticisms of the qualities of American culture and education, the course of the development of ideologies of left and right, the persistence of American racism, and the new threats of antimodern fundamentalisms, all revolve around important theoretical principles, which are often not considered publicly because of an easy substitution of cynical explanation and manipulation for democratic reasoning and contestation. I try to remedy this situation by analyzing the poverty of cynicism and illuminating present political and cultural principles, using nontechnical language and avoiding insulating scientistic jargon.

An important part of my argument is its form. I have consciously tried to analyze and criticize social science, literature, journalism, popular culture, and politics in a way that addresses both the current debates in sociology and political and cultural theory, and in the politics of our lives. In doing this, I have had a few works particularly in mind: Alexis de Tocquevilles's *Democracy in America,* Walter Lippmann's *Public Opinion,* and Robert N. Bellah, Richard Madsen, William M. Sullivan, Ann Swidler, and Steven M. Tipton's *Habits of the Heart.* Though I do not agree with everything these authors argued, the way they made their arguments I find exemplary. They contributed to the discourse about contemporary issues without compromising intellectual seriousness or political principles. Such work stands as proof that cultural quality and democracy need not be incompatible, and that there is an alternative to cynicism.

Cynicism has been a central but neglected aspect of modern political culture. As I analyzed it intensively in my previous work, *Beyond Glasnost: The Post-Totalitarian Mind,* cynicism was a key component of Soviet totalitarianism. In the present work, I investigate the parallels between cynical totalitarian practices and the cynical practices of ideology and mass manipulation in American society. While the differences between modern tyrannies and democracies should not be minimized, the significance of cynicism in our political and intellectual life indicates that the defeat of Communism does not represent a simple victory for democracy and freedom. Now that the cold war is over, critical democratic appraisals of American politics and culture are necessary. If we look closely at our everyday practice, as I try to do here, celebrations of the end of history or the victory of the West appear to be inappropriate, to say the least.

This and other judgments made in this essay emerged over many years from a series of conversations and collegial relations too numerous for me even to recall, let alone acknowledge. I began the research on this book in a certain broad sense while I was still in college and, like many in my generation, active in the antiwar movement. The critique of the New Left is a critique of my own activities and those of my friends. The basis of the critique was developed in what used to be called the socialist world, which I have been studying now for nearly twenty years. I did not travel to the Soviet bloc to see the future, and I "knew" that what existed there was not really socialism; still, from it, I learned something I did not expect—a deepened respect for democracy, and a renewed appreciation of the importance of political and cultural freedom in any political project. Without naming them individually, I wish again to thank my colleagues in the developing democracies for their invaluable contributions to my education.

More closely related to the actual writing of this book were the conversations I had with colleagues in the Graduate Faculty of the New School for Social Research, and in the newly constituted Sociology of Culture section of the American Sociological Association. I have had a hard time convincing my fellow sociologists that a concern for cultural quality is a democratic necessity. I hope this study demonstrates my position, which has been informed by their criticisms. I also hope that my skepticism concerning the value of certain grand theoretical schemes is further substantiated here.

Differences in intellectual opinion, coupled with mutual respect, have provided me with an optimal learning situation. For presenting me with such situations, which contributed to the making of this study, I thank Andrew Arato, José Casanova, Ferenc Fehér, Liah Greenfeld, Ira Katznelson, Elzbieta Matynia, Eugene Rochberg-Halton, Eli Sagan, Donald Scott, Charles Tilly, and Vern Zolberg. Most of the ideas and research developed for this book are an outgrowth of courses and seminars I have conducted in the Sociology Department and the Committee on Liberal Studies of the Graduate Faculty. Although I realize some might respond cynically to the declaration, I have learned at least as much from my students as they have learned from me. I gratefully recognize them as my teachers, particularly Anne Bowler, Blaine McBurney, Nancy Hanrahan, Margaret Heide, Dorothy Mullen, Martha Reiss, and Dennis Torreggiani. It has been my privilege to have early access to their insights into the problems of sociology and cultural theory. A broader public is already discovering their contributions.

Finally, I would like to make a simple observation about the making of books. Serious intellectual exchange between editor and author is becoming a rarity. Too often in commercial publishing, editors have become marketing executives, and in academic publishing, they have become bureaucrats who circulate manuscripts among the experts. In marked contrast, Douglas Mitchell of the University of Chicago Press is a man of intense intellectual curiosities and commitments. We have now fruitfully worked together on three books. His commitment to a principled pluralism, and his support, without complete agreement, of my distinctive way of contributing to pluralistic discourse, were crucial in making this essay available to the public. For this I am profoundly grateful.

ONE

Cynicism and the
American Way of Politics

I believe that the single most pressing challenge facing American democracy today is widespread public cynicism. The major political parties contribute to the problem, as do the various parties and movements of the left and right margins. The conventions and forms of news reporting and commentary play significant roles in the cultural formation of cynicism, and a broad spectrum of the social sciences contributes, by ignoring or being insensitive to cynicism and even by using cynicism as a key theoretical proposition. In this study, I will examine the role cynicism plays in contemporary American political and social life. I will also show how specific living cultural traditions provide democratic alternatives to the cynical malaise.

I

Cynicism in our world is a form of legitimation through disbelief. There exists an odd but by now common practice. Leaders use rhetorics which neither they nor their constituents believe, but which both leaders and followers nonetheless use to justify their actions. In the United States, the astute public and politicians may have known that in the fall of 1988 a tax increase was highly likely in the near future, but presidential candidates in the election campaign competed with each other to deny this likelihood, and the candidate who most effectively denied the generally recognized inevitability won public support. Yet the general public, or at least significant portions of it, disbelieved all the denials. The press reported these facts and judged the relative effectiveness of fictive claims; social scientists who documented how socioeconomic groupings accepted or rejected different claims did so without judging the validity of the claims. In this way disbelieved rhetorics seemed to be natural and fortified the powers that be.

The actions of political (and cultural, economic, and religious) leaders, the general public, the media, and the scholarly academic community all constitute the fundamental character of the cynical society. But they do this without much reflection. Cynicism dominates the assumptions of our political and cultural life. We not only do not recognize the cynicism ; we confuse it with democratic deliberation and political wisdom. American reaction to American party politics and Soviet political struggles, reveals the dimensions of the problem.

II

In the spring of 1988 a special conference was held by the Communist party of the Soviet Union. In the summer of 1988 nominating conventions were held by the Democratic and Republican parties in the United States. Many observed a striking paradox—the American gatherings were carefully orchestrated, while the Soviets openly expressed political diversity. Despite the intriguing irony, drawing the logical conclusion—that the Soviets are democratizing, while we are bureaucratizing—is not only mistaken but dangerous. It represents a fundamental blindness to primary political facts. It also typifies the cynical mentality.

American political conventions, both Republican and Democratic, though flawed by cliché, sentimentality, and media manipulation, still are exercises in a great democratic experiment. The Soviet party conference, on the other hand, was not in any significant sense a democratic gathering. If we are to keep our experiment alive, we must carefully observe the connection between contemporary political practices and political experience. The real differences between the Soviet and American political meetings reveal too often overlooked fundamentals of distinct political traditions.

The Communist party conference presented a front of diversity within a political context of enforced unity. This epitomizes the most profound weaknesses of the Soviet order. It is a variation on an old totalitarian theme. The Democratic and Republican conventions presented a front of unity within political diversity. This draws upon a long and distinguished tradition of unifying diverse political forces in the pursuit of a common good.

The participants of the Soviet conference adhered to a politically sanctioned ideology. "The truth" and the will of the prevailing powers of the state apparatus were identical. At the conference, the official line included perestroika and glasnost. Thus, hardliners and liberals, conservative representatives of the interest of the vast political bureaucracy and their opponents led by Gorbachev, expressed their competing interests using the new official line. And the party leader interrupted, cajoled, encouraged, and silenced others as it served his interest. There was diversity. But it was used to solidify Gorbachev's political might.

In recent years, the American political conventions have had little to do with the actual nominating process. This has been centered in the primaries. But the conventions still are serious democratic affairs. They provide the forum within which emerging political leaders articulate distinctive political visions based on the shared political principles of each party. The success or failure of candidates and their parties depends on the clarity and cogency of their political visions for the general public.

Before he gave his acceptance speech, Michael Dukakis appeared to be an expert manager, a political technocrat with questionable capacities for leadership. In his speech, notably lacking specific program details, he articulated a broad Democratic political vision—somewhat distanced from the liberal policies of the past, but identifying with the problems of ordinary people; supportive of free enterprise, but understanding that sometimes the invisible hand of the market can be quite cruel and must be controlled. This son of Greek immigrants celebrated the "American Dream," but emphasized the role the Federal government can play in making the dream possible for the less fortunate. All segments of the party, from Michael Harrington and Jesse Jackson to Albert Gore and Lloyd Bentsen, enthusiastically supported the governor's vision. Dukakis unified the party not simply to increase the likelihood of victory in November. He articulated a vision based on shared principles which distinguish Democrats from Republicans.

George Bush articulated a different vision. In his party, too, the unity to be presented was not based on actual or coerced uniformity. Fiscal conservatives, libertarians, neoconservative anticommunists, and moral majoritarians had to be brought together in the convention and given a shared sense of common destiny through Bush's speech and actions. Bush had to present himself as the heir apparent to the reign of Reagan, but also as his own man. Thus his emphasis both on his individual toughness and his call for a "kinder and gentler America." As with the Democrats, party unity was not realized through ideological formula—an American perestroika. Rather, a common political ground was found.

The election was reported as a struggle between personalities, campaign strategies, and advertising gimmicks. But it also was about political philosophy. Bush benefited, as did Ronald Reagan before him, from a new, vigorous, conservative critique of the "liberal" welfare state. Dukakis did not even seem to realize that he desperately needed to seek a philosophy, so the voters could make sense of who he was and what he wanted. Dukakis focused on his innovative programs, medical care provided through the workplace, long-term government-backed loans for college education, and so on. He hoped the inherent value of these programs would convince the public that new approaches would yield an improvement in the quality of life. When Bush attacked him as a liberal, Dukakis rejected the attack without defending the liberal tradition through much of the campaign. His reticence was never publicly explained. Many commentators, strategists, and Republican and Democratic partisans observed that this made him seem weak, deceptive, and ultimately unpresidential.

But the most significant theoretical and practical point is that Dukakis was not a liberal in the old statist, social welfare, and internationalist mode. He, like the neoconservatives, knew that state bureaucracy is now part of the problem, not simply a solution to the heartless avarice of the industrial plutocrats (as Franklin D. Roosevelt would have put it). He, as a post-Vietnam War politician, was skeptical about the efficacy and even desirability of commitments to making the world safe for democracy, to "Pay any price, bear any burden," as John F. Kennedy put it. But Dukakis was a liberal, or at least not a conservative, in that he could not happily accept the gross and growing inequities and suffering that have characterized the longest economic boom in the postwar era. He knew that for 60 percent of the population it has been a bust, with no improvement in their personal economic lot. Dukakis's programs, his reticence concerning big government but also big business, and his identification with the recent experiences of the bulk of the population, all had important popular support. Yet these themes, as they are linked, were not clearly communicated to the voting public. How do we explain this? Clearly it was not because Dukakis lacked the intelligence or desire. Rather it was because of a fundamental crisis of political imagination, a patent outgrowth of cynicism.

Politicians and the public have grown accustomed to cynicism. It is regularly confused with reason and deliberation. A debate raged after Dukakis's defeat. How to explain it? Did the Democrats lose because of Dukakis's personality, his inexpert campaign strategy, because he was too closely associated with Jesse Jackson and his "radical" campaign for social justice, or not enough associated with black Americans and the concerns of the oppressed? Can a Northern liberal win? Must presidential politics be the politics of video display, sound bites, and patriotic machismo? These were the questions raised in the inner sanctums of the party elites and in the open forums of talk shows, newspapers, and magazines.[1] But these all are cynical questions. They assume politics is essentially about winning and losing, campaign strategies, and getting out the vote. Real politics is about all of this—of course—but is this what it is all about? Missing in these discussions is that which distinguishes even present-day American politics from Soviet politics, even in the age of glasnost.

The news accounts of the American primaries, nominating campaigns, election campaigns, and election aftermath report the cynical political veneer, overlooking democratic substance. George Bush speaks about environmental issues (especially the dumping of untreated waste) in a boat off the New Jersey coast. This is duly reported by press and TV. Earlier his travels around the world while vice president were carefully filmed by his partisans; for example, in Israel at the Wailing Wall, in Poland at Auschwitz and with Lech Walesa. The press and political commentators explain the importance of the campaign speech as another photo opportunity, like those in Israel and Poland, pitched at a specific voting cohort. They explain the sensitivity of New Jersey residents to ocean pollution and tell about the closed, polluted oceanfronts, the ruined summer for both vacationers and the vacation industry. The details of Bush's speech on the boat are not analyzed. The big news is the constituency appeal. Almost all election-campaign news reports are focused in this fashion.

Of course such reporting is accurate. The choice of location and the appeal of the speech are primarily expressive and not substantive. Bush visually presents his sentiments on the environment—he is certainly against pollution. This is aimed at the New Jersey voters. Bush and his handlers are most concerned with the visual presentation. Bush is there at the Jersey shore and on New Jersey's side. The news media report the event for what it is, and face a standard journalistic dilemma. If they report the event as framed by the Bush campaign, they become little more than Bush's public-relations agents.[2] Yet, the norms of journalistic objectivity preclude refutation of Bush's expressive appeal, i.e., that he is on New Jersey's side. In news reports and broadcasts, they can add a substantive piece on Bush's environmental record (which is not too good) and program (which is rather vague), and an explanation for the presentation of such a piece in such a place.

From the point of view of the Bush campaign, positive press is without such additions, negative is with them. Both campaigns and their partisans then monitor the media to make sure that negative and positive reports are at least evenly distributed. Inevitably, partisans of both candidates complain that the reports are to their disadvantage, while these same partisans map out strategies to yield favorable overall reports to their advantage. But note that, despite all this, substantive approaches to pressing political problems are not reasonably being discussed.

Critics complain that this lack of rational discussion is because of the candidates' lack of substance. Thus, "none of the above" was the most popular candidate in both the primaries and the elections. Critics of broadcast television, especially in newspapers, maintain that the absence of substance is an outgrowth of the formal TV requirements for good, succinct visuals and sound bites for summarizing the day's politics in two minutes. Broadcast journalists defend themselves. They maintain that they do periodically present in-depth reports on the nightly news and in news specials. Yet, the in-depth reports and the critics of TV and the candidates all focus on cynical campaign appeals, their veracity and effectiveness, their link with polling practices, rather than with the quality of mind and practical vision of one candidate or another, or on the pressing issues of the day.

Not surprisingly, then, when George Bush won, few observers had any idea what direction his presidency would take. It seems to be a reasonable question whether he did. Would he be a "kinder and gentler president," i.e., a moderate mainstream Republican, or a flag-waving patriot who speaks derisively about the "L word" and emphasizes his commitments to capital punishment and anticommunism? Would he subtly turn from Reagan's agenda or extend it? His campaign literature, his election ads, and his debate performances did not indicate answers to these fundamental questions. Americans elected a man to the presidency without a rational knowledge of who he was or what he would do. We have a cynical president, elected in a cynical campaign, reported by a cynical press, to a cynical society.

We would have found the same result, of course, if Dukakis had won. Would we have had a liberal or merely a competent president? Would he be against trade barriers (as he opened his campaign) or for them (as he closed it)? Would he fundamentally rethink the logic of foreign and defense policy, as his past commitments indicated, or would he continue within the mainstream course (whatever that might mean) as he claimed during the campaign?

III

Nonetheless, though our political life is strikingly imprecise and emotional rather than rational, it still is democratic. A fog of cynicism surrounds American politics, but they are still animated by fully institutionalized democratic norms and traditions. The difference between the American democratic tradition and political culture and the absence of such a tradition and culture in the Soviet Union is substantial. Americans did deliberate democratically in the 1988 election, and the voting public was not simply an object of political manipulation, even though cynical manipulation shaped campaigns, reporting, and citizens' decision-making. Effective political manipulation and cynical campaigns may or may not have made the difference in the election, yet clearly there were other significant differences as well, more substantial differences, which very well may have been as consequential in the election outcome, and should be more consequential in the political long run.

I have in mind the differences in political philosophy and political principles, not ideology. Dukakis claimed that the campaign issue was competence, not ideology. Bush knew this not to be the case. He declared the campaign was and should be about ideology. They both, in my judgment, were wrong, strategically and theoretically. Dukakis confused technocracy with democracy. He thought if he presented himself as an expert manager, Americans would vote for him. But a political executive is not a business executive, and Americans clearly knew this. Bush certainly took advantage of Dukakis's position. He aggressively declared that ideology indeed was the issue, and he proceeded ideologically. This empowered his campaign, and such empowerment, together with aggressive and expert campaign strategy, turned George Bush, the Wimp of the Summer, into George Bush, President of the United States. But during the course of this empowerment, he undermined the democratic terrain. Following the Reagan of 1980 and 1984, he presented his political ideas ideologically, weakening both his opponent and potentially himself as well.

First, note the positive element of the Bush campaign. It was a campaign based on general and understandable ideas, while Dukakis's was not. Bush had a direct and understandable position. He endorsed the "Reagan revolution." He expressed positive commitments to supply-side economics, fundamentalist moralisms, and the neoconservative critique of the welfare state. In foreign affairs, he followed Reagan's lead, combining resolute anticommunism and a commitment to a strong defense (i.e., peace through strength) with a developing flexibility toward the substantial signs that Mikhail Gorbachev is a new kind of Soviet leader. His position was not only understandable but meaningful to a significant portion of the American population. It spoke to the experiences of their daily lives, and to their most fundamental and cherished ethical and political commitments. Following Reagan, Bush spoke about the fundamentals of family, community, and church; for patriotism and pride in America's comeback; against crime and government bureaucracy; for individual initiative and entrepreneurship. Thus he expressed the fundamental post–New Deal, post–Great Society, and post–Vietnam conservative position. Of course he did fudge the inherent contradictions in the conservative position—the contradiction between libertarianism and Moral Majoritarianism, even between new cold-war Reaganism and the Reaganesque version of detente. Despite this, though, Bush presented a meaningful political message, a conservative Republican one with which he openly identified. The contrast with Dukakis was striking and decisive.

Dukakis seemed to present a new broad neoliberal vision in his acceptance speech. But he never crystallized his position. He did not even dare to name it. He seemed to think that the elements of his message naturally came together. He never clearly articulated his overall position. He never clarified his distinct political vision for the public. Bush's success in doing this, along with Dukakis's failure, may very well have been the key to the outcome of the election. To be sure, neither Bush's nor Dukakis's political philosophy was examined by the press or public, and Bush's clearer position was mostly inherited. Yet Dukakis's failure to present a clear overall position was so great and so evidently connected to other often-mentioned failures—the inconsistent ad campaign, the suspicion of his positions on defense, the economy, and environment, the lack of enthusiasm for him both from the white ethnics and blacks—that it was a fundamental cause of the Democratic failure and the Republican victory.

In the battle of general political ideas and principles, Bush was the decisive winner. From the point of view of this inquiry, his victory has very positive meaning. Despite all the cynicism and political manipulation, Bush won as the candidate with a more meaningful and understandable program. Without regard to partisanship, the candidate with the more coherent political position, more understandable to the general public, prevailed.

IV

Yet, as should already be clear to the reader, I do not believe we can or should be too satisfied with this conclusion, both because of the cynicism surrounding the campaigns (the strategy, news reports, and social-scientific analysis) and because the idea of a set of political principles as the center of party politics has been undermined by the rise of ideology in American political practice. This rise might be viewed as cynicism from within.

The new liberal Democrats went from Gary Hart's new ideas with little substantive content to a candidate without general ideas, or at least one who did not and perhaps could not clearly articulate them. The Republican challenge to this was clear and forthright—1980s' conservatism, epitomized by Ronald Reagan and, in Great Britain, by Margaret Thatcher. But in their able hands, something strange happened to conservatism. It became radicalized, ideologized, running very much counter not only to the conservative tradition but also to the Anglo-American culture of politics.

Modern conservatism has been distinguished by its distrust of a highly rationalized politics. Since Edmund Burke, the best conservatives have chosen custom over reason as the most appropriate guide to political life.[3] Yet, both Reaganism and Thatcherism are informed by a few fundamental propositions, deductions from which political policy is determined. For example, government is part of the problem, not the solution, sapping entrepreneurship and individual initiative. Therefore, government regulations are bad. Therefore, without regard to the consequences for worker health, the environment, air-travel safety, and even economic competition, deregulation is in the public interest. Those who support regulation, then, are by definition, i.e., by ideologized deduction, self-interested bureaucrats or advocates of special interests. Such ideological reasoning has been integral to the Reagan and Thatcher regimes and appropriated by George Bush in his election campaign. This, more than Bush's character, in my judgment, explains the particular meanness of the 1988 presidential campaign.

When one thinks ideologically and acts ideologically, opponents become enemies to be vanquished, political compromise becomes a kind of immorality, and constitutional refinements become inconvenient niceties. Liberalism, the great political tradition at the very root of the American idea of politics, becomes an ideological vulgarity—as we heard in Bush's derogatory emphasis on the *liberal* governor of Massachusetts, and his reference to the "L word." The coresponsibility of executive and legislative branches of the federal government in the hands of Reagan became an excuse to vilify the Congress for all existing social problems. He even closed his presidential term with a denunciation of the "iron triangle" of the press, special interests, and the Congress. (We find ourselves remarkably distanced from Eisenhower's principled warnings of the military-industrial complex.) Not only opponents, but the basic American republican principles of free speech and the separation of powers are ideologically denounced. Turning ideological anticommunism into a new form, ideologized antiliberalism, George Bush repeatedly denounced Michael Dukakis as a card-carrying member of the American Civil Liberties Union, and this apparently won him votes.

Such a denunciation can be easily dismissed as normal electioneering hyperbole, a kind of expression deeply rooted in past election practices. Indeed, the outrageous statements made about the "Founding Fathers" in their day make present-day political rhetoric seem to be the height of civilized discourse. Further, it can also be objected that the campaign slogans and jingles of the nineteenth century were very much equivalent to twentieth-century advertising. That is, political manipulation and its cynicism are as American as apple pie.[4] The recent intensification of these practices and the cultural framework of ideology present new and profound challenges to American democratic practice, suggesting the formation of a cynical society.

To appreciate the dimension of the challenge requires a systematic study of the cultural and sociological bases and implications of cynicism in American life, the task of this inquiry. But before we turn to this, I should account for my conviction that there are alternatives to cynicism, that a belief in the possibility of a principled democratic deliberation and contestation is not hopelessly naive.

V

Cynicism has its philosophic basis in relativism. When we no longer know that our way of life is the best way, we learn to respect others, but we also begin to doubt ourselves. Our positions on political, social, and even religious issues come to appear accidental, more the product of who we are—our class position, nationality, and limited interests—than a product of how well we think and act. Thus the quality of what we say and do and what others say and do come to be understood cynically. Words and actions are interpreted as manifestations of the limited positions of specific individuals and groups, not believed or judged on their own terms. Democracy, then, appears to be little more than a particularly civilized version of social conflict. A major question is why the competing parties continue to play the game by the rules when some know that they will consistently lose. A significant social-scientific literature explains this as a complex problem of the interaction of limited interests, rationalities, and choices.[5] More traditional political philosophies see the problem of relativism and cynicism, and the social-science literature addressed to it, as a modern one, to be overcome by going back to the ancients, discovering their original intent and value, and making their wisdom ours.[6] But because this nostalgic position so easily ignores, dismisses, or even condemns modern accomplishments, from democracy itself to civil rights and feminism, and romanticizes past glories, for all but the most narrowly elitist it is much worse than the problem it proposes to resolve. It is not, however, the only alternative to relativism and cynicism. The active constitution of democratic values is readily observable in our history and in contemporary social, political, and cultural life (as I have illustrated in the case of the nominating conventions). Such constituted values provide a most substantial alternative to the prevailing cynicism.

The observation of American democratic values in historical and contemporary practices requires an anti-utopian political sensibility, what I have elsewhere called a post-totalitarian mentality.[7] Collective memory must be a central political and theoretical concern, contrary to that well-known malady, American amnesia. The political climate of mindless patriotism and anticommunism must be discarded, as must be the truisms of simple left-right political categorization. Irony and self-limitation must inform the analysis. These key components of post-totalitarian culture developed in East Central Europe as a democratic project for deconstructing the political culture of totalitarianism, a culture that emerged from the experiences and legacies of the French and Russian revolutions. In America, with a very different political culture and revolutionary legacy, a distinctly nontotalitarian one,[8] the same cultural components can be used to perceive an embedded and institutionalized democratic political culture that provides significant alternatives to cynicism.

De Tocqueville, in considering the culture of America, asserted that Americans are natural Cartesians, though they do not read Descartes. Likewise, I believe that despite the fact that we are heavily burdened by a ubiquitous cynicism, Americans are in a sense natural post-totalitarians, even though we have not confronted directly either the experience of totalitarianism or seriously considered the democratic struggles for alternatives to modern tyranny. But we must work at discovering our natural post-totalitarian culture, or more precisely our nontotalitarian culture, for a primary aspect of totalitarianism is ideological thinking, and ideological thinking is becoming a part of American politics in the final decades of the twentieth century. This is perhaps the most consequential implication of the cynical malaise.[9] Cynicism is most manifest in the straightforward manipulations of our political and economic life, in political and commercial advertising campaigns. But the latent cynicism of ideology is the most dangerous political result of the societal cynicism.

Cynical manipulation as well as democratic deliberation, and principled political reasoning as well as ideological declaration and deduction, are all part of American politics and culture. They arise out of the American experience. They are observable not only today but as a part of the two-hundred-year American experience, built into the deep structure of our society. To discover the deep structure in the pages that follow, I take memory to be the primary cognitive resource for avoiding cynicism. We must remember democratic accomplishments and their components so that manipulation and its political clichés do not seem to be the essence of politics. Using this cognitive resource effectively requires irony and self-limitation. To characterize American society as "The Cynical Society" or as "The Democratic Society," an alternative I believe to be sound is not to engage in totalized or literal descriptions. Both democracy and its culture, and cynicism and its implications, are delimited parts of the American experience. The ironic and sometimes tragic combination of democracy and cynicism defines our present-day situation. The two should not be confused or combined. If we are overwhelmed by cynicism, our democratic hopes diminish. If we celebrate our democracy, overlooking the implications of our cynicism, the results are no different. Thus we must understand the social and cultural foundations of democracy and cynicism, and their relation to one another.

T W O

Cynicism as a Cultural Form

Cynicism, in a certain sense, is an understandable and rational response to our present-day circumstances. Television, our major form of society-wide communication, is saturated with lies and manipulations. Our political leaders are more concerned with reelection than political accomplishment. Social justice, demanded in the civil-rights era, and promised in Lyndon Johnson's "Great Society," is more distant than ever. For many, proclamations of the American Dream accomplished seem simply to cover up a wide range of American nightmares. And pieties about the values of democracy appear quite empty. For those who look closely and critically at the American way of life, there is much about which to be cynical.

Cynicism is shared by the haves and the have-nots; in the language of the 1980's, by the yuppies and the underclass. With stock-market speculation, junk bonds, and corporate takeovers, capitalism has reached its logical conclusion. Now it is not simply that the workers are alienated from the fruits of their labors, capital accumulation has become distinct from production and entrepreneurship. New, innovative rules of the financial game are disengaged from the game's point. The connection between getting rich and societal wealth is remote. During the Reagan era, as the number of millionaires multiplied, the nation's relative wealth in the world economy precipitately dropped. And for the underclass, on the other side of the social coin, there are only closed doors. The breakdowns in family and community life, the failures of public education, and the deindustrialization of the American economy make it so that the low men and women on the economic totem pole have fallen off the pole. Hence the proper word describing their situation is underclass, not lower class or working class.

Viewing life at the top and the bottom, those in the middle are prone to dismay. They observe a social surrealism of wealth not earned and poverty that threatens. They sense that the hotshots of Wall Street make millions for themselves without earning this wealth. And, they know that many among themselves—workers in the heavy industry of the Rust Belt, in the agriculture of the Farm Belt, and in the petrochemicals of the Sun Belt—have lost everything. The old work ethic, Max Weber's "Protestant Ethic and the Spirit of Capitalism,"[1] seems to be out of order, if not in complete disrepair.

Cynicism, then, has distinct economic foundations. For the yuppie, anything goes. Wealth is accumulated, but so is anomie—a commitment to nothing at all. Yuppie cynicism is a cynicism of power without culture. For the underclass, the absoluteness of poverty testifies to the absence of value in the way things are. Their cynicism constitutes a culture of powerlessness. Yet, as we will see, the struggle of power versus powerlessness is crucially fought among the middle class. Cynicism of the middle is where democratic capacity may be lost.

I

When we observe that a ubiquitous cynicism is in a certain sense rational and understandable, we are perceiving the positive and ancient philosophic roots of the term and the impulse. To appreciate this, we must have a sense of the broad cultural meaning of cynicism. It has both positive and negative connotations, which are rooted in the very history of the word.[2] Cynicism as a distinct and positive political philosophy began as a chosen project of poverty. In Hellenic Greece, Diogenes debunked the pomposity of philosophy and social conventions with a willful denunciation of worldly goods, not through theory but primarily through action. Anecdotes about his life (he left no written works) reveal a radical critique of the world of his time, emanating from the intellectual power of the powerless. Diogenes, the archetypical cynic, was a social satirist and radical social critic. His actions demonstrated a set of moral principles concerning the human condition applied to the particular situations in which humans found themselves.

On the human condition, Diogenes suggests that the good life is one that renounces excessive expectations, that takes pleasure as it comes, but does not distort the proper balance between natural circumstances and human existence. If one needs nothing, or at least very little, one can be happy with what one gets. Thus real individual autonomy and freedom can be achieved. To prove it, Diogenes lived in a tub. He purposely lived life stripped down to necessity. For this reason, Athenians called him "dog." But he adopted this term of derision as a positive credo. Cynicism is the dog philosophy, a philosophy of simplicity critically applied to the excesses of society and its powers.

On the powers, a story is told about Diogenes and Alexander the great:

> Legend has it that the young Alexander of Macedonia one day sought out Diogenes, whose fame had made him curious. He found him taking a sunbath, lying lazily on his back, perhaps close to an Athenian sports field; others say he was gluing books. The young sovereign, in an effort to prove his generosity, granted the philosopher a wish. Diogenes' answer is supposed to have been: "Stop blocking my sun!"[3]

The most politically ambitious man of the ancient world seeks the wisdom of a philosopher. A prince of power meets an intellectual prince (whose castle is a bathtub). But when the man of power not only grants the intellectual access but the actual power to get something done, this philosopher, unlike Aristotle, Confucius, Machiavelli, and today's policy analysts, who did and do all they can to have influence, tells the personification of power to get out of his way so that he can enjoy a simple natural pleasure. Intellectual autonomy requires a simple life uncompromised by political ambition. In this way, social critique can be kept alive.

On the nature of prevailing social order, Diogenes is brutal. "One day the philosopher lit a lamp and, as he was asked on his way through the town what he was doing, his answer was, 'I'm looking for an honest person'." Diogenes needs the assistance of a lantern to seek an ideal of humanity not easily found among his fellow citizens. Through his way of life, he exemplified that people should be in control of their desires and live in harmony with nature. Using manmade light during daylight, he showed how far reality was from the ideal. In numerous stories, he reveals the existence of the ideal and the sorrowful state of convention. He emphasizes the animal side of the political animal in order to question its politics.

The philosophy of cynicism has taken twists and turns since the time of Diogenes, alternating among critique, resignation, and apology.[4] In the late Roman Empire cynicism became a cult, resigned to the status quo. The critical focus of "Lucian the Mocker" (born 120 C.E.), was a cultivated attack upon the uncultivated moralists (Christians among them). Those who naively sought to live a moral life were shown to be fools. Lucian did not mock the false pretenses of social convention and the powers, but those who were trying to morally avoid the pretenses.

Then and now mocking cynicism expresses resignation, if not support, for the way things are. When convention is mocked from the point of view of the powers, the powerful use their disregard for convention to further accumulate power. When the powerless observe this, their sense of powerlessness increases, and when despite this sense they try to act according to moral principles that reveal the problematic nature of the way things are, mocking cynicism ridicules their effort. Such was the experience of antiquity, and it is our experience too.

II

The cynicism of the powers is justified with power. The extreme modern case in point is totalitarianism.[5] In totalitarian orders, power and reason are absolutely conflated. There is an official truth concerning just about everything, and it is enforced through the powers of the state. The social order is legitimated when the state's subjects act according to the official script, whether or not they believe it. Thus, at least theoretically, there is a symbiotic relation between those who believe their power constitutes reason and those who conform to the whims of the powerful without recourse to reason. One day the Chinese "People's" powers decide that "socialist reformers" are "capitalist inroaders" and they become enemies of the people, not only to be reviled but imprisoned. Ordinary people comply with the new script, not because they necessarily believe in such transformations, but because they know the price to be paid for publicly expressing disbelief. Yet disbelieved convictions, cynically expressed publicly, become social realities, a totalitarian normality.

In less extreme modern circumstances, there is greater distance between power and reason. Nonetheless, the cynicism of the powers is justified by and also justifies power. The cult of "the bottom line" in our economic and extra-economic life demands that the rule of profit-making, the core steering mechanism of our capitalist social order, as Jürgen Habermas once put it, not only steers all aspects of social life but dominates them. From the point of view of this power, if something is profitable it is true, real, and good; if it is not, it is without true meaning. The implications of this are broad, and deeply penetrate our daily life. To argue against profit maximization is practically impossible, and has even been defined by certain economists and political scientists as irrational.[6] Social customs, cultural accomplishments, and the law are to be discarded in pursuit of profits. The powerful, thus, "pursue" and those without power "know" that they all do it: corporate capitalists and trade unionists, preachers and politicians, con artists and fine-arts critics. Everyone is in it for the money or the political power which is too easily translatable into money, and which money easily buys. People do not necessarily think all this is for the good, but their mocking cynicism tells them that this is the way things are, and they act accordingly. Again a social reality is legitimated not by believed principles but by their operation.

Yet there is something missing in this account as it is applied to our social and political reality. Unlike in the totalitarian situation, other human relationships operate in addition to the ones that exist between ruler and ruled. From the point of view of the American political project, there is not only domination of polity and market, there is as well an institutional democratic culture and system. Imperfect as they are, they have a meaningful social reality, even if they are cynically understood by those in power as obstacles to be overcome or mechanisms to be manipulated.[7] From the point of view of the underclass, democratic culture and institutions may seem to be beside the point, or worse—a set of cultural practices and institutions which control their lives but which they do not understand and over which they have little control. Still, for the great bulk of ordinary people, democratic culture in America has both justified their dignity and empowered them. If we abandon this democratic sense and resort to cynicism, power and domination are all that remain.

III

Modern cynicism in general is a much more complex phenomenon than the cynicism of antiquity. Diogenes was concerned with the mores and foibles of a relatively simple society. Modernity brings complexity. Now the relationships between rulers and ruled are articulated within a highly complex social order. Modern democracy is a constitutent part of this order, as are other social institutions and practices. These are supported by such positive modern values as individual liberty, and freedom of speech and association, religion and property. Cynicism can and does undermine both the values and the institutions and practices they support.

Cynicism is a long-term aspect of modern democracies which in

recent years in America has reached crisis proportions. As an enduring problem, cynicism emerges as the cultural underside of democratic cultural commitments, which are centered around our individualism, as Alexis de Tocqueville so forcefully argued. In explaining democratic culture and its underside, Tocqueville focused on individualism. He understood that individualism was both a key to the constitution of our democracy and the possible cause of a new tyranny which could replace it. Democracy, as the rule of the people, requires the reasoned autonomy of equal citizens. Individuals must be able to make up their own minds, make their own judgments. They must be free agents. But as free agents they can become atomized egoists, disconnected from their traditions and fellow citizens and unconcerned with the common good.

Tocqueville believed that the atomizing effects of democracy could be avoided with the development of an individualism of broad horizons, what he called "individualism properly understood." With such an ethic, Tocqueville sensed, American citizens would appreciate that their own private interests as individuals could only be realized in their democracy when they took care for the overall well-being of society. Private interests and the public good must be, and are, developed in tandem. We will closely analyze these two sides of the individualistic coin in Chapters 3 and 4. Here we simply note that a perpetual cynicism is produced and reproduced in democracies because the necessary balancing act between individual interests and the common good provokes suspicions and differences in judgment. People suspect that actions in the name of the public good actually serve individual private interests. Thus the notion that politicians are all corrupt, that they are all "in it for themselves," is a recurring theme of American political discourse. And such suspicions are also focused on competing definitions of what actually constitutes the public good. One man's common good is another man's special-interest group. For New Deal Democrats, for example, Republican concerns with economic growth and productivity are but smokescreens for the special economic interests of big business; while for the Republicans, Democratic concerns for social equity simply serve the interests of big labor, civil-rights groups, corrupt big-city political machines, welfare-rights organizations, and so forth. In the face of such suspicions, the line between Tocqueville's "narrow individualism" and "individualism properly understood" is not easily drawn. This is a constant refrain of modern democratic politics.

This issue cannot and should not be decided definitively or philosophically.[8] Deciding about such issues is the stuff of politics. Cynical attitudes will always be with democratic politics. But something more than this has developed in the past twenty years in America. The long history of cynicism has been compressed into our most recent past. We have rapidly replaced cynicism as a critical sense, a form of ironic satire, with a mocking cynicism that does little to upset the status quo. After World War II America moved from the American century, to the Cold War and its anticommunist hysterics, to the atomic age, to the hopes and disappointments of the civil-rights era, to the turmoil of the Vietnam War and the antiwar movement, to Watergate, to the "new dawn" of Reagan's America, with America "riding tall" again, to Irangate and George Bush's attempt to constitute a "new era of good feelings." Wild swings of excessive optimism and pessimism, exaggerated by politicians' public-relations campaigns, have characterized an amorphous national mood. Depending upon one's political and aesthetic sensibility, alternative scenarios have been formulated to account for the apparent radical shifts in national character: rise and fall (primarily constructed around military and economic might), rise, fall, and rebirth (primarily constructed by New Right moralists and Reaganites), rise and fall with a potential rebirth (primarily constructed by Democrats of so-called liberal and moderate persuasions). Yet all of these scripts have cynicism in common, moving from a critical cynicism in the fashion of Diogenes to a cynicism that is mocking and enervating.

The American century, proclaimed by Henry Luce in the middle of World War II, has provoked a critical cynical response. From William F. Buckley, Jr.'s, *God and Man at Yale*[9] to Abbie Hoffman's *Steal This Book*,[10] the limitations of American pomposity have been subjected to critical ironic attack from both the left and the right. Prevailing sureties, secular liberalism on the one hand and consumer capitalism on the other, have been criticized in the fashion of Diogenes. Buckley played the role of a conservative clown, writing (during the McCarthy era) a diatribe against academic freedom. Though his political judgment is surely questionable, and its place in the development of American political culture requires critical appraisal (see Chapter 7 below), he did reveal the distance between the American academic culture and the general political culture in striking and amusing ways. Likewise, Hoffman was a jokester, a one-man guerrilla theater. Using the techniques of mass marketing and consumer culture, he denounced them, calling for a youth rebellion and revolt against all those over thirty when he himself was thirty.

His political antics were ridiculous, but they ridiculed the powers that turned away from the project of realizing the goals of the civil-rights movement to half-heartedly pursue a war that had little justification. Hoffman and other critical cynics of the New Left revealed and attacked the striking contradictions of the New Deal political consensus, though the form and content of their actions should be questioned in light of subsequent New Left nihilism (the Weatherman underground and the spread of a stultifying drug culture). But before considering the specific strengths and weaknesses of satirists and cynics of left and right, we must observe the central significance of a mocking cynicism that in the last twenty years has ridiculed critics more than the powers.

IV

Satirists and social critics with political ambitions reveal the distance between social ideals and social practices in hopes of instigating changes in social practices.[11] Modern (mocking) cynics reverse this critical impulse. They satirize or raise doubts about social critics and their criticism, and about the possibility of social change. The distance between ideals and realities discourages rather than encourages efforts to enact change or reassert fundamental principles. The distance between ideals and realities stands as proof that forces behind the scenes control the human order, and that there is little or nothing ordinary mortals can do about it. As a very important American case in point, let us briefly consider the fate of patriotism in the wake of the Vietnam War.

Animating the great bulk of the antiwar sentiments during the war was an American critique of American practices. Americans held the conviction that the United States should be on the side of the colonized, the dominated, and the oppressed. In World War II our international task was to engage in the good fight for freedom for others as well as for ourselves. But throughout the 1960s there was a growing sense that this was not the case in the dirty little war in Southeast Asia. Our allies included authoritarian dictators and their corrupt lieutenants, and there was mounting evidence that the people of Vietnam hardly appreciated (or understood) our "assistance," while official rhetoric proclaimed that we were fighting for freedom and democracy. Critics pointed out the distance between a typically American patriotic rhetoric and our actual practices, which included liberating villages by liquidating them and napalming agricultural settlements. The realities behind political appearances led first to the questioning of the realities (the war), and then of the appearances (the patriotic rhetoric). The American military engagement in Vietnam was so severely and universally criticized that even the argument between the war's supporters (the "hawks") and its foes (the "doves") became an argument about how we could disengage from the universally condemned ("un-American") war—with the hawks promoting "peace with honor" as an alternative to the doves' call for an unqualified "peace."

But for the most critical New Left radicals, the deceptive qualities of official rhetoric were confirmed by the war's realities. Radical critics, then, moved from patriotic critique to a rejection of patriotism. American democracy itself appeared as the enemy. The mainstream political debate, for the radicals, was only a facade for global imperialism. Political rhetoric was then viewed as a front constructed both by the conservative hawks and the liberal doves.

In a parallel fashion, the hawks knew that the doves essentially provided aid and comfort to the enemy, despite protests to the contrary by liberal doves; i.e., the doves were America's enemy. Both liberals and radical doves were viewed as actually being traitors.

And from the point of view of liberal doves, radical critique undermined legitimate political discourse. Radical critique compromised loyal opposition from this viewpoint, but it was also understood as being symptomatic of how an illegitimate pseudo-patriotic war was alienating the most promising young Americans from American ideals. Conservatives, liberals, and radicals, then, both doves and hawks, came to interpret publicly articulated political disagreements as "mere rhetoric."

As a consequence, the very ideals of democracy were not only rejected, or at the very least overlooked by the radical fringe, but such was the case at the very center of power in Richard Nixon's White House. Those with different political judgments were put on enemy lists, and the high ideals of American democratic life as they are formalized in the Constitution and operationalized in constitutional governance and political practice were systematically attacked. Not only the outs but also the ins became cynical about democracy. They questioned both the appearances and the realities of central American ideals.

When this sort of cynicism dominates a democratic political culture, as it has done in the post–Vietnam War era, democracy is threatened from many directions, mainly because it is not taken seriously. People use democratic political rhetorics where necessary, but they do not necessarily believe them, and even if they believe them, they are not necessarily believed by others. We observed this in the preceding account of the 1988 presidential election campaigns. But the problem goes beyond electoral politics; it penetrates everyday social life. A legitimation of disbelief supports and constitutes authoritative relations throughout American social life, from our political life to our religious life, from New York's Wall Street to Berkeley, California, from urban housing projects to suburban school boards.

V

The primary task of our inquiry is to examine how cynicism has been confused with political wisdom, and to explore cultural bases for alternatives. This will take us through a deliberate sociological analysis of both the relationship between American democracy and mass society, and the dialectics of American political commitments—tragically, from principled politics to ideological politics. I take this tragic story as it is produced and reproduced in our political and cultural life to be of fundamental importance for the vitality of our republic. For this reason, I focus on the culture of American politics and the politics of our culture. But before we examine these problems directly as they are linked in the structure of mass society, I believe that the reader should have a stronger sense of the form of cynicism as a legitimation of disbelief typical of our society.

As we have observed, cynicism was originally a particular (dog) critical philosophy. In our time and historically it has become a mocking attitude that is in fact the opposite of critical. The mocking cynic knows that life is a sham, but the knowledge is so universal that alternatives no longer exist. ("They all do it.") And in fact everywhere ideals are but facades for ugly realities. This attitude has ironic implications in everyday social life. Primary among these is the implication that the attitude becomes a self-fulfilling prophecy. If we believe that all those in authority justify their actions through elaborate rationalizations of privilege, then the principles upon which authoritative actions are at least sometimes based will disappear.

Teachers today, for example, are an endangered species. They face the normal skepticism of youth; more significantly, they are inundated with the cynical attitudes of adults. Their job is not held in high regard, as is indicated by their salaries, and there is a general understanding that the truly able do not choose such a semiprofession. With these cynical insights in mind, curriculum developers and school administrators increasingly seek to make the American classroom teacher-proof. Information and basic skills are to be taught through textbooks and workbooks, while teachers become little more than overseers who make sure that students complete a specified number of pages of assigned tasks. In such a view, teachers are judged with even more suspicion. Though obviously they still do teach, and in a great variety of ways, traditional and experimental, progressive and conservative, with varying degrees of success, the cynical attitudes toward teachers deprofessionalize them. The most significant representatives of learning to our children are socially defined by us, their parents, not as authorities but as incompetents.

When the authority due teachers wavers, so does the respect for learning itself. Teachers are symbols of learning. The social degeneration of their status not only compromises their specific life situations but constitutes a direct attack upon the representation of learning and enlightenment. The ideals of learning, as a significant end in itself and as a key to the constitution of liberty and democracy, are abandoned. We will consider in Chapter 8 how such abandonment must be addressed in order to understand the nature of the crisis in American education. Here we analyze the general pattern—how an institutional cynicism detaches a society from a key normative commitment. Such is the case in education and beyond.

Cynicism is not simply an attitude of criticism or apology; it is now a component of the social structure. Both ideally and practically, the primary goal of education is learning. It should link student with teacher, and both with society as a whole. Cynicism has displaced the goal. Teachers know they are held in low regard, and consequently they themselves view their profession in this way. Some come to education cynically. Such teachers choose teaching as an easy way out of the job race. With a moderate amount of education, and no special expertise, they can be called professionals, have lengthy vacations, and contribute to a middle-class standard of living in a two-income family. Other teachers learn their cynicism the hard way. They choose teaching because of a love of learning and a love of the process of educating our youth, but taxpayers, school administrators, politicians, and business elites attack their initial motivation directly.

Taxpayers "know" that school taxes are the ones over which they have the most control. They convince themselves that the schools are wasteful, teach the wrong things, encourage disorder among youth, and overpay their employees. They "know," as former President Reagan "knew," that throwing money at the problems of education only makes matters worse. Thus financial support for schools in America has often been unsteady and uneven.

Given this situation, school administrators "know" that they cannot attract the best and the brightest into teaching. Thus they promote teaching strategies and educational programs which are the most immune to incompetence, and rationalize those programs according to one dubious educational theory or another. Consequently students read predigested textbooks rather than books, and become skillful readers of reading-comprehension paragraphs, instead of prose and poetry. When business leaders and politicians react to the result—a growing cultural illiteracy along with the expansion of schooling—they deplore the state of affairs, appointing blue-ribbon panels and making public pronouncements as if their own emphasis on immediate profits, low taxes, and popularity had not contributed to the cynical malaise.

One frequent answer to the situation only hardens the cynical glue. Knowing that there is a problem in education, all too many observers agree that those implicated must be held responsible for their actions. Students must account for their learning in the form of scores on objective, usually multiple-guess national tests. Teachers must account for their performances through the test scores of their classes, as must administrators, elected school boards, and politicians. So education becomes directed toward test results rather than learning. Cynically, education, from preschool through high school and beyond, becomes a grand adventure in test taking. I will try to demonstrate more closely below how this direction in education is linked with national and local political trends. The point here is that a cynical attitude toward teachers and education has become a constituent and fundamental norm in schooling as a social institution; an institution intended to further learning has become instead an elaborate system of quality control.

It was the lifework of Michel Foucault to show how such reversals are produced in all modern institutions.[12] Though we may be critical of his radical judgments—because, for example, even the abysmal American welfare institutions provide support for the poor as they control them—it is beyond doubt that social control over the unruly is a significant part of psychiatry, education, medicine, criminal justice, and so forth. And such social control is produced and reinforced by an institutionalized cynicism.

VI

The cynical attitude exists throughout American society. Perhaps the most striking portrait of American cynicism can be found in Tom Wolfe's *The Bonfire of the Vanities*.[13] Wolfe's best-seller is a comedy of manners. He ridicules the demeanor of a wide variety of American social types, in a cross section of America's urban social structure. We meet yuppies and political activists, assistant district attorneys and church bureaucrats, journalists and a motley assortment of representatives of the underclass, the WASP upper class and Irish cops, a Jewish mayor and a civil-rights leader as black hustler. There is something for almost everyone to laugh at, to ridicule. All characters are presented as exaggerated stereotypes. In the exaggeration, there is comedy. If the reader is offended by one cynical representation or another, it is likely that the next one will hit the mark for him or her. A dark, cynical view of everyday life brings the characters together and strengthens the thin story line.

The novel takes place in New York City. It is about class, ethnic and racial relations, about the failures of criminal and social justice. Sherman McCoy, a quintessential yuppie and WASP, while bringing his mistress back to the upper East Side from the airport, gets lost in the South Bronx. In a tragedy of errors, McCoy is involved in a hit-and-run accident which leaves a young black man in a coma. Uncertainties and ambiguities surround the accident.

It is not absolutely clear to McCoy that his mistress, while driving the car, hit the young man, nor is it clear whether the two black men approaching their car were offering assistance or trying to rob them. A black minister and civil-rights leader turns the case into a political cause, purportedly out of empathy for the victim's mother, but also because of the publicity value the event provides. The Reverend Reginald Bacon attacks the media and the white power structure. He also enriches himself through phony black-enterprise front corporations, and empowers himself through the presentation of political protests to television cameras. A white district attorney uses the case to further his reelection, demonstrating (without regard to evidence) that he is on the side of the underclass (his electorate). For Abe Weiss, television image defines political reality. An assistant district attorney basks in the attention the case provides him. Larry Kramer usually prosecutes the wretched of the earth. Now he not only observes the world of Park Avenue but manages to destroy someone imbued with its aura, to the appreciation of his superior, two tough street-wise New York cops, the general public, and a sexy juror (with brown lipstick). Vanity of one sort or another motivates the action of these and other characters, urging them to the pursuit of power and privilege but leading to their downfall.

For Wolfe only image is reality, and it is pretty foolish. Though he covers the worlds of business, politics, civil rights, church, print and TV journalism, and state justice, all his characters seem more concerned with the salience of the social images than with their social or personal responsibilities. Indeed, the pursuit of image masks irresponsibility. McCoy, a bond salesman, pursues wealth. He is a million-dollar-a-year man who cannot pay his bills. He claims the one worthwhile part of his life is his six-year-old daughter, but he chooses to sneak out to his mistress rather than read his girl a bedtime story. When the daughter asks him what he does for a living, he has no answer.

Peter Fallow is a British expatriate journalist. He smugly observes the lack of style of all about him, as he brings himself to his daily alcoholic stupor. He marginally supports himself on American anglophile stupidity until his big scoop arrives. Writing for a tabloid scandal sheet, he disregards journalistic standards as he is fed his big story by Albert Fogel, an aging white radical working in the service of the Reverend Bacon. Fallow's new, easily won fame supports him in the manner to which he has grown accustomed. He continues to feign his superiority over Americans as he is willingly manipulated by our worst elements.

Even Henry Lamb, the black victim of the hit-and-run, is not what he appears to be. As the story unfolds, Wolfe reveals that the victim was an innocent, while his companion was a hoodlum. Lamb was probably offering assistance to McCoy and his mistress, while Lamb's "friend" not only looked menacing to their racist eyes but was a threat. Yet the victim was less than he seemed. Because of the publicity needs of Fallow, the Reverend Bacon, Abe Weiss, and Kramer, a decent but ordinary young man who managed to avoid problems was portrayed as an honor student, the pride and hope of his community, a future leader. Wolfe portrays the youth's transformation in an interview between Fallow, the journalist, and one of Lamb's teachers:

> ". . . I'm calling to inquire about one of your students, a young Mr. Henry Lamb."
>
> "Henry Lamb. Doesn't ring a bell. What's he done?"
>
> "Oh, he hasn't *done* anything. He's been seriously in-

jured." He proceeded to lay out the facts of the case, stacking them rather heavily toward the Albert Vogel-Reverend Bacon theory of the incident. "I was told he was a student in your English class."

"Who told you that?"

"His mother. I had quite a long talk with her. She's a very nice woman and very upset, as you can imagine."

"Henry Lamb . . . Oh yes, I know who you mean. Well, that's too bad."

"What I would like to find out, Mr. Rifkind, is what kind of student Henry Lamb is."

"What *kind*?"

"Well, would you say he was an *outstanding* student?"

"Where are you from, Mr.—I'm sorry, tell me your name again."

"Fallow."

"Mr. Fallow. I gather you're not from New York."

"That's true."

"Then there's no reason why you should know anything about Colonel Jacob Ruppert High School in the Bronx. At Ruppert we use comparative terms, but *outstanding* isn't one of them. The range runs more from cooperative to life-threatening." Mr. Rifkind began to chuckle. "F'r Crissake, don't say I said that."

"Well, how would you describe Henry Lamb?"

"Cooperative. He's a nice fellow. Never gives *me* any trouble."

"Would you describe him as a good student?"

"*Good* doesn't work too well at Ruppert, either. It's more 'Does he attend class or doesn't he'?"

"Did Henry Lamb attend class?"

"As I recall, yes. He's usually there. He's very dependable. He's a nice kid, as nice as they come."

"Was there any part of the curriculum he was particularly good—or, let me say, adept at, anything he did better than anything else?"

"Not particularly . . ."

"Let me ask you this. How does he do on his written work?"

Mr. Rifkind let out a whoop. "*Written* work? There hasn't been any written work at Ruppert High for fifteen years! Maybe twenty! They take multiple-choice tests. Reading comprehension, that's the big thing. That's all the Board of Education cares about."

"How was Henry Lamb's reading comprehension?"

"I'd have to look it up. Not bad, if I had to guess."

"Better than most? Or about average? Or what would
you say?"

"Well . . . I know it must be difficult for you to understand, Mr. Fallow, being from England. Am I right?
You're British?"

"Yes, I am."

"Naturally—or I guess it's natural—you're used to
levels of excellence and so forth. But these kids haven't
reached the level where it's worth emphasizing the kind
of comparisons you're talking about. We're just trying to
get them up to a certain level and then keep them from
falling back. You're thinking about 'honor students' and
'higher achievers' and all that, and that's natural enough,
as I say. But at Colonel Jacob Ruppert High School, an
honor student is somebody who attends class, isn't dis-
ruptive, tries to learn, and does all right at reading and
arithmetic."

"Well, let's use that standard. By that standard, is
Henry Lamb an honor student?"

"By that standard, yes."

"Thank you very much, Mr. Rifkind."

In this passage cynicism prevails, both as Wolfe's subject matter
and method. A cynical journalist interviews a cynical teacher from a
cynical school using a cynical program, and the journalist draws the
cynical conclusion. But the victimization is much more complex
than Wolfe permits himself or his reader to explore. In this slick passage we observe how the distance between appearance and reality is
formulated. The formula is repeated throughout *The Bonfire of the
Vanities* (Wolfe's first novel), and in his numerous journalistic reports.[14] We are repeatedly turned away from the real tragedy. There
is no education in Lamb's life, no way he can make use of his apparent goodwill for self-improvement, surrounded as he is by schools
without learning, courts without justice, journalism without the
pursuit of truth, churches without morality, and politicians who operate without the common good or collective interests in mind.
Lamb is the one character in Wolfe's cast who reveals this dark situation, and the author puts him in a coma. Wolfe, then, substitutes for
tragedy in its complexity a comic series of happenings which, when
revealed, imply a superiority of the author and his reader. Cynicism
is confused for wisdom.

This is an American tragedy, for the form and dimensions of
Wolfe's 700-page best-seller represent a new American condition,
one in which cynicism has replaced positive democratic and cultural
ideals.

Now we move from this fictive portrayal to cynicism's historical embeddedness in the structured relationship between democracy and mass society. We must appreciate how and why cynicism appears to be everywhere, so that we can then illuminate the possibilities of cultural and political alternatives.

THREE

Mass Society as the Underside of Democracy

Cynicism promotes acceptance of the existing order of things. In the post-Stalinist Soviet order, in the era before glasnost, just about everyone used official ideology to get on with official business, though practically no one believed the official rhetoric they were compelled to use. Through a complicated process, this led to a totalitarianism without terror and shaped in a significant way the alternative rhetorics of post-totalitarian culture.[1] Cynicism gave an extended life to totalitarianism. In the post–World War II American order, a parallel but much more complicated process can be observed. Cynicism supports and is a product of mass society. It makes economic, political, and cultural domination invisible, and casts serious doubts on cultural and political alternatives. *The substitution of cynicism for critical reason supports the mass-society underside of democracy.* The primary goals of this inquiry are to illuminate the processes by which this substitution occurs, and, in order to strengthen democracy, to explore means by which these substitutions can be reversed. We must, then, be clear about the distinction between democracy and mass society, and about their relationships. I consider the social structure of mass society and democracy in this and the following chapter. This will lead to an appreciation of the social and cultural formulations of cynicism, and their alternatives.

As a new concept, mass society gained critical currency among conservatives and radicals in response to late nineteenth- and twentieth-century social change. Today it rarely appears in public and theoretical discourse. It is strikingly unfashionable. This turn in fashion has ominous meaning. In my judgment, it represents the triumph of cynicism and the social fact of mass society. To turn the tables, political and linguistic confusion must be addressed. Here I describe the emergence of the notion of mass society in its social and political context and analyze the use and loss of the notion of mass society in sociological inquiry, attempting to demonstrate the cogency of a specific conceptualization of mass society for an understanding of American economic, political, and particularly cultural life.

I

The crowding of civilized institutions, the special structures of cities, characterizes Ortega's mass society.[2] For Canetti, the ubiquitous and spontaneous formation of crowds constitutes the mass order.[3] Daniel Bell views mass society as the heavily populated, developed, and differentiated institutional structure of the modern social order.[4] And Edward Shils sees that mass society is the inclusive structure of ever broader portions of the population into central authoritative institutions.[5] Mass society, for Ortega and Canetti, represents a normative problem. It is viewed with apocalyptic fear. Bell and Shils, in contrast, view mass structures with hopefulness. Shils in fact, as we will observe more closely below, believes the notion of mass society is a confused formulation for democratic society, properly understood.

Sociologically, the differences of usage can be readily explained. Aristocratic attachments and acute sensitivity to the rise of European totalitarian social movements give shape to the formulations, observations, and judgments of Ortega and Canetti. Though they differ in their precise specification of mass society, both are centrally concerned with the overwhelming population pressures upon the cultural and political institutions of Western civilization. Twentieth-century barbarism looms behind their judgments. The relatively peaceful development of mass democracy in America and its conflation with the normative ideals of the Enlightenment and democracy inform Bell's and Shils's conceptualizations. For them, the crowding of societal life indicates the spread of cultural and political opportunities for the formerly disenfranchised. The "American century" provides the backdrop for their judgments.

The facts of twentieth-century barbarism and the American century are directly related. While totalitarian terror practically extinguished European civilization, it laid the groundwork for American political, economic, and cultural predominance in the world. Executing the war fueled the American economy, while the European economies were left in ruins. Winning the war left the U.S. as the undisputed geopolitical superpower. During the war, America became the refuge for the arts and sciences of the world.

Americans understood that they truly had an international cultural mission in welcoming intellectual and artistic refugees; the mission was not only to assimilate European civilization but, as a democratic nation, to advance upon it. John Peale Bishop, in 1941, observed:

I shall begin with the single conviction that the future of
the arts is in America. . . . Without waiting for the outcome [of the war], or even attempting to predict it, it is
possible even now to say that the center of western
culture is no longer in Europe. It is in America. It is we
who are the arbiters of its future and its immense responsibilities are ours. The future of the arts is in
America. . . . The presence among us of these European writers, scholars, artists, composers is a fact. It
may be for us as significant a fact as the coming to Italy
of Byzantine scholars, after the capture of their ancient
and civilized capital by Turkish hordes. The comparison
is worth pondering. As far as I know the Byzantine exiles did little on their own account after coming to Italy.
But for the Italians their presence, the knowledge they
brought with them, were enormously fecundating.[6]

For Europeans, the coming of the masses brought Nazism, fascism, Francoism, and Stalinism. For Americans, it brought mass
politics, mass production, and mass consumption, along with
world hegemony. It undoubtedly represented, as it was appreciated
at the time, an American triumph. To be sure, a few "Byzantine exiles," seeing the silver lining, perceived the cloud. Thus, Hannah
Arendt saw proto-totalitarianism in the development of mass politics,[7] and the Frankfurt school theorists saw incipient fascism in the
mass-culture industry.[8] Such perceptions, though, were dismissed,
e.g., by Shils, as manifestations of an intellectual elitism, even if
sometimes leftist, which ultimately betrays a distrust of the demos.[9]

European social theorists had little reason to judge mass society
as benign. They experienced firsthand twentieth-century terrors.
For them, total power and powerlessness obviously went hand in
hand. Mass movements and atomization were understood as two
sides of the same coin. This could be perceived simply as a personal
experience. In the face of mass social movements, recourse to reasoned deliberation and established privileges no longer could hold
sway. Mass racism overwhelmed Central European universities and
cities. Individual representations of the collective irrationalism of
redemptive politics exiled individual representatives of refined
culture.[10]

Personal experience gave form to theories of mass developments.
The prospective view of the coming of the masses clearly involved a
relatively undisguised fear of the formerly disenfranchised hordes.
In Stanislaw Witkiewicz' vanguard play *The Shoemakers*, for exam-

ple, it is not what the empowered shoemakers will do, but the fact that they are shoemakers (and not aristocrats) which represents the apocalyptic vision.[11] Witkiewicz committed suicide when the vision was realized with the Nazi and Soviet invasion of Poland. For those with less romantic flair, a more sober and specified theoretical appraisal ensued, especially from the vantage point of exile.

The social carrier, the "masses," came to be viewed with less suspicion. The social structure of mass society became the object of investigation. Common to mass movements and mass social structure is that their conglomerated constituencies hold little in common. They were understood as being massed together with little social interaction. For Adorno, along with his colleagues of the Frankfurt school, the manipulations of mass culture and the mass politics of fascism were identified. Societal domination was ensured. Atomized individuals interacted only with the leader. For Arendt, mass structures led to the breakdown of the common public world and the loss of collective identities, most specifically class identities. Atomization and the loss of the capacity for concerted collective action were viewed as the necessary prelude to totalitarianism.

Disturbingly, for those who identify American social arrangements with the ideals of modernity and democracy (e.g., Daniel Bell, Edward Shils, and Talcott Parsons),[12] these more refined critics of mass society and its culture recognized common elements of mass structures and atomization not only in fascism and Soviet style socialism but in American consumer society as well. Though Parsons, Shils, and Bell, and Arendt, Horkheimer, and Adorno, make similar observations, they differ radically in their judgments. The critical appraisal of atomization in the hands of these American sociologists becomes the positive attribute of individualism. The critical appraisal of mass society becomes simply the operationalization of democracy—social, cultural, and political.

The despair of the exile may be used sociologically to account for the mass-society and mass-culture critiques. Their currency among certain American intellectuals in the 1940s and 1950s may be accounted for by these intellectuals' status insecurity.[13] Indeed, such argumentation seems to have been accepted in American academic circles. Thus the term "mass society" has generally dropped out of sociological investigations. Analysis focuses instead upon the operations of democracy and modernity in existing social institutions.

But in my judgment such analysis does not represent intellectual progress. A richly textured social complex is analyzed empirically, tendentiously, and apologetically. The facade of the social edifice is confused with its architecture. The behavioral manifestations of individualism and the "two-party system" are misperceived as the normative promises of liberty and democracy, fostering a general (mocking) cynicism. Those who question the perception are explained away as frustrated status-insecure intellectuals who are overly committed to an adversary culture.[14]

II

Most common, among critics of contemporary American political and cultural practices and among the apologists for these practices, is the identification of liberal democratic norms with given American practices. Critics dismiss the norms too readily. Apologists celebrate the practices too easily. Without an analytic framework to distinguish democratic practices from mass manipulation, the built-in ambivalences of modernity are ignored. The critic of bourgeois or formal democracy with cynical glee unmasks the hypocrisies of representative institutions, free speech, and the rights of the individual, and in the process becomes a political pilgrim to totalitarian worlds.[15] The neoconservative happily and cynically condemns this turn, ignoring the distance between the normative promise of Western ideals and actual Western practices, which stimulated the totalitarian journey.

An earlier, often misunderstood political pilgrim, Alexis de Tocqueville, realistically but without cynicism addressed these issues. While contemporary political pilgrims imagine a tension between capitalism and socialism, or a transition from one to the other, Tocqueville, as a nineteenth-century political pilgrim, understood himself to be between aristocracy (and its cultural and social forms) and democracy (and its cultural and social forms). He was neither a tendentious democrat nor a conservative aristocrat. His ambivalence about the world he saw passing and the one he saw coming refined his judgment of democracy's value, and of its underside. In the language of our day, he understood the distinction between democracy and the mass society.

Tocqueville recognized the promise of American society perhaps more than any other European social observer. To appreciate the promise, he analyzed democratic norms and their relation with American practices. Conservative critics and liberal observers today tend to focus on his appreciation of America's democracy. Indeed, his American contemporaries for this reason judged volume 1 of *De-*

mocracy in America quite favorably and were cool to volume 2, because in the second volume the undersides of American life and democracy were critically examined.[16]

Often missing, both then and now, is an appreciation of Tocqueville's nuanced approach. At times he is a conservative, e.g., in his positive approval of the impact of religion, tradition, and the family; at times he is a liberal, e.g., in his defense of political and civil liberties. At still other times he seems to be quite a radical democrat, e.g., in his investigation of the importance of participation for democracy. The one thing Tocqueville is not is a cynic. Thus, centrally, Tocqueville distinguishes individualism from egoism (mere selfishness) and analyzes them as they pose special problems for democracies. Democracy provides for the positive norm of individual autonomy. Since all citizens are equal, no greater authority other than the individual or a collection of individuals "naturally" constrains individual activity. The individual, for his or her own life, becomes the authoritative judge and jury. The positive constraints of cultural norms, religion, family, and locality all reach beyond the individual, and therefore are undermined. Social cohesion in a democracy becomes problematic.[17]

Tocqueville examines enlightened individualism (or, in his terms, "individualism properly understood") as the ongoing means to resolve the problematic. If individualism is unenlightened, i.e., if the individual does not take into account his or her place in a larger society, a democratic society provides the groundwork for a new and most severe tyranny. The tyranny, he predicted, would be characterized by:

> An innumerable multitude of men, all equal and alike, incessantly endeavoring to secure the petty and paltry pleasures with which they glut their lives. Each of them, living apart, is as a stranger to the fate of all the rest; his children and his private friends constitute to him the whole of mankind. As for the rest of his fellow citizens, he is close to them, but does not see them; he exists only in himself and for himself alone.
>
> Above this race of men stands an immense and tutelary power, which takes upon itself alone to secure their gratification and to watch over their fate. That power is absolute, minute, regular, provident and mild. It would be like the authority of a parent if, like that authority, its object was to prepare man for manhood; but it seeks, on the contrary, to keep them in perpetual childhood: it is

well content that the people rejoice provided that they think of nothing but rejoicing. For their happiness such government labors . . . it everyday renders the exercise of the free agency of man less useful and less frequent; it circumscribes the will within a narrower range and gradually robs a man of all the uses of himself. . . . Such a power does not destroy, but it prevents existence, it does not tyrannize but it compresses, enervates, extinguishes and stupefies a people.[18]

The enervated will of an egalitarian people legitimates the centralization of power in the new tyranny of mass society, Tocqueville reasons. The collective self-determination of the people, a fundamental normative premise of democracy described by Tocqueville as public freedom, will have dissipated. Tocqueville did not expect this of America. In comparing continental Europe with America, he was deeply struck here by the traditions and capacity for public freedom in voluntary associations and among enlightened individuals. Without the commitment to and activity based upon public freedom, and without the voluntary association of enlightened individuals, his version of what we recognize as mass society results.

Mass society looms as the ever-present potential underside of democracy for Tocqueville. I maintain, following the insights of Edward Shils, that the terms of inclusion and participation in society determine democratic and mass structural outcomes.[19] A successful democracy requires the active participation of equal citizens in state and civil (social) institutions. When such participation is manipulated or when citizens no longer seek to participate (in classical terms, when there is no semblance of republican virtue), social atomization and a new form of political tyranny result.

In America, the archetypical nineteenth-century democracy, Tocqueville saw both the positive realization of classical democratic-republican norms and the potential for a mass society. This is the root of his ambivalent judgments. His ambivalence suggests a twentieth-century analogue: the analytic distinction between democratic and mass societies.

Propensities toward the realization of both democratic norms and mass structures can be observed in contemporary Western society. By viewing society as an amalgamation of these propensities, without differentiating them, both the promise of democracy and the dangers of mass society become imperceptible. A cynical attitude toward democracy then becomes the common wisdom.

Thus, for example, the pluralist theories of American democracy,[20] as well as neocorporatist democratic theories,[21] observe "interest group" interactions empirically. They assert that these interactions constitute modern forms of democracy, since interest groups in conflict, and corporate groups through negotiated cooperation and coordination, explain their activities with democratic rhetorics and operate within formally democratic political structures. But the undemocratic constitution of these groups most often is not examined, nor is the undemocratic nature of their social construction analyzed (e.g., political parties and trade unions). Robert Michels long ago analyzed the fundamental dimensions of these problems.[22] In order to achieve efficiently the most democratic of ends, democratic union and party life must be sacrificed, he maintained. Even the major empirical study, *Union Democracy,* by S. M. Lipset and his colleagues, undertaken to refute Michels' so-called "iron law of oligarchy," suggested that democratic unions are the exception that seem to prove the oligarchic rule.[23]

The studies of the neocorporatist and interest-group theorists, and of elite theorists such as Michels, miss the central analytic point, though, and in doing so they lose a critical clarity. Democracy, especially in the American tradition, as an end is a means. As such, in modern Western society it is one central normative component of a complex social structure. As Tocqueville observed, along with the potential of broad democratic achievement comes the possibility of tyranny. Following his line of argument, to define democracy operationally with mass structures and processes, in the way the corporatists and interest-group theorists do, eliminates the possibility of democratic critique. To avoid such a cynical conclusion of political theory, the theoretical and practical grounds for mass society as a critical analytic concept must be reconsidered.

III

We are now in a position to explore the sociological distinction between mass society and democracy. Edward Shils, the conservative social theorist, serves as our guide, as we consider the sociological literature.

In 1962, Shils declared, "A specter is now haunting sociologists. It is the specter of 'mass society.' "[24] He explained that the notion of mass society is not of contemporary sociologists' own making. In his rather skeptical view, the notion has its origins in the ancient Roman historians' conception of the tumultuous populace and was given its modern life in the aftermath of the French Revolution, becoming properly part of sociology by those who made a strong distinction between Gemeinschaft (community) and Gesellschaft (society). All these elements were synthesized, according to Shils, "in the quasi-Marxist assessments of the regime of National Socialist Germany."[25] With the emergence of mass communications, this critique and technological developments resulted in a new image of mass society. Shils questions the critical thrust of those who employ the image, while he attempts to explain its constitution in recent societal developments. He notes the image of a:

> territorially extensive society, with a large population, highly urbanized and industrialized. Power is highly concentrated in this society, and much of the power takes the form of manipulation of the mass through the media of mass communication. Civic spirit is low, local loyalties are few, primordial solidarity is virtually non-existent. There is no individuality, only a restless and frustrated egoism. It is like those states of nature described by Thomas Hobbes, except that the public disorder is restrained through the manipulation of the elite and the apathetic idiocy of the mass.[26]

Shils absolutely rejects this view of contemporary life. He believes it distorts central features of large-scale liberal democratic societies; it is empirically blind to fundamental aspects of the modern order; and it cannot theoretically account for how such a social order could possibly reproduce itself. Yet, and the qualification is a crucial one, he does concede that "the conception of mass society has the merit of having responded, however erroneously, to a characteristic feature of [the] recent phase of modern society; namely, the entry of the mass of the population into greater proximity to the center of society."[27]

Shils turns the critics of mass society on their heads. He maintains that these critics have addressed something novel in the history of human society but are fundamentally wrong about its causes and significance. Here, I turn things around a bit more, taking seriously Shils's account of the causes of mass society and his general description of it, but drawing very different theoretical and practical conclusions.

Shils shows how democracy and mass society are linked through the process of social integration. Using an analysis of one of the central concerns of modern sociology, the concern about social order and integration, he addresses the political problems of democracy and mass society. He provokes a reconsideration of the sociological classics of Marx, Weber, and Durkheim and their programs, and suggests a different view of past and present.

In the past, Shils maintains, large-scale societies were rather tenuously integrated; now they are more tightly and democratically bound. Then, the distance between town and country, the few highly educated and the many illiterate, the very wealthy and the poor, and the politically powerful and the powerless was great. Integration was achieved through the legitimized domination of the powerless by the powerful, and the justification and acceptance of huge differences in social condition. Today's democratic and mass societies are distinguished by their novel means of inclusion and integration, with domination transformed, along with political rhetorics and cultures.

We must remember that the differences of social condition have been depicted, justified, and condemned in a variety of ways by social theorists and political activists. Modern European conservatives such as de Maistre and Burke, reacting to the French revolution, view the differences as natural, inevitable, and even desirable.[28] Liberals are divided between the nineteenth and twentieth centuries. The earlier liberalism (which still goes by this name in Europe) views the differences as inevitable even if undesirable, fearful that attempts to ameliorate the differences will diminish liberty. The later (twentieth-century American) version of liberalism attempts to increase liberty for broader segments of the population by diminishing the differences.[29] Modern radicals, especially in the Marxist tradition, view the lessening of the differences as the primary goal of political action.[30] These political traditions do not conceive of inequities as modes of social integration.

Twentieth-century social scientists do. Modern sociologists from Emile Durkheim to Max Weber to Talcott Parsons, C. Wright Mills, and Alvin Gouldner, link the problems of social difference and inequality with the problem of integration vs. disintegration.[31] Shils's innovation is to utilize the sociological approach for understanding the political problems of democracy and mass society in the tradition of Tocqueville. By doing so, he provides for sociological investigation. He addresses a major gap in the sociological tradition.

For Durkheim and Weber, at least in their more scholarly writings, democracy and mass society are not perceived as problems. Domination based on inequalities constitutes the political for Weber. It is justified by the special qualities of the political leader (charismatic authority), by the ways of doing things in the past (traditional authority), or by rational means/ends calculations and formal legality (bureaucratic authority). Different allotments of scarce resources (power, privilege, and status) are linked to the types of authority and are justified. Missing is an appreciation of a politics among equals—a democratic politics with democratic authority. Also missing is an accounting of how people of different qualities politically react to the changing grounds of their social interactions, in Weberian terms when one sort of dominant-subordinate interaction (traditional) is replaced by another (bureaucratic). Durkheim too does not address these issues. For him, differences and inequalities within a given population are either functional or dysfunctional (in his terms, abnormal). A natural evolutionary view of human development tells him that the dysfunctional differences are transitional. Integration is axiomatically linked to the differences in complex societies. The differences foster mutual dependence leading to social cohesion. The types of integration charactertize human development—the primitive ("mechanist solidarity") based on sameness, and the advanced ("organic solidarity") based on differences. The bringing together of different people with different resources and capabilities is viewed as politically and sociologically unproblematic. The problem of inclusion for Durkheim is a technical rather than a political one.

Parsons develops this point, synthesized with Weber's view, to its logical conclusion. The social system is reified. It is given lifelike holistic qualities requiring structural solutions. Integration of society is a systemic response to social differentiation. With this much Durkheim would agree. But Parsons addresses greater complexities. He accounts for a broad variety of integration mechanisms—on grounds of sameness and difference, but also on grounds of affection, rationality, religion, art, and so forth. He further explains differentiation as a complex response of adaptive upgrading to the environment, as well as a response to the social needs of integration.

The details of Durkheim's, Weber's and Parson's approaches to social differences and integration need not concern us here. We simply need to observe that they do not view the relationship between social differences and social differentiation politically, specifically in terms of the development of mass society.

Alvin Gouldner and C. Wright Mills were distinguished as critical sociologists in that they rejected the aforementioned social-scientific justifications for inequalities and set the theoretical and research agendas for American critical inquiry of the past twenty years. Both wrote major works critical of the then dominant Parsonian sociology as an ideology for the powers that be. Gouldner sought to substitute an alternative social science that avoided the weaknesses but drew upon the strengths of the academic (Parsonian) and the critical (Marxist) traditions.[32] This effort did not address the problems of democracy and mass society since it synthesized two approaches that did not do so either. His work promoted a broadened acquaintance with critical Marxism over the past decades. It turned inquiry toward a consideration of class, the relative importance of the state, and the relative autonomy of politics. Those primarily influenced by his synthesis did not consider the issue of mass society.

Mills, though, did centrally address the issues of democracy and mass structures. Indeed, he was one of the theorists of mass society who received Shils's attention. In Mills's major work, *The Power Elite*, democracy, the political rule of the people in publics, has been replaced by the rule of a "power elite" over a mass society. Shils's characterization of the critiques of mass society, quoted above, fairly represents Mills's view. The elites of business, government, and the military rule America, as a mass society. Mills sharply distinguished such a society from democracy.[33] The transformation of democratic society into mass society he explains as a simple but effective domination by those with economic, political, cultural, and military resources. The social integration of the elite and the disintegration of the public into a mass accounts sociologically for the effectiveness of the domination. Here is where the most serious flaws in his work become evident.

It has often been observed that Mills's account of the power elite's cohesion is overly social-psychological and conspiratorial.[34] According to Mills, the leaders of business, politics, and the military coordinate their activities through interpersonal ties; they seek the same ends because they grew up in similar families, went to the same schools, and belong to the same clubs. Such interpersonal ground is an unlikely primary source for the functioning of a complex social structure. His notion of mass society is even more problematic.

Mills's contrasting images of masses and publics graphically depict the concerns and observations of mass society's critics—such as those of Tocqueville and the turn-of-the-century critics of massification. He perceives major changes: "an enlarged and centralized political order [has made] modern societies less political and more administrative," with "mass communications that do not truly communicate." Unlike in previous participating liberal publics, there is "an absence of voluntary associations that really connect the public at large with the centers of power," as they had in the past.[35] But apart from the assertion that this absence is enforced by a power elite (whose coordination is not sufficiently explained), he does not analyze the social forces that explain the mass structures which he describes. He and his theory of mass society, then, could be, and were, rather easily dismissed. Even the confusions and excesses of the New Left of the 1960s have been explained as being a consequence of the sharpness of his contrasting images of mass and public, without explanation of their connection. It is said that the student activists too readily dismissed American society as an undemocratic mass society, seeking "real" participatory democracy in reconstructed publics. When their utopian vision failed, it is observed, they became fanatics.[36] Clearly Mills's ideas themselves did not cause such problems, but the starkness of his contrast between mass and democratic publics, without any accounting of how they are connected, does have both negative theoretical and negative political implications. This is where Shils's critique of the mass-society critics and his analysis of mass society are crucial.

IV

Following the tradition of political inquiry into democracy and mass society outlined above, Shils links the analysis of mass structures with the negative evaluation of aspects of democratization. He adds to the tradition by showing how democratization is a process of social integration. He does this by proposing a distinctive view of social structure.

Society may be conceptualized in a variety of ways. Major schools of social inquiry and political philosophy are distinguished by the way they conceptualize society. For Durkheim, society is not simply like an organism, it is studied as an organism. For theorists such as Talcott Parsons and Jürgen Habermas, society is analyzed as a systemic whole with its own internal logic and structural dynamics.[37] For Weber, society is a summation of individual meaningful actions. And for Marx, society or a social formation is most prominently characterized by class formation, action, and conflicts arising from productive relations. Shils proposes an alternative view, which can be characterized as a social ecology of authority.

Shils observes that every large-scale historical social order has a central zone. This zone, not necessarily geographical, is where the prevailing power and ultimate valuative justification for it are concentrated. "The center of society [is] the central institutions governed by the elites and the central value systems which guide and legitimate these institutions."[38] Most people in most social orders do not take part directly in the central workings of power and valuative justification. They live and work at the peripheries. "The mass of the population in all societies stands at some distance from authority. This is true with respect both to the distribution of authority and to the distribution of the secondary qualities associated with the exercise of authority."[39] But nonetheless it is the central authority and the degree and type of consensus around the central values which Shils believes orders a society. No matter how differentiated and unequal a society, certain fundamental values transcend class and factional differences and identify that society. The values of freedom, democracy, and equalitarianism are such values in American society. They justify the prevailing authorities and existing social institutions. The mass of the population accepts the values and engages in conflicts over how they might be realized. Those in the center, the political, economic, and cultural leaders, use the values both to justify their positions and to engage in their societal activity. Those on the periphery are affected by authority but do not directly take part in its exercise. Societies differ according to the character of their centers and their peripheries, and the character of the relationships between centers and peripheries. But despite these differences, which Shils uses to explain the distinction between democratic and authoritarian regimes, between pluralistic and unified orders, between traditionalism and modernity, and much more,[40] the central values and the actions of central authorities are the keys to social integration even in complex societies. Shils explains:

> The central value system is constituted by the values which are pursued and affirmed by the elites of the constitutent subsystems and of the organizations which are comprised in the subsystems. By their very possession of authority, they attribute to themselves an essential affinity with the sacred elements of their society, of which they regard themselves as the custodians. By the same token, many members of their society attribute to them that same kind of affinity. The elites of the economy affirm and usually observe certain values which should govern economic activity. The elites of the polity affirm and usually observe certain values which should govern

political activity. The elites of the university system and the ecclesiastical system affirm and usually practice certain values which should govern intellectual and religious activities (including beliefs). On the whole, these values are the values embedded in current activity. The ideals which they affirm do not far transcend the reality which is ruled by those who espouse them. The values of the different elites are clustered into an approximately consensual pattern.[41]

But the central values also may lead to changes in the patterns of order and integration, and thus to transformation. Shils observes:

> Implicitly, the central value system rotates on a center more fundamental even than its espousal and embodiment in authority. Authority is the agent of *order*, an order which may be largely embodied in authority or which might transcend authority and regulate it, or at least provide a standard by which existing authority itself is judged and even claims to judge itself. This order, which is implicit in the central value system, and in the light of which the central value system legitimates itself, is endowed with dynamic potentialities. It contains, above all, the potentiality of critical judgment on the central value system and the central institutional system. To use Mannheim's terminology, while going beyond Mannheim, every "ideology" has within it a "utopian" potentiality. To use my own terminology, every central value system contains within itself an ideological potentiality. The dynamic potentiality derives from the inevitable tendency of every concrete society to fall short of the order which is implicit in its central value system.[42]

Now the fundamental structure of democratic and mass societies can be clearly and simply described. They are societies where those on the periphery "in mass" come much closer to the center and even regularly take part in central activities. Citizen armies, the use of vernacular, the spread of literacy, the development of modern parliamentary democracy and the spread of the franchise are evidence of this as a modern propensity. In the postwar period, this form of integration rapidly intensified worldwide. In Shils's view, this spread of democracy has been denounced improperly by its critics as mass society.

Yet, Shils fails to analyze the different forms of inclusive processes and their various social consequences. The terms and

methods of integration have definite impact upon the power relations among social groups and on the fundamental structure of the
social order, potentially transforming democratic society into mass
society. The inclusion and participation of the populace (the demos)
into ever broader aspects of social life constitute both democracy
and mass society as related but different social forms.

This is where I part ways with Shils, as I suggested I would. His
discussion of center and periphery and of mass and democratic society treats integration in neutral terms. It does not adequately
consider various modes of participation. Manipulation may not be
as raw and interpersonal as C. Wright Mills suggested, but it has
been a significant, even systemic, component of the integration of
those at the periphery into the center. In the next chapter, we first
observe this in American economics and politics. Then we will see
how the realm of culture is even more striking. Changes in the cultural realm point to the fundamental distinctions and relationships
between mass and democratic practices, between cynicism and
democratic culture.

F O U R

Democracy in America

The Beardian progressive eco-
nomic interpretation of the American Constitution has come in and
out of fashion.[1] But even its most harsh critics must and do recognize that the political prelude to the Constitutional Convention was
the Annapolis Convention of September 1786, which was called explicitly to regulate commercial conflict among the states.[2] The
delegates of the earlier, sparsely attended convention could not address the specifically commercial issues. Too many states were
unrepresented. Nonetheless, they accomplished a great deal. The
New Jersey delegate, Abraham Clark, was commissioned by his
state "to consider how far a uniform system in their commercial
regulations and *other important matters,* might be necessary to the
common interest and permanent harmony of the several
states . . . effectually to provide for the exigencies of Union."[3] The
Annapolis delegates, apparently maneuvered by Hamilton and
Madison, used the New Jersey mandate to call for another convention with a more broadly conceived mandate. The need for
economic regulation instigated a reconsideration of political constitution. Politics were at the very core of the commercial and
economic conflicts.

It was clear that economic integration was the order of the day. At
issue were the terms of integration. Debtors and creditors, bankers
and farmers, tradesmen and craftsmen, from the southern and
northern states, and from the interior and the coasts and the river
basins, were being brought into an integrated economic system.
Their conflicts, as citizens and as economic agents, over economic
and political matters had less to do with the facts of integration than
its terms. There were serious class conflicts. Thus, support and opposition to ratification of the Constitution ultimately divided along
class lines.[4] The opponents of the Constitution, the anti-Federalists,
expressed anti-aristocratic positions in the interest of those with
moderate means, who were often in debt and were rarely politically
or socially prominent. The Federalist supporters and leaders were

society's privileged, who had interest in debt parity, hard currency, and a stable centralized banking system. Significant and conflicting economic interests found political voice.

The constituting authorities understood that they were insuring proper social (class) relations in the social order. Reactions to Shays' Rebellion reflect this. Madison, for example, wrote to his father: "They [the insurgents] profess to aim only at the reform of their constitution and of certain abuses in the public administration, but an abolition of debts public and private, and a new division of property are to be suspected to be in contemplation."[5] Similar reactions furthered the drive for a new political constitution.[6] For the present purposes, the issue is not whether class and economic divisions determined the contours of the political constitution. Rather, it is to observe that the terms of inclusion into central economic life were motivating a differentiated society in its politics.

Debates over the terms of economic inclusion continued through the nineteenth and twentieth centuries. The Jacksonian attacks on the national banks, the populist support of paper money in the post–Civil War period, the social reforms of the New Deal, and Reaganomics all are struggles over the terms of inclusion of the populace into central economic life.

The economic democratization described here, as Shils would understand this inclusion, may not seem very democratic in the positive normative sense. Indeed, it is not. Inclusion has been considered without reference to participation. Representatives of both debtors and creditors took part in the constitutional debates, but the creditors won. A politically supported economic system was established that markedly disadvantaged the unpropertied. That this was the case is not surprising. The unprivileged did not have the political and cultural resources to realize their interests. The franchise was still quite limited. Educational resources were unequally distributed. Society was still led by its "betters," and in colonial America this was generally accepted.[7]

The struggle for economic democracy and justice is predicated upon political and cultural dimensions of democratization. But here too inclusion does not automatically yield equal capacity to participate. The development of the so-called two-party system exemplifies this.

Today it is axiomatic, at least in the West, that democracy requires a multiple-party system. The loyal opposition must be permitted to organize in pursuit of its understanding of the interests of its constituency and the common good. But in the early days of the American republic, this was not generally accepted. Factions or parties were viewed as undesirable. While factions were understood to be "natural," they were also understood as things that needed to be controlled. The early struggles between the Federalists and the Democratic-Republicans suggested political failure to the "founders." Organized opposition seemed indistinguishable from sedition. Factions suggested disunity. Disunity laid the groundwork for tyranny. The Alien and Sedition Acts were natural outgrowths of contemporary political theory.

In the 1820s and 1830s, views changed.[8] It became clear to a newly emerging political leadership that competition among parties supported liberty and that loyalty to a party, whether in or out of power, was an important support for democracy. The propertied elite constituted the early American political leadership. Thus, for example, though the anti-Federalist argument supported the interests of the less advantaged, its spokesmen still were predominantly from the propertied elite. Only they had the resources to take up political leadership.[9] In the 1820s and 1830s, a new sort of leadership emerged—professional politicians such as Martin Van Buren, who were committed to party life. The leadership was open to broader segments of the population, and, with the expansion of the franchise, they sought the support of broader popular circles. But the terms of participation in party life can undermine democratic quality.

I

In traditional justifications of representative democracy, constituencies choose representatives, and members of a party choose their leadership. The representative either acts according to his or her own best judgment, or seeks to act according to the desires of his or her constituency. Though the desirability of these alternatives is much debated, a fundamental shortcoming of party practices is that neither is often the case. Rather, quite often, parties and their leaderships create constituencies that serve party interests. Party leaders seek to develop a program to keep the party in power. Here we observe the emergence of mass structure in political parties.

The rightward shift of the Democratic party in the 1980s, for example, involved strategies for the party's predominance at least as much as changes in political judgments and convictions. The party leadership reacted to Ronald Reagan and his popularity. It formulated policies seeking to counteract Reaganism. In 1982 the traditional Democratic strategies worked. In the throes of the worst economic depression since the 1930s, the traditional Democratic coalition was sustained. But by the mid-1980s, with the anticipation of the next presidential election, things changed.

Reagan's appeal to key segments of the Democratic coalition had to be addressed. The Democrats sought to compete with the Republicans over fiscal responsibility, the sufficiency of their anti-communism, their willingness to use military force in the Third World, and their pro-growth economic policy. Policies were changing in the hope of creating a new democratic majority. A new conservative national mood apparently demanded new conservative politicians. Thus, the conservative Southern wing of the party, which previously was kept in the fold as a subordinate minority wing, became ascendant.

But the "conservative mood" was not directly a natural creation of autonomous individuals. It was constructed and manipulated most forthrightly by Reagan himself. While Reagan's policies had clear ideological content, his candidacies were of personality and sentiment. People voted for "the Gipper," the "nice regular guy," willingly working for them, getting the government off their backs, and restoring America's pride and position in the world. To this end, military spending expanded exponentially while real welfare spending was slashed. The government became an instrument for private economic accumulation, the summation of which was the newly defined common good. The ravages of poverty, disease, homelessness, and age no longer were seen as primary governmental concerns. Educational problems were addressed with calls for discipline, school prayer, and privatization.

There is nothing wrong or inconsistent in this relationship between candidate appeal and ideological governance. Reagan did not present himself as anything other than what he was, both personally and ideologically. But his package brought together a new combination of symbols and policies. His success required Democratic party reaction. Fetal rights, a balanced-budget amendment, advanced nuclear armaments, tax and social-welfare cuts, and anti-communism, do not *necessarily* combine. Reagan combined them, though his supporters did not do so consistently.

The Catholic bishops both strongly affirmed his position on abortion and condemned his positions on military spending and economic policies, while Catholic laypeople may have reversed the judgments. The majority of union workers and their leaders supported his foreign policies, but condemned his union-busting labor policies, which created an age of labor "givebacks." Great numbers of union workers, nonetheless, voted for the man who restored American stature, while the union leadership campaigned aggressively against him. Most corporate managers affirmed his economic policies but found his position on moral issues bizarre, while fundamentalist farmers from the American heartland may have supported his moral agenda, but sensed that his farm policies were part of an international oligarchic conspiracy. As the satirical columnist Russell Baker glibly put it, some supported Reagan so that he could be Reagan (the ideologues—this was the well-known refrain of the New Right), others supported him so that he could be the Gipper (the nice guy he portrayed in an old Hollywood football film).[10] But both sorts of supporters, who fundamentally were in conflict, created the new conservative mood. They constituted the Reagan mandate. Reagan did not represent this diverse constituency. He created it as the political majority.

The Democratic party sought to create an alternative majority. They needed to deconstruct the Reagan majority and reconstruct a new Democratic majority. FDR's lasted for fifty years, first firmly (until 1968), then tenuously until 1982. Then, apparently, it was finished. As the different Democratic presidential hopefuls competed in the 1988 primaries, they offered alternative projects for the reconstruction of a Democratic majority. In 1984 Mondale tried the old coalition and failed. Then the so-called moderate and progressive wings of the party competed with an amalgamation of new ideas. Some, such as Albert Gore, combined a post-racist Southern social policy with a frank criticism of the failures of the New Deal and the War on Poverty. Others, such as Michael Dukakis, proposed "new ideas," which included a strong commitment to both old-fashioned military defense (with an emphasis on relatively "low-tech" conventional armaments) and the development of a postindustrial economic order. Still others, such as Jesse Jackson, combined old-fashioned moral appeals for self-reliance with strong commitments to state-enforced social justice. The personalities and policies differed radically. Some of the policy proposals seemed to come from deep conviction, others seemed to more directly involve a cynical constituency construction. Conviction and construction combined in each case.

It is striking how public discourse, reported in newspapers and journals and on radio and television, focused on the cynicism, on the constituency appeals, and not on reasoned debate between those with opposing opinions. In the 1984 presidential primaries,

Mondale appealed to "compassion" and the particular concerns of blacks, trade unionists, teachers, and others, and Hart called for "new ideas" and railed against special interests. Important differences and judgments seemed suggested by their alternative slogans, but they could not be discerned precisely. The dimensions of the problem became clear in the Reagan-Mondale presidential debates. Reasoned political discourse was notably absent. Little political interaction could be observed. All that existed were cynical candidate appeals to broaden their constituencies. Reagan's statements all seemed to be to the "left" of Mondale's. Mondale purposely positioned himself toward the right. Reagan was soft on communism, according to Mondale. Reagan emphasized the expansion of welfare spending under his administration. This is the language of mass politics, i.e., a language of *cynicism*. Everyone knew Reagan was to the right, so he made leftist statements. Everyone knew Mondale was to the left, so he made rightist statements. Add this to the thirty-second political commercials packaged by those who make cola ads, and the cultural problems of mass politics come into view. Politicians carve out their support from the depoliticized mass. They do not represent socially constituted constituencies.

The demarcation of democratic representative politics and mass politics is both subtle and gross. The politics of the common good, that of the old republican model, emphasized reasoned deliberation, but tended to be elitist. The party politics of the nineteenth and twentieth centuries democratized political institutions. More people participated and the less exalted could lead. But such democratization provided the framework for mass manipulation, most strikingly apparent in recent years. People are called to affirm their prejudices in elections. Political differences are masked by the sentimentalities of prejudice and only partially hidden private interest appeals. Cynicism prevails. The simplest evidence is within the culture of the mass media.

Mass politics forms and is formed by a mass culture. Such culture has developed over a long time. Its social institutions are a response to political and cultural problems raised by democracy, but as a response they represent the most fundamental challenge to democracy's viability. The major problem of mass society is its cynical culture. This culture attacks the reason required for democracy, as is most evident in the conduct of political campaigns. But we must recognize that mass culture is a response to the underlying tensions in democratic ideals and practices.

II

For most of human history, a great deal of cultural life has been closed to large portions of the population. The great works of civilization were products of those at the center and accessible primarily to them. This is most clearly the case in written cultural forms—works of philosophy, science, and poetry. Access to such works depended upon literacy and often knowledge of the esoteric language of letters—e.g., Latin in Europe and Mandarin in China—not the language of daily life. Clearly, then, the culture of the center was extremely remote from those at the periphery.

In the modern age this remoteness has been radically minimized. The terms of this transformation have been both democratic and fundamentally antidemocratic. The spread of literacy and more generally the democratization of cultural life are necessary prerequisites for both the conceptualization and the practice of modern democracy. Yet the way literacy has spread and the terms of popular inclusion into cultural life fundamentally have undermined the realization of modern democracy's promise.

Key to the modern (enlightened) notion of democracy is the idea that the people can know what is in their interests. Advocates of aristocracy and monarchy made their claims, one way or another, on the grounds that governance is a refined craft which can only be successfully practiced by the refined elite or most refined individual. Democracy's answer to this (not generally accepted even in North America until the nineteenth century) is that enlightenment need not be the privilege only of the few. When the populace is properly educated, when it is literate and has access to central cultural works, it governs best because it knows best its own circumstances and prospects. Thus, diminishing the distance between those at the center and those at the peripheries of cultural life is a key to both the theory and practice of democracy. The mode of inclusion, and especially pseudo-participation, significantly complicates these matters.

Here C. Wright Mills's strong distinction between mass and public life is most compelling; Tocqueville's contrast between democracy as a successful form of governance in America and democracy as a potential prelude to a new tyranny is particularly salient, and the importance of contrasting the reactions of European and American observers of the "coming of the masses" can be drawn upon in a nonreductive manner.

When I opened the preceding chapter, I maintained that in discarding the mass-society critique, contemporary social inquiry has mistaken the facade of the social order for its architecture. By considering the massification of the American cultural realm, I am in a position to demonstrate this. I will interpret Mills's distinction as analytic rather than empirical, and Tocqueville's contrast in terms of continuing underlying propensities, not in apocalyptic terms. I will utilize European reactions to clarify and strengthen an American critical democratic commitment, to replace an American apologetic.

The American apologetic is rooted in American cultural practices and their mass structure. Parsons's sociological theory has been understood as an elaborate ideological justification for American priorities, as has Daniel Bell's notion of "the end of ideology"[11] (which was a coded attack on Marxism and the critics of mass society). Such American ideology is not only a recent phenomenon. It is tied to the emergence of the American mass society and its culture. While democratic political culture is at the center of American experience, it has faced serious challenge in the developing form of a cynically formulated mass culture.

At first, the notion of democracy was not generally accepted. An open rule by society's betters, its "natural aristocracy," in Jefferson's terms, was the ideal. Between the writing of the Declaration of Independence and the Constitution, desirable republicanism and undesirable democracy were distinguished. The goal was to avoid the "rule of the rabble." In Shils's terms, entrance to the center was restricted, and distance between center and periphery was deemed not only inevitable but desirable. A stable social order was assured, based on principles of hierarchy. Political contention, first between the colonials and the colonial power and then among the states and citizens, was about the location and forms of actions within the center. The conflicts between monarchy, aristocracy, and republicanism were about how the elite would govern, according to which principles of action and selection. The issue of independence concerned the location of the center, the breaking away of an old periphery, and the formation of a new center. With the formation of political machines and the developing breakdown in the established colonial hierarchies in the early nineteenth century, democracy as a central value was ascendant. This presented a fundamental challenge to the politics of culture and the culture of politics.

Republicanism based on hierarchy was supported by and was supportive of a finely reasoned political discourse. The most spectacular evidence of this is the subtle seriousness of the *Federalist Papers*. Americans of the twentieth century, if and when they read this classic American contribution to political philosophy, read it with awe.[12] It appeared in New York newspapers as part of a systematic campaign to ratify the Constitution. It was written to convince the voting public. Comparison with late twentieth-century "media campaigns" clearly indicates how far political discourse has declined.

More than decline is involved here. Then, the most literate debated and argued the political issues of the day. These gentlemen at the societal center, as the economic, military, political, cultural, and religious elite, despite occasional humble affectations, led their fellow citizens, according to strict rules of deference and hierarchy. Republican political discourse was the discourse of a political elite.[13] Those on the periphery "naturally" followed. They knew no other way. In fact, they were more a part of things than their counterparts in Europe.

Obviously, between then and now much has happened. The social base of politics is much broader, but the quality of political discourse is much poorer. For those with an elitist bent, democracy itself accounts for the decline. Yet Shils, who as a political conservative would probably agree, provides us with a way to perceive that this is not necessarily the case.

The relationship between the refined center and the periphery proceeded through custom in the eighteenth century. In the twentieth, center and periphery interact through the institutional structures of mass society. People are brought into the center but in a highly mediated fashion. They are brought in according to cynical formula.

When the customs of class privilege no longer led to the natural assumption that reason would fully inform politics, when those of privilege became alarmed that their greatest fear was coming true—republicanism was leading to the rule of the rabble—those in the center responded by attempting to bring to those in the periphery the necessary knowledge of the arts and sciences. Community centers for democratic practical knowledge were established. Lecture circuits were developed so speakers of "practical knowledge" could reach a broad public. Public school education became a broad societal commitment. Land-grant colleges were formed, as were public libraries.[14] All of this and more represented a concerted attempt throughout the nineteenth century on the part of Americans to support democracy through a broadened knowledge of the arts and sciences by the general public. As the distance between center and periphery in the political realm was narrowed through the expansion of the franchise, a similar attempt was made in the cultural realm.

But the way those at the periphery were brought in, involved significant inequalities. The political and literary publics of the eighteenth century were comparatively equalitarian; the broadened democratic public was inequalitarian. In the old elite literary circles, the relationship between writers and readers, between speakers and audience, was relatively symmetrical. Though the writers of the political pamphlets in the revolutionary period, for example, were probably more literate than their readers, the differences in literary knowledge between writers and readers were not that great. They were part of the same cultural world, with shared experiences and knowledge of fundamentals in Protestant theologies and classic and contemporary political theories.[15] With the acceptance of democratic principles in politics and culture, the differences among those who took part in political and cultural life increased. The relation between speaker and audience, and between writer and reader, became ever more asymmetrical. The degree of cultivation of expressive facility and literary knowledge, of interpretive and judgmental capacity, became much greater among speakers and writers in comparison with their audience. Different sorts of institutions were established to address this imbalance. The imbalance presents a twofold challenge. Those who revere the full development of the arts and sciences fear that they will be diluted. Those who know that democracy requires an enlightened citizenry fear that the unequal distribution of knowledge will undermine democracy.

First, consider a note of realistic skepticism. The institutions established to facilitate the participation of the previously excluded public were, no doubt, also established to sustain privileges of the past. When governance as a gentlemanly affair was being questioned through democratization, education and the creation of an American culture necessary for democracy became the preserve in which "gentlemen" (and "ladies") could still assert their symbolic position of superiority in the social order. Those who worked to educate the masses naturally had advantage over them, not only because they were educated and their audiences were not, but also because they could decide what would be brought to the relatively uneducated populace, and how it would be brought. Their control over a scarce resource created a self-interest in maintaining mass concern with cultural matters, while also maintaining an unequal distribution of knowledge of cultural affairs. The complex way such cultural superiority has been used to assert class privilege is a primary concern of cultural sociologists.[16] But much more significant and damaging from the point of view of democratic commitment is that cultural accomplishment may be compromised, and that democratization may be replaced by mass structures.

The cultural public of the old republican hierarchy was a small elite of equals. The cultural public in the democratizing American society was a creation of mediators—people and institutions connecting an ill-informed audience with central cultural products. The mediation over the past two hundred years has not been neutral. Consider the early nineteenth-century case of the lecture circuit at the very beginning of mass mediation.[17]

Initially, the lecture halls were established by community leaders to bring "practical knowledge" to the local citizenry, so that they could function efficiently and contribute to the management of practical affairs. Local elites brought the best American cultural life had to offer to the citizens of cities, towns, and villages. The lectures on topics of foreign travel, politics, philosophy, and ethics opened up new worlds to the citizenry. The lecturers arranged for a series of presentations, going from town to town. In this way, local presentations took on national scope and were reported by major journals and newspapers. A broad network of lecture circuits developed. Decision-making was localized, but the localized decisions added up to a national network of public culture, open to broad segments of the population. By participating in this circuit, major intellectuals of the day, such as Emerson, supported themselves and reached a broad public (particularly broad when compared to the older literary circles). Such public lecturing became one of the primary ways intellectuals supported themselves financially.

We should not overlook the limitations of this democratization. Lectures were chosen by community leaders—essentially the representatives of the old elites in Shils's center. Yet, those at the periphery were beginning to take part. This nationalized network was both a great accomplishment and a looming threat. As accomplishment, it represented Mills's ideal of a large-scale democratic public. He observes, "in the community of publics, discussion is the ascendant means of communication, and mass media . . . simply enlarge and animate discussion, linking one *primary public* with the discussions of another." But this very idealized structure also fostered the development of Mills's notion of the public's opposite—mass media and audience. Mills continues: "In a mass society, the dominant type of communication is the formal media, and the pub-

lics become mere media markets."[18] In the lecture circuit, the
nationalized network became a formal medium.

At first, lectures were booked by local elites. But when the lecture
circuit was firmly established, a new vocation emerged, that of the
nineteenth-century media agent. The agents saw a potential way to
greatly enlarge the income of the most popular lecturers and by taking a percentage, to enrich themselves. They booked lecturers in
localities, renting public halls at a good price. They provided enlarged audiences for their clients. They created large "media
markets" for lecturers, rationalizing the contact between speaker
and audience. Though the lectures did not radically change, at least
at first, there was significant local resistance. Local elites were challenged by the new arrangements. They no longer defined,
controlled access to, and profited from practical culture. It was taken
from their hands. All they did was rent halls.

More was involved than a shift in political and economic power.
Those who witnessed the change knew that the primary concern of
the agents would be to maximize their profits, not to satisfy particular needs for cultural enrichment. The ideal of democratic practical
knowledge, they foresaw, would yield to lectures as entertainments. More people would take part, but lectures appealing to the
broadest of audiences, as perceived and constructed by the agents,
would prevail in the "lecture market." In our terms, democratic
culture recedes and a mass culture prevails.

We observe in the position and actions of the media agents, then,
a new social role, and the beginnings of a fundamental transformation in the social relation between center and periphery. In the
lecture circuit as it first emerged, those on the periphery were
brought into the center by the localized elites who took part in central cultural life. The central values of culture and republicanism
informed the process of inclusion. With the ascendancy of the
agents, they specialized in the inclusion. They linked the product of
the center—the lecture—with the audience. Profiting from the linkage, they were less concerned with both the audience and the
product. As such, the agent of the lecture circuit is the nineteenth-
century precursor of the industry of mass culture in the twentieth
century. Both the agent and the industry institutionalize cynicism in
the social and cultural order.

Note that the ideals of culture and the democratic public are not
necessarily destroyed by the changed cultural relations. They simply become secondary—of less importance to the media agent than

the linkage between audience and cultural product. Mass culture and the ideals of democratic culture coexist (in tension) within cultural institutions such as the mediated lecture circuit.

The American apologetic identifies such mediated culture with democracy itself. It does not critically examine the effects of mediation. The European critics, such as those of the Frankfurt school, dogmatically assert that the negative effects of mediation are overwhelming. Critical inquiry and informed democratic action should investigate, make judgments, and act reasonably.

To do so requires an understanding that mass society and its culture are real. Mediated mass culture has been perfected over a long period; it coexists with the ideals of democracy and culture, as the underside of democratization. To identify the two is a fundamental theoretical and political mistake.

III

The mistake, as we observed, is common to the left and right and to European and American intellectual traditions. By failing to examine the workings of cultural institutions, such commentators confuse democracy and culture with their opposites.

The logic of a mediated mass culture structures our world much more than it did when mass culture first emerged as a threatening underside of democratization. Now, the social structure of cultural life is the same as in the nineteenth-century lecture circuit. Those on the peripheries are brought into the center, not by central authorities, but by the mediators. But by facilitating inclusion, they restructure the cultural order. The mediating function is one of the major social practices in our society.

Such diverse commentators as C. Wright Mills and Edward Shils, indeed almost all observers of mass society, explain that it is a consequence of size and complexity. Mediated culture allows for public access to cultural life in a rational fashion. Without mediation, there would be chaos, with too many "speakers" addressing masses of people who do not know how to listen. Mediators, from book-club directors to TV network executives, link cultural products to their appropriate cultural audiences. The crucial issue is how the mediating activity creates specific audiences and specific cultural products to the exclusion of others which may have developed. Is the mediation fulfilling cultural or democratic ideals, or some other system of values?

This problem is a pressing one. A most interesting and crucial example is our practices of reading and writing. More people are writing, buying, and reading literature than ever before in American history. Yet the relationship between reading and writing is not a simple one. Ideally, we imagine a liberal model of the literary order. Writers write books, stories, essays, theses, for the reading public. These works are received and appraised, and those with the greatest worth gain the greatest reputation and the most serious attention. We may recognize that some readers' appraisals are more important than others—e.g., editors, critics, and experts. Their judgments help the less-informed discern what is worth considering. But we imagine with the free exchange of ideas, worthy literary works will receive public attention. Realistically, we must very critically appraise the liberal model. Specifically, we must consider how certain mediators create types of literature as well as literary audiences.

IV

The *New Yorker* magazine presents a certain type of writing.[19] It is highly refined, "upscale," descriptive, moderate in its politics and religion, rather prudish. The writing, along with the design of its production copy, intentionally appeal to a specific range of readers, the very same people who are potential consumers for the goods and services advertised in the magazine. Of all the possible readers of serious poetry, fiction, and essays which the *New Yorker* certainly does publish, wealthy consumers are the ones most important to the magazine's continued existence and profitability. Knowing this, many of the magazine's writers and staff vigorously protested changes in its management practices, when it was bought up by the Newhouse conglomerate. The fear was that the mediation between writing and reading accomplished by the *New Yorker* (i.e., the audience it creates for good writing and good consuming) would be oriented primarily toward profitability, compromising literary excellence. This is an instance of a fundamental struggle against mass culture.

The *New Yorker* is far from a perfect magazine. Its sophistication represents a challenge to writers. On the one hand, the magazine pays relatively well and reaches a large audience in comparison with other publications of refined writing. On the other hand, it is an editor's magazine. There is a *New Yorker* style, which is certainly not the only way to write. Yet if writers want to reach the broad *New Yorker* audience, they must not only accept the editorial changes of the *New*

Yorker; in order to have works even considered, they must write in the required style.

The *New Yorker* editors know who makes up their audience and what they expect to read. Even if a writer imagines a different way to reach the same audience, it is unlikely that this would be acceptable by the *New Yorker*. Some sensibilities, the very critical and the very pessimistic, some approaches, the philosophical and the analytic, and some topics, the erotic and the esoteric, are lost to the broad public because of this. Indeed important works are not even being written as a consequence. Writers self-censor themselves, knowing the *New Yorker* today provides one of the very few forums reaching a broad, intelligent audience. They will produce what the editors want in hopes of reaching that audience.

This situation represents a fundamental challenge to cultural freedom.[20] Certain cultural traditions could be silenced, e.g., the tradition of the philosophically sophisticated public intellectual.[21] Would the *New Yorker* publish John Dewey? Certain publics may not develop a self-identity, the intelligent reading public may be replaced by the upscale reading audience. Are the potential readers of today's John Dewey the same as the *New Yorker*'s audience? And, as already suggested, certain works may never be written. Are the criteria for a good short story or philosophical essay the same as the criteria for a good *New Yorker* story or essay?

Yet, the challenge these questions suggest has more to do with the absence of many significant alternatives to the *New Yorker* than with problems with the magazine. It has more to do with the overall structure of cultural life. The worlds of painting, poetry, dance, film, theater, politics, and more are seriously presented by the magazine to a broad audience. The problems the magazine faces and creates, as described thus far, are the problems of a contemporary democratic culture, amplified because mass-culture outlets overwhelm outlets for serious cultural work.

The problem of mass culture arises when the process of mediation dominates the culture for extracultural purposes. I use the awkward phrase "extracultural purposes" instead of marketing or capitalist purposes because politics as well as economics can transform cultural worlds, in the United States to some degree, but especially in totalitarian orders of the left and the right.[22] In the United States, though, mass mediation primarily serves market and capitalist relations.[23] This was the case of the "media agents" for the nineteenth-century lecturers. The *New Yorker* staff appropriately is concerned with the cynical bottom-line mentality of corporate America.

The *New Yorker* is a highly successful magazine. It gains its primary revenues from advertising. Sociologically, this means it sells commercial access to its audience. The staff is concerned that the new management will change editorial policy in hopes of making its audience more attentive to advertisers. There are two ways this might be accomplished: by making the writing more "readable," i.e., more easily understood by a broader audience; or by shaping the contents of the magazine more to economic and political elites, less to cultural elites. A specialized readership of more likely consumers or a broader readership of consumers both would serve the magazine's "profitability." In the case of the *New Yorker*, given its success, neither strategy is likely to be pursued. Despite this, the staff rightly understands the potential dangers of an intensified cultural cynicism.

To perceive the dangers, consider briefly *People* magazine and *U.S.A. Today.* In these publications, we observe the epitome of cynical culture. They are clearly business enterprises, creating copy to create readerships to sell to advertisers. Little else matters. Both publications are innovative, intentionally turning TV audiences into readerships, using TV marketing techniques and cultural forms. Fragmented short bits of information, homogenized to appeal to people from all regions of the United States and all classes, following highly standardized formats, using repetition of presentation and color to create an attractive familiarity, make up this magazine and this newspaper. The mediation is their message, or at least their primary purpose. A mass audience is created, but it is a modern market, not in any way a democratic cultural public. Cultural products are presented, but these products are means to ends. Like prime-time TV programs, which have as their main purpose gaining the attention of large groups of people so that they will view and be persuaded by commercials, these are vehicles for creating potential consumers. Directed primarily to selfish concerns of individuals as consumers, such newspapers, magazines, and television programs instruct their readers and viewers in exactly the sort of selfish individualism that Tocqueville feared would lead us from democracy to tyranny.

V

Here we face the central dilemma of our mass society. It is through exactly such cynical cultural forms that the fundamental contours of political and economic life are defined. Today the mediators of mass culture shape practically all components of our social order to the point that what is on or in the mass media is the real, i.e., it appears to have a primary claim to truth and reality in an age of relativism. Such diverse activities as international diplomacy, domestic political contestation, and even serious intellectual debates are conducted through and gain a reality in the mass media.

When Anwar Sadat sought to transform Arab-Israeli relations, he did so not through diplomatic channels but through American television. He gave an interview suggesting a changed approach, and then, before his trip to Israel, the preliminaries of changed relations between Egypt and Israel were explored and publicly aired on TV. Though contact between Israel and an Arab head of state, King Hussein of Jordan, in fact, had occurred previously, the televised diplomatic exploration and then the visit to Jerusalem made such contact a social reality for all those who supported and opposed it.

If something appears on television, it is real as a consequence. The diversity of political opinion in newspapers, magazines, specialized journals, and books in the United States is rich and broad. The publication of an opinion broadly at odds with White House policy rarely elicits an official response. But when critical opinion or reporting implying criticism is aired on network television, the response over the last twenty years has been immediate and severe. It has been reported that Lyndon Johnson realized he lost the battle for the hearts and minds of the American public concerning the war in Vietnam when Walter Cronkite presented a series of reports strongly suggesting the war was not proceeding as official accounts purported. Jimmy Carter clearly lost his hold on the presidency when Americans were reminded each day on TV how many days "America [had been] held hostage." The Irangate scandal undermined Ronald Reagan's authority more than any other episode during his presidency. But when it turned out that one of the chief agents of the scandalous policy, Colonel Oliver North, played well on television, Reagan's popularity rebounded.

When opinion is divided on political issues and when partisan leaders compete, the battle must appear on television for it to have consequence. But the battles fought are the battles most effectively presented on television. Though there were serious differences between George Bush and Michael Dukakis, concerning such issues as armaments, foreign and domestic policy, and approaches to problems of the family, education, the judiciary, and the environment, these intelligent men did not confront each other primarily on their differences during their campaign. Rather, each cynically competed to associate himself more directly with attractive media symbols.

Each sought to be tough, forthright, manly. The concern was with TV "media" image more than with political issues, judgment, or orientation, even when serious issues were raised. Each candidate questioned his opponent's honesty. For Bush, Dukakis's position on military matters was not debated but dismissed. According to Bush, Dukakis did not really believe what he was saying. He was just trying to mask his true dovish beliefs. Likewise, for Dukakis, Bush's speeches on the environment were not to be taken seriously. They were represented as an election-year conversion, attempts at trying to hide the Reagan administration's anti-environmental record. A confrontation between opposing views became competing media performances, more or less appealing, more or less believable. The former governor of California, Edmund G. Brown, Jr., a Democrat, while expressing concern over the quality of the election, explained that the Democrats were reticent in addressing difficult issues because their positions are more complicated and difficult to communicate to the electorate.[24] This may be the case, but it simply documents most dramatically the great cynical divide that separates us from the Federalists and Anti-Federalists, who published debates and appeals to the electorate which were not only very complicated and carefully reasoned, but stand as classics in the history of political theory. Media demands and mass appeals now primarily constitute our political culture and discourse, not reasoned democratic excellence.

And when men and women of reason attempt to break out of the TV media bind, they too only get public attention through the mass media. They become intellectual celebrities or they are ignored. Media pundits replace essayists. Instead of journals of arts, letters, and politics, there are TV "magazines" and talk shows. The most widely read books are written by celebrities of film and TV or the occasional intellectual or artist who joins them on the talk-show book-promotion circuit. Serious intellectual reflection continues to exist, of course, but it is becoming a specialized market, along with surfing, skiing, and gourmet cooking, consistently not reaching a general public. And on one of the rare occasions when serious discussion does reach the general public, it does so through the logic of mediation which, as we have observed, threatens to overwhelm the distinctiveness of reason in the nation's newspapers.

Shouting, partisan, talking heads are replacing the pluralistic search for the common good. To understand the nature and dimension of the threat, we must reconsider mass society and its culture as facts of contemporary life. We must strongly distinguish democracy

and culture from their opposites. The theoretical task is to illuminate the distinction as it concretely manifests itself in ongoing
political and cultural life. The practical task is to strengthen democracy and culture, especially as they are mutually supportive. In the
remaining chapters of this inquiry, we will engage in the theoretical
task and consider instances of the practical one, so that a living but
embattled American tradition of democratic culture may be appreciated and extended. We now turn to a consideration of recent
attempts to account for the decline of our democratic culture, and,
implicitly, the rise of cynicism.

F I V E

The Decline and Fall
of American Culture?

Allan Bloom, E. D. Hirsch, Jr., and Russell Jacoby are oddities. They have reached broad publics, as they seriously critique elements of cultural cynicism. This is significant for two reasons (at least). Their writings themselves illuminate pressing problems, and the size of their publics indicates a broad awareness of the problem. The works of Bloom, Hirsch, and Jacoby are part of the solution in that they have stimulated public debate about serious matters, contrary to the usual state of affairs. But they are also part of the problem in that their specific formulations of the problem (especially Bloom's and Hirsch's) include cynical mass appeals. Here we untangle their contributions from their confusions.

I

Bloom, Hirsch, and Jacoby concur—American culture is in decline. They agree on little else. Bloom's sense of decline emanates from a very conservative, even reactionary sensibility, bemoaning the twilight of a golden age, a primordial utopia. E. D. Hirsch's sense of a Fall is coupled with hopefulness—if students study his required lists. His is a tale of fall and rise. Jacoby presents a more complex story. He mourns the lost world of our (intellectual) fathers (and mothers?), disappointed by his peers and colleagues, but he also attempts to explain how the intellectual loss is connected to changing material conditions. From a sociological point of view, his is the most serious approach.

His *The Last Intellectuals*,[1] like Hirsch's *Cultural Literacy*[2] and Bloom's *The Closing of the American Mind*,[3] can easily be caricatured and in my judgment too readily dismissed. Though these are works which are fundamentally flawed by excess, cynically designed to reach a mass audience, they do highlight enduring cultural problems, too often overlooked by more moderate commentators and more disciplined scholars. Each of these works in highly idiosyncratic ways explodes current cultural clichés and calls for deliberate discussion. As we have observed, such discussion must address the problematic relationship between culture and democracy as one of the central dilemmas in the American tradition of politics and culture.

Bloom most explicitly addresses the issue, as he is also the most cynical. His is a study of "How Higher Education Has Failed Democracy and Impoverished the Souls of Today's Students." He ranges broadly, defining his primordial utopia. The good cultural life, for Bloom, was and ought to be personally experienced. He nostalgically remembers his initiation into the world of ideas, his awe and sense of excitement, and regrets that his students do not experience the world as he did. The seriousness and power of the Western tradition seem to have been lost to them. Instead of the pursuit of truth, there is an adolescent certainty that all is uncertain.

Bloom laments the banality of popular culture, denounces feminism and the black-power movement, criticizes the "Germanization" of American social sciences and the "Nietzscheanization" of the American left, and deplores the personal narcissism of his students and the decadence of love and friendship in our society. But most of all, he rages against relativism. In his mind, American society and especially its universities have shamefully contributed to a decline in standards and a loss of the pursuit of truth, which was the great legacy of Western civilization. And now only an "I'm okay, you're okay" mentality remains.

Judgments of Bloom's essay have been primarily based on political prejudice and cultural sensibility. From Saul Bellow, who wrote the foreword, to William Buckley, Jr., the media arbiter of things elitist, conservatives approve. Bloom recognizes the symptoms of decline and he defends enduring Western accomplishments. For those on the left, this is not only a defense of privilege, its form represents a self-parody. Robert Paul Wolff has gone so far as to review Bloom and his book as if they were creations of Bellow's demonic irony.[4]

The lack of seriousness in Bloom's defenders and critics is, no doubt, a reflection of Bloom's own writing. He is cranky and prejudiced. He declares rather than reasons. He presents his readings of politics and culture as correct; those who disagree are ignorant and worse. He gives us a grand reading of the history of ideas, with many flaws in the details—from his reading of the classics and social sciences to his interpretation of the politics of the 1960s. However, and this reservation is most important, he has clearly illuminated a profound cultural problem that resonates with a broad public. "The souls of our students" are impoverished, if we take the pompous phrase to mean that there is a crisis in modern (American) culture, and Americans know it. Bloom, Hirsch, and Jacoby, taken together, point to the dimensions of the crisis, while they ignore the fundamental causes.

Bloom highlights the problems of relativism and the reductionism of social science, under the shadows of mass culture. At times this may seem pretty silly. From a position of cultural contempt, he observes Mick Jagger:

> Mick Jagger. A shrewd, middle-class boy, he played the possessed lower-class demon and teen-aged satyr up until he was forty, with one eye on the mobs of children of both sexes whom he stimulated to a sensual frenzy and the other eye winking at the unerotic, commercially motivated adults who handled the money. In his act he was male and female, heterosexual and homosexual; unencumbered by modesty, he could enter everyone's dreams, promising to do everything with everyone; and, above all, he legitimated drugs, which were the real thrill that parents and policemen conspired to deny his youthful audience. He was beyond the law, moral and political, and thumbed his nose at it. Along with all this, there were nasty little appeals to the suppressed inclinations toward sexism, racism and violence, indulgence in which is not now publicly respectable. Nevertheless, he managed not to appear to contradict the rock ideal of a universal classless society founded on love, with the distinction between brotherly and bodily blurred. He was the hero and the model for countless young persons in universities, as well as elsewhere. I discovered that students who boasted of having no heroes secretly had a passion to be like Mick Jagger, to live his life, have his fame.[5]

This passage reveals Bloom's position precisely. Note how the writing form is a mockingly cynical posture. He does not really consider Mick Jagger as a cultural figure, musician and hero, nor does he analyze the contradictions of the mass-culture industry and its construction of celebrity status. Rather, he belittles the concerns of youth in the name of a privileged virtue.

Earlier Bloom observed that his students, when asked, could not name a hero whom they emulated. Then he observes that though Mick Jagger goes unnamed because it is not fashionable to have heroes, he is the hero of the young. "Mick Jagger played the role in their lives that Napoleon played in the lives of ordinary young Frenchmen throughout the 19th century."[6] Here Americans do indeed seem impoverished and the consequences seem great. Instead of a man of military genius who changed the political world, they emulate a rock musician who sings songs with questionable musical and moral value. And, things even get worse, according to Bloom:

> My concern here is not with the moral effect of this music—whether it leads to sex, violence or drugs. The issue here is its effect on education, and I believe it ruins the imagination of young people and makes it very difficult for them to have a passionate relationship to the art and thought that are the substance of liberal education. The first sensuous experiences are decisive in determining the taste for the whole of life, and they are the link between the animal and the spiritual in us. The period of nascent sensuality has always been used for sublimation, in the sense of making sublime, for attaching youthful inclinations and longings to music, pictures and stories that provide the transition to the fulfillment of the human duties and the enjoyment of the human pleasures.[7]

Even though the sentiment expressed here is repugnant to me as a "child of the 60s" who attempts to sensitively teach students of the nineties, I maintain that we must recognize that these are important points, which must be seriously considered. Refined sensibilities are important for the fate of a civilization and for the success of a democratic society. It very well may be the case that wasting time with the banalities of mass culture distracts attention from and undermines an appreciation of great cultural works of past and present. Further, in that democracy requires the general enlightenment of the people if their rule is to be reasonable, the shaping of minds by mass-consumer culture does seem to fundamentally undermine democratic practice. Now we choose presidents as we choose our rock stars, as we choose designer jeans. The challenge to democracy and culture is indeed great.

And Bloom does address the challenge. He understands that the university and the education of students should be insulated from the business of daily affairs. The university should supply an alternative to the lessons drawn from the struggles for sustenance and the pursuit of consumer goods. The university should introduce its students to the great debates about the good, the beautiful, and the true. Yet, for all but the most committed conservative or Straussian,[8]

Bloom makes these points oddly. He believes the logic of today's daily life is the logic of democracy. His notion of philosophic reflections, both general and specialized in the particular arts and sciences, seems to be the purview of an elitist, almost secret, society. Nonetheless, he shows clearly that the university ought to be a special place. The issue is how to constitute, support, and defend this special place.

When stripped of posturing and prejudices, Bloom's position is both simple and important. American higher education and scholarship are not sufficiently self-consciously grounded in the great tradition of Western inquiry. Education and scholarship in America are challenged by an imported German nihilism, a native democratic ethos, and the false promises of the modern Enlightenment. The nihilism comes in the form of the antidemocratic traditions of Nietzsche and Weber, as they have transformed our understanding and practice of politics in the names of realism and the natural. Thus reasonable politics seems impossible. The democratic ethos as it questions distinctions among people, also undermines significant distinctions among cultural artifacts. Thus, cultural refinement is insecure, as Tocqueville maintained. The Enlightenment promises that a realistic politics, true to and based on human nature, can create a new democratic culture superior to aristocratic decadence. Thus, a privileged place for reason and culture may be lost. Bloom forcefully maintains that Weber and Nietzsche, as well as Marx, Dewey, and Rousseau, mislead. We must go back to the ancients to overcome the modern philosophical crisis.

This much is the well-known position of Bloom's teacher, Leo Strauss. Bloom's innovation is to articulate the position in the shadows of the culture and politics of the sixties. Feminism, black power and student radical movements of the late sixties and early seventies are treated with intense ridicule and contempt in Bloom's text. His account of the fate of Western civilization is very much filtered through his personal experiences in the sixties, particularly at Cornell University. The shocking events of western New York State reveal for Bloom the dimensions of the decline of the West. As Saul Bellow's hero in *The Dean's December* gives the reader a philosophic and comparative political distance for interpreting the state of urban culture and race relations when he thinks about Chicago while visiting East Central Europe,[9] Bloom's philosophic concerns are enlivened through the things he saw and heard at Cornell and his conviction that they have had lasting effects. As with a great deal of social, political, and cultural theories in the last two decades,

Bloom's work is a theoretical reflection on and critique of the 60s.

For Bloom the sixties are summarized in one event. During the campus unrest, black students at Cornell not only engaged in the prevailing theatrics of "non-negotiable demands" for black separatism, separate dorms, cultural centers, and academic programs, at the height of the confrontation they brandished guns and threatened the lives of individual professors when making their demands. The university reacted timidly, accommodating the protesters rather than steadfastly defending the law and the academy. "The professors, the repositories of our best traditions and highest intellectual aspirations, were fawning over what was nothing better than a rabble, publicly confessing their guilt and apologizing for not having understood the most important issues, the proper response to which they were learning from the mob; expressing their willingness to change the university's goals and the content of what they taught."[10] It is this conviction which animates Bloom's cultural critique. Its rhetorical power is compelling, but its narrowness of vision undermines his criticism.

The narrowness is primarily a consequence of his dogmatic understanding of the Western tradition and its powers. He has in mind not only a very select, very Western, very male, and very white tradition of great works, he presents us with a limited interpretation of the significance of the Western tradition. Understanding great works in their historical contexts is dismissed as historicism (a minor relativistic disorder), attempting to reinterpret great works in terms of the present is a sort of adolescent blasphemy. Bloom writes:

> Imagine . . . a young person walking though the Louvre or the Uffizi, and you can immediately grasp the condition of his soul. In his innocence of the stories of Biblical and Greek or Roman antiquity, Raphael, Leonardo, Michelangelo, Rembrandt and all the others can say nothing to him. All he sees are colors and forms—modern art. In short, like almost everything else in his spiritual life, the paintings and statues are abstract. No matter what much of modern wisdom asserts, these artists counted on immediate recognition of their subjects, what is more, on their having a powerful meaning for their viewers. The works were the fulfillment of those meanings, giving them a sensuous reality and hence completing them. Without those meanings, and without their being something essential to the viewer as a moral, political and religious being, the works lose their essence.[11]

As for his fellow Straussian Judge Robert Bork, for Bloom works must be interpreted according to their original intent. Here he clearly, if unintentionally, reveals the limitations of his approach. The complexities and profound spiritual qualities of modern art are not recognized. The value of viewing the history of art from the viewpoint of the twentieth century is dismissed. That a student might be able to do this is not celebrated but condemned.

E. D. Hirsch, Jr., views these things differently. Hirsch shares with Bloom a concern for the preservation of a common (Western) culture, but he is much less dogmatic about what the works should be and what we should get from them. His notion of "what every American needs to know" is, in fact, quite minimalistic, and his project is pragmatically democratic. Whereas Bloom sees the crisis in American culture as a manifestation of lost elite skills, Hirsch is concerned with the American everyman. Bloom focuses his attention on the intellectual life of the great universities; Hirsch concerns himself primarily with secondary students. Bloom laments the loss of esoteric skills. Hirsch pragmatically proposes educational reform for the general population. In the final analysis, Bloom condemns democratic influence while Hirsch's modest proposal is for cultural reform in support of a democratic society. It is therefore somewhat startling that the work of Hirsch and Bloom have been received as mutually supportive.

William Bennett, when secretary of education, praised Hirsch's book as crucial to the reform of "what goes on in our nation's classrooms." And upon Bennett's retirement as secretary of education, he formed a private educational foundation with Bloom. It, therefore, appears, at least for the politically observant, that though Hirsch's book is on fundamental schooling for the bulk of the population while Bloom's is about elite universities for the privileged few, their positions may be two sides of the cultural transformation of the Reagan era, as personified by the former secretary of education and chairman of the National Endowment for the Humanities. Yet Mr. Bennett's actions have been inconsistent, dictated more by cynical partisanship than scholarship. For him, educational reform means privatization, discipline, and less federal funds. All attacks on progressive education (and its expense) are ammunition for political battles. Since Bloom and Hirsch attack progressive education, they can both be supported. But since their criticisms are motivated by fundamentally opposing principles, and the objects of their attacks are fundamentally different, this support makes little theoretical sense. It is more sensible to appreciate that their political commitments and cultural sensibilities differ, while they are appraising two dimensions of the same problem—the crisis in American culture. For Bloom the greatest significance is the challenge the crisis poses for the elite; for Hirsch, the challenge is a democratic one. Both seek a common culture to resolve the crisis.

II

Hirsch opens his inquiry by defining cultural literacy as a necessary condition for full citizenship in the modern world. He declares:

> To be culturally literate is to possess the basic information needed to thrive in the modern world. The breadth of that information is great, extending over the major domains of human activity from sports to science. It is by no means confined to "culture" narrowly understood as an acquaintance with the arts. Nor is it confined to one social class. Quite the contrary. Cultural literacy constitutes the only sure avenue of opportunity for disadvantaged children, the only reliable way of combating the social determinism that now condemns them to remain in the same social and educational condition as their parents. That children from poor and illiterate homes tend to remain poor and illiterate is an unacceptable failure of our schools, one which has occurred not because our teachers are inept but chiefly because they are compelled to teach a fragmented curriculum based on faulty educational theories. Some say that our schools by themselves are powerless to change the cycle of poverty and illiteracy. I do not agree. They *can* break the cycle, but only if they themselves break fundamentally with some of the theories and practices that education professors and school administrators have followed over the past fifty years.[12]

For many people, especially the economically disadvantaged, the rudimentary information needed for participation in public life is lacking, according to Hirsch. Cultural illiterates, in Hirsch's sense, do not know enough about the economic, political, and cultural worlds to compete in the marketplace or engage in political deliberations. It is not that they necessarily lack intelligence. They lack knowledge about the fundamental components of a common culture.

Hirsch's central concern is not with the domain of esoteric knowledge. Rather, it is with fundamental cultural, particularly linguistic, ability. His concern does not primarily focus on expertise—the advanced specialized knowledge we as a nation must master in order to survive in the age of high-tech. He is concerned with the basic components of cultural life. The components are understood as being part of a language. Just as one must know the referent of the word "orange" to speak about a painting, one must know some fundamental phrases concerning our cultural world to be in a full sense a citizen taking part in conversations in social life. One cannot act politically, for example, without knowing what the phrase "New Deal" refers to. One must know the names Richard Nixon and Thomas Paine; have some idea what NATO and the PLO are. Hirsch underscores that a citizen need not know much about such programs, organizations, and persons, but he or she must know at least vaguely their referents.

Although he is not cited by Hirsch, George Herbert Mead's theoretical investigations of social behavior and symbolic interaction lend significant support to Hirsch's position.[13] Mead proposes that we understand the socialization of the individual into a society as being a process of adopting the attitudes of the other towards the self. One learns who one is and how one is supposed to act by fulfilling the expectations of others. Further, one fits into the society and understands how the society works as a whole by understanding the expectations people share. Such understanding is achieved through symbolic exchange. The words "police officer" (and the person) symbolically constitute a system of social control and action. In such a way words and symbols regulate and provide a framework for social action.

What Hirsch argues is that we must share symbols and the expectations and understandings which surround them in order to act effectively in our community and society. When certain spheres of life require knowledge of certain symbols and people lack them, both the societal sphere and the people suffer—the sphere because of the noise the ignorant create, either using the appropriate symbols without understanding, or by using the inappropriate symbols. The people suffer because they act in a state of constant bewilderment, without the resources to pursue either self-interests or the common good. Consider the view that the language and meaning of the Declaration of Independence, the Bill of Rights and civil liberties in general are subversive and un-American. People who hold this view, based upon a misunderstanding of our political constitution, can more easily be deprived of their rights and deprive others of their rights.

Hirsch delineates a long list of key words that a culturally literate person should know. This has subjected him to easy ridicule. He seems to argue that all one must do to be culturally literate is to be vaguely familiar with his list of dates, names, places, movements, ideas and works, from *abolitionism* to *Old Mother Hubbard* to *Zeitgeist*. Satirists suggest that his notion of a proper education would be the study of the definitions on his list. But if we keep in mind the Meadian framework, it should be clear that his educational ideal and his cultural critique are actually much more serious.

Since he emphasized the importance of shared knowledge of meaning for successful social, political, cultural, and economic practice, education must disseminate this important knowledge. Here Hirsch launches a frontal attack on progressive education. The chief object of the attack is John Dewey, with passing barbs thrown at Jean-Jacques Rousseau.

In Hirsch's rather odd reconstruction of the history of ideas, Rousseau and Dewey make up a modern progressive school of educational thought, which emphasizes the process of learning over the object of learning, i.e., its cultural content. Hirsch ignores the important differences between Dewey, the American pragmatist, and Rousseau, a representative thinker of the European Enlightenment. Rousseau's central concern with the natural is quite different from Dewey's focus on practical knowledge and knowledge through practical action. For Hirsch, they are identified because both seem to deemphasize educational content. Clearly Dewey and Rousseau are serving primarily rhetorical purposes in Hirsch's argument. He is positioning himself along with Bloom and Bennett against modern education. But such cynical positioning, while it attracts attention and provides ammunition for various educational fundamentalists, confuses Hirsch's argument, which ultimately is quite pragmatic and liberal. He is arguing not for a literary canon to conservatively assert status distinction, but for a cultural common ground which makes a democratic social and political reality possible.

He cogently argues on pragmatic grounds that a democratic politics is predicated upon cultural literacy. He observes:

> Illiterate and semiliterate Americans are condemned not only to poverty, but also to the powerlessness of incomprehension. Knowing that they do not understand the issues, and feeling prey to manipulative oversimplifications, they do not trust the system of which they are supposed to be the masters. They do not feel

themselves to be active participants in our republic, and they often do not turn out to vote. The civic importance of cultural literacy lies in the fact that true enfranchisement depends upon knowledge, knowledge upon literacy, and literacy upon cultural literacy.[14]

He approvingly cites Jefferson, who asserted:

Were it left to me to decide whether we should have a government without newspapers, or newspapers without a government, I should not hesitate a moment to prefer the latter. But I should mean that every man should receive those papers and be capable of reading them.[15]

Hirsch underscores the importance of the capability which is often dropped from this much-cited quote. He, then, is following the great Jeffersonian tradition in emphasizing the literacy that is necessary for democratic politics. Further, he very much is an American pragmatist, following Mead (and Dewey) in pointing out that the requisite literacy requires a basic knowledge of a common world of cultural discourse.

The concern with the common world can easily be confused with Bloom's call for a canon, especially since Hirsch, like Bloom, emphasizes the need for a standardized language,[16] the formation of a local high culture[17] and the importance of imparting nationalist values.[18] But it must be kept in mind that for the conservative Bloom, the standard language, high culture, and nationalism serve a comfortable elite. For Hirsch they are means to a democratic end, not only political but also social.

Hirsch points out the centrality of cultural literacy for social mobility and social democracy. The striking correlation between class, education, and personal success for Hirsch is understood not as an inevitable sociological relationship but a sign of educational failure. Education, in his judgment, should facilitate social mobility and equality. Literacy is a resource for the less advantaged to improve their situation. Without the resource, the improvement is an impossibility.

Literacy must be understood as demanding competence and background information necessary for communicating in a complex industrial society. Hirsch favorably quotes Orlando Patterson:

The people who run society at the macro-level must be literate in this culture. For this reason, it is dangerous to overemphasize the problems of basic literacy or the rele-

vancy of literacy to specific tasks, and more constructive
to emphasize that blacks will be condemned in per-
petuity to oversimplified, low-level tasks and will never
gain their rightful place in controlling the levers of
powers unless they also acquire literacy in this wider cultural sense.[19]

Patterson, a committed social democrat and critical sociologist,[20]
recognized that in order for subjugated groups to overcome sub-
jugation, both individually and collectively, they must be broadly
familiar with the discourse of the dominant culture. To act otherwise
involves an acquiesence to subordinate roles, "becoming literate to a
specific task," and to political ineffectiveness. Even the most radical
critics of the social order and advocates of the most fundamental
transformations use their cultural literacy as the basis for their positions. Thus Hirsch notes that in the Black Panther party platform,
the Declaration of Independence is quoted verbatim, justifying the
party's position, but only for those who are culturally literate.[21]

Such cultural literacy, Hirsch maintains, is in marked decline. He
blames the supermarket high schools and public schools which in
the pursuit of teaching critical thinking forget about the acquisition
of vital information. Hirsch declares:

> Cafeteria-style education, combined with the unwilling-
> ness of our schools to place demands on students, has
> resulted in a steady diminishment of commonly shared
> information between generations and between young
> people themselves. Those who graduate from the same
> school have often studied different subjects, and those
> who graduate from different schools have often studied
> different material even when their courses have carried
> the same titles. The inevitable consequence of the shop-
> ping mall high school is a lack of shared knowledge
> across and within schools. It would be hard to invent a
> more effective recipe for cultural fragmentation.[22]

With such fragmentation, the democratic educational project is
lost. Hirsch hopes that a concerted effort to create a prescriptive core
body of knowledge will reverse the trend to fragmentation. But the
effort may face much more serious obstacles than Hirsch recognizes.
The problems he analyzes are not simply a consequence of poorly
fragmented educational policies, as he seems to believe. They are
imbedded within the institutional structure of cultural life in America. This is most clearly the case in our universities. Bloom shows us

how their independence has been undermined. Russell Jacoby highlights academic isolation.

III

Academic intellectuals, according to Russell Jacoby, in a major way
contribute to cultural fragmentation. They do this by being isolated,
narrow, overly technical, concerned with career more than intellectual mission, preoccupied with displaying their refinement rather
than communicating their insights to a general public. Jacoby concerns himself particularly with critics of the left who have
abandoned their public role in pursuit of academic careers. His image of the university mirrors Bloom's. Both regret the presence of
leftists at the university—Bloom because of the harm this has done
to the university, Jacoby because of the harmful effects the university
has had on critical intellectual life and its relation with a general
public.

Whereas Bloom is concerned with the elite and esoteric culture,
and Hirsch is concerned with the general population and a common
culture, Jacoby is concerned with bohemia and its critical culture.
He observes a real decline in critical capacity, which opens the cultural field to cynicism. Jacoby tells the nostalgic story of past
heroes—C. Wright Mills, Lionel Trilling, Lewis Mumford, Richard
Hofstadter, Irving Howe, and Edmund Wilson, among others, and
he notes something strange about their successor generation. He
tells us his concern clearly and simply:

> This book is about a vacancy in culture, the absence of
> younger voices, perhaps the absence of a generation. The
> few—extremely few—significant American intellectuals
> under the age of thirty-five, even forty-five, have seldom
> elicited comment. They are easy to miss, especially be-
> cause their absence is longstanding. An intellectual
> generation has not suddenly vanished; it simply never
> appeared. And it is already too late—the generation is
> too old—to show up.[23]

It is Jacoby's blunt thesis that there are no "public intellectuals" of
the younger generation. He maintains that the restructuring of cities, the passing of bohemia, and the expansion of the university are
the primary factors accounting for this new lost generation. His con-
tentions are easily refutable. First we can note the existence of one
younger intellectual or another—Marshall Berman? Richard Flacks?

or Jacoby himself? That they are not household names may have more to do with the structure of publicity than the nature of their writing. We thus may not be as assured as Jacoby that the factors he analyzes as accounting for the apparent disappearance of young critical intellectuals are the most important ones. The dominance of mass culture and the impact of television in political and cultural discourse clearly are not given enough attention in Jacoby's analysis. Jacoby's focus on urban decline, the disappearance of bohemia and the rise of the university seems to be dictated as much by sentiment, nostalgia, and resentment as by empirically informed judgment. He is one of a rare species, an independent scholar unattached to any university. Is his but a highly elaborate defense of a dying breed?

Though there may be some element of truth in such a simple sociology-of-knowledge explanation and though fine individual public intellectuals can be identified, and mass culture's impact is greater than Jacoby recognizes, he does, in my judgment, highlight a major problem facing American democratic culture—the rupture between the most reflective elements of the public and the public itself. He analyzes two dimensions of a three-dimensional problem. He tells us a great deal about changes among intellectuals and the breakdown in the media that facilitated their connections with their publics. He does not consider the transformations of the public into mass audiences and the forces that have structured these transformations.

Jacoby compares the work of three distinct generations of critical intellectuals, those born in the years around 1900, 1920, and 1940. He notes that the careers of these generations represent distinct modes of intellectual life. Those born at the turn of the century "represent classical American intellectuals; they lived their lives by way of books, reviews and journalism. They never or rarely taught in universities. They were superb essayists and graceful writers, easily writing for a larger public."[24] He cites three archetypes: Lewis Mumford, Dwight Macdonald, and Edmund Wilson. He labels the next generation (born around 1920) as transitional. "They grew up writing for small magazines when universities remained marginal; this experience informed their style—elegant and accessible essays directed toward the wider intellectual community. Later in the 1950s, they often accepted university positions, which looked better and better as the nonacademic habitat diminished. . . . In their mastery of public prose they are loyal to their past; in a precise sense they are obsolete."[25] Alfred Kazin, Daniel Bell, and Irving Howe are the primary examples of the transitional generation. Those who were born after 1940 bear "the full weight of academization." For them (us), nonuniversity intellectuals hardly exist:

> To live from selling book reviews and articles ceased to be difficult; it became impossible. The numbers of serious magazines and newspapers steadily declined (and the pay scale of those remaining hardly increased), leaving few avenues; the signs all pointed toward the colleges. If the western frontier closed in the 1890s, the cultural frontier closed in the 1950s. After this decade intellectuals joined established institutions or retrained.[26]

Jacoby observes the beauty of earlier intellectual prose, its political immediacy and intelligibility, and goes on to analyze the erosion of nonacademic intellectual habitats. Cheap apartments in urban centers were lost to the ravages of urban decay and gentrification. The marginal life of the bohemian in cafés was replaced by the academic life of committee meetings and cafeterias. He clearly prefers the former intellectual life on aesthetic grounds, though he does recognize that the transitional generation freely chose the academic life for the security, stability, and comforts it provided. His is a cautious romantic account, he appreciates the style of life and prose of the starving artist, but he understands why, given a free choice, most will (in the language of the romantic) sell out.

But Jacoby is no structural determinist. Though the natural conditions for the bohemian intellectual have been relegated to the dustbin of history, buried under the waste of urban decay, he recognizes that young academics as autonomous agents could conceivably choose the intellectual path of their predecessors. The transitional generation chose to go to the university and maintained a critical, publicly intelligible character. Why hasn't the younger generation? Jacoby does not really have a straightforward answer to this question. He simply observes the sublimated critical impulses. Critique has turned into alternative, established, academic genres— academic Marxism, technically superb new social histories which do not address general publics,[27] radical political economies with jargons which make them useless for the public,[28] critical literary and cultural studies which are not only often based on the dubious notions of linguistic breaks but are written in languages that are impenetrable to all but refined initiates.[29] His is the lament of an old New Leftist.

But the lament itself is its own undoing. Jacoby's romantic account of the "Last Intellectuals" does in fact embody the very qualities he feels have been lost in the age of academe—both the strengths and the weaknesses. He, along with Bloom and Hirsch, presents accessible texts for general audiences. In Jacoby's case, the prose is even elegantly written. These works successfully highlight fundamental problems in American culture. But in that they are each impressionistic, lacking the (academic) discipline of more esoteric studies such as the ones that Jacoby criticizes, they resemble intellectual postures to be bought and sold on the (trade) book market. They are consumed, i.e., bought and read, but their challenges are not easily digested, i.e., understood, refined, and acted upon. They are as much a manifestation of the problems they analyze as a remedy to the problems.

In a fundamental way, Bloom, Hirsch, and Jacoby are all addressing the same problem—the erosion of democracy and cultural excellence with the ascendancy of mass society and its culture. But they each turn away from a direct and careful analysis. Bloom does not distinguish between democracy and mass society. Ultimately, all that is wrong with the world can be blamed on the moderns, without carefully distinguishing between modern horrors (totalitarianism), modern challenges (primarily relativism), modern accomplishments (such as liberalism), and modern dreams (particularly democracy). Each of these "modernisms" is denounced because, Bloom asserts, they undermine the zone for the study of the Great Books, the autonomous university. Though he ridicules particular pieces of mass culture, he does not recognize it as a social systemic challenge to democratic as well as elite practice. As he sees it, democracy is part of the problem. Hirsch and Jacoby, on the other hand, know that the mass media have caused problems. But they simply assert that other factors are more important. For Hirsch, more important are the obvious failures of our public schools. For Jacoby, it is the negative effects of academic life. But Hirsch never asks about the relationship between the schools, the ill-conceived curriculum, and mass social and cultural structures, nor does Jacoby analyze the relationship between these structures and the problems of the university.

Serious discussion of the important problems raised by Bloom, Hirsch, and Jacoby must, in my judgment, start with an analysis of the problems mass society poses. Without such an analysis, these critiques and the responses to them will be received by the public and critical community with a combination of false adulation (as has been the case with the works of Bloom and Hirsch) or cynicism (as has been the case with their professional academic critics). Without studying the mass-society underside of democracy, as Tocqueville and the later critics of mass society would, the whole problematic relationship between democracy and culture necessarily must be confused.

In the final analysis, Bloom, Hirsch, and Jacoby pose questions which they leave unanswered. Bloom asks, is democracy compatible with cultural excellence and autonomy? While his answer must be dismissed as little more than conservative posturing, we must seek a sound theoretical and practical strategy (see Chapter 9). Hirsch asks, how can the common ground which might make democracy and culture mutually supportive, be supported? But while his idea of cultural literacy seems to suggest little more than an upper-middle-class Trivial Pursuit, we must critically appraise how ideological approaches of the left and right have addressed the problems of cultural illiteracy (see Chapters 6, 7, and 8). And Jacoby asks, can public intellectuals raise their voices so that the problems and potentials of our society are discovered and communicated to a general public? To answer this question adequately requires a clear and literate voice such as Jacoby's. But more is needed. Jacoby's questions must be addressed along with Hirsch's and Bloom's as part of a general critique of mass society and its culture. Without such a general critique as the one formulated in Chapter 3, their analyses become but components of a cynical culture, the object of their own criticism. Bloom and his publishers sell him as a celebrity, very much like record producers sell Mick Jagger, and Bloom enjoys the celebrity status.[30] Now there is a new board game modeled after "Trivial Pursuit" entitled "Cultural Literacy." Jacoby has not been so successful in the mass culture game, but because he has not frontally analyzed the dynamics of mass society his cogent observations can be (and have been) dismissed as little more than the complaints of an intellectual excluded from the academy. We should not accept such cynicism.

Ideology and the American Left:
The Pursuit of Obscurity

The cynicism that culturally threatens the prospects for an independent and excellent democratic cultural life emanates, in my view, from two sources. Contrary to Allan Bloom, one of these is not democracy. Contrary to most of his critics, the other is not elitism. The threats are, rather, the cynical manipulation of a mass democracy and the ideologies of new elites. Mass manipulation, as we have already observed, has to do with the *undemocratic* inclusion of the population into central authoritative economic, political, and cultural institutions. Ideology can more profoundly transform the core values of social life. It arises from the problems of mass structures but can directly erode the normative basis of a democratic political and social order.

Ideology is one of those odd modern terms, like totalitarianism and bureaucracy. It implies a great deal, has positive meanings, but it is most often a negative epithet. Its ambiguity suggests it should not be used in careful political and cultural analysis, but its ubiquity suggests it must be. For the purpose of this inquiry, ideology is considered primarily as a distinctive type of political thought, not just any type, as seems to be the supposition of the popular press, especially since the debates between Dukakis and Bush in the 1988 presidential campaign. We will observe in Chapter 9 another secondary referent of the term, as in "ideological critique." This activity, I will attempt to show, is a kind of academic "bad think."

Ideology, deductively, connects a simple rationalized absolute truth (e.g., the history of humanity is a history of class struggles) to a totalized set of political actions and policies (past, present, and future), which are understood as acting upon and realizing the simple truth. In the U.S. it is usually thought that ideology, for the most part, is a kind of cognitive infantilism of the left. Thirty years ago when Daniel Bell announced "the end of ideology," he was referring to the end of such leftist infantilism.[1] He observed that the appeal of

Marxist ideological simplifications no longer made sense to even most leftist intellectuals. Ideological enthusiasm seemed to Bell to have a future only in non-Western societies. Though the reports of the death of ideology were indeed premature, Bell was clearly on to something. Today ideological exhaustion is dramatically apparent in the Second and Third Worlds. Ironically, in right-wing politics and among left-wing academics, ideology is again alive and all too well in America.

In my judgment, Daniel Bell was right: leftist ideological politics were exhausted by the late fifties, but they started anew in the sixties when the New Left reached its limits and the New Right began to ascend. In this chapter we consider the left, showing the ineffectiveness of its ideology in addressing the problems of mass structures. Then we will observe the centrality of a pseudo-counter-revolutionary ideology in the politics of the New Right (Chapter 7) and its institutionalization in the case of education practice (Chapter 8). All of these ideological developments foster a cynicism which has undermined democratic culture. As we will see, ideology both oddly answers the political questions posed by mass society, particularly that of cultural illiteracy, and stimulates increased development of mass structures.

I

The ideological left has always been weak in America. There is not and never has been a significant socialist challenge to American capitalism (at least in comparison to leftist ideological European experiences). To be sure, at the beginning of the century many socialist mayors were elected. Eugene Debs did build a significant national third-party movement, and radical socialist labor unions, most spectacularly the IWW, were broadly supported. But governance did not go beyond localities. The nationwide socialist movement expressed discontent and influenced the major parties but never came close to policy implementation. The radical labor unions which directly challenged capitalism were overshadowed by unions which sought social justice within the context of capitalist relations. There was good reason for the German social democrat and social scientist Werner Sombart to ask his classic question, "Why is there no socialism in the United States?"[2]—even if the question is illogical.

Sombart's question assumes that socialism naturally follows capitalism, and therefore its absence must be explained. But the necessary development of socialism in America was apparent only to those on the peripheries of political and economic life. This, nonetheless, is not the case for intellectuals. Among writers, artists, and scholars, socialism has been very much on the agenda. While there has been no substantial leftist challenge to American capitalism, there have been very significant cultural movements, which have indirectly affected our politics.

In the opening decades of the century, the combination of a large immigrant population, fundamental struggles over workers' rights, and severe economic conditions did produce a public for the intellectual left. Political repression was sometimes severe, particularly in the immediate post–World War I period, with the Red Scare and the Palmer Raids. The IWW for all intents and purposes was destroyed. Yet until the New Deal amelioration of the harshest aspects of working-class life, many ordinary people identified with the program of the left-wing political parties and unions.

Following World War II, this public disintegrated. The development of the Cold War and McCarthyism, the cumulative effects of the growing knowledge of the Stalinist excesses of the thirties, the Hitler-Stalin Pact of 1939, and the resurgence of Stalinist terror, isolated in the public mind not only the Communist party but all those associated with the left. During the early Cold War, even "New Dealers" were suspect. A growing chasm developed between the general public and the cultural worlds where the intellectual left was still significant. In the fifties, sixties, seventies, and eighties, the politics of left-wing intellectuals and the politics of the general public developed in separate though related ways.

For the Old Left, the left that still identified the working class as the primary agent of social change, struggles were increasingly sectarian: between socialists and Communists, Trotskyists and Stalinists, anti-Stalinist liberals and anti-anticommunist liberals. The struggles were often defined by international politics but had mostly symbolic importance on native grounds. Theirs became a politics of moral accusation and defense, one that was born in the thirties, flourished during the McCarthy period, and echoed through the subsequent years. The main political issues on the domestic front centered around how to react to the anticommunist hysteria. On the foreign front, the main issue was the orientation towards Stalinism. The foreign and domestic issues were obviously related. The struggles were ideological, but in the postwar period they had little connection to social movements for social change. Rather, tests of moral courage and ethical judgment abounded.

From the thirties onward, such "ethical politics" of the Old Left revolved around the Soviet Union. For the Communists and those who in one way or another aligned themselves or found themselves aligned with the Communist party or the Soviet cause, the thirties were a decade of opportunity, great hope, and severe challenge. The strategy of the Popular Front brought together a broad array of leftists committed to a broad range of political causes, from artists' unions to support for the Spanish Republic. Ignorance about the Soviet Union (much of it self-imposed) made it possible for many to believe that Soviet socialism provided a model for transcending the contradictions and tragedies of capitalism. When news of the Stalinist purges, the gulag, and induced starvations reached the outside world, simple ideological belief and certainty led to denial. The carriers of the facts were denounced, so that the facts would not be scrutinized. Thus Robert Lynd, the renowned sociologist, while admitting that the Soviet Union had not yet achieved "the socialism that fulfills all our dreams," criticized Dwight Macdonald for his "reckless complacent namecalling." He attacked the messengers and made light of the message, declaring, "The thing that I am stumped by is the apparent imputation of nothing but malevolence to the Kremlin by some of you fellows. It's all . . . a matter of personal deliberate intent, with no quarter even for mistakes, the tight coercions of circumstances and with the Soviet Union constantly measured against a perfectionist yardstick."[3]

The most difficult public and undeniable fact was the Soviet pact with Hitler. Since antifascism was the chief slogan of the Popular Front throughout the thirties, the pact led to the disillusionment of many, but, amazingly, many others steadfastly supported the turnabout. Thus, for example, the leftist Almanac Singers, including Woody Guthrie and Pete Seeger, released a record album in 1941, "Songs for John Doe," with explicit antiwar lyrics imposed on popular tunes.[4] Since the working class represented the transcendence of the history of previous class struggles and exploitations, and since the Communist party was the workers' vanguard in power in the Soviet Union, Soviet policy represented the truth, both when it led the antifascist alliance and when it made alliance with the major fascist power. At first the Soviet Union as the true progressive force was clearly the strongest bulwark against the world forces of fascist reaction. Then, during the pact, the Soviets astutely established the need to protect itself from the Nazi regime because it could not get support from Britain and France. And then when Germany invaded Russia, it all turned out to be a refined gambit by Stalin, biding time to fortify military resources. Antifascism, appeasement, and then again antifascism were each progressive, following the timing of official Soviet policy. The force of the Soviet state did not coerce certain American progressive intellectuals, it defined their reasoning. This ideological configuration is the epitome of totalitarian culture.

II

Though there was much public support for the Soviet Union during the war, it was not as a result of such ideological gymnastics. The Soviet Union was supported by the U.S. government and by the general public as an ally fighting against the common enemy. When the Americans first joined the war effort, for a brief period there was a convergence of interests between the American government and the pro-Soviet left. Official propaganda goals and the left's ideological rhetoric called for the same manipulative message—making the Soviet Union appear as a trustworthy fellow democracy, with enlightened leadership and goals quite similar to those of the United States and England. During this period, it was difficult to publicly criticize the Soviet Union. Bennett Cerf, the publisher of Random House, not a leftist ideologue, even proposed an industry-wide withdrawal from sale by publishers of all books critical of the Soviet Union.[5] Hollywood produced a number of films which appeared to be little more than pro-Soviet propaganda, the most notorious of which was *Mission to Moscow,* based on a best-seller of the same title by Ambassador Joseph P. Davies.

Since the release of *Mission to Moscow,* marred both by its blatant propaganda and its mediocrity, coincided with the turning point of the war (the Russian victory at Stalingrad), criticism of the film marked a turning point in American political culture.[6] The film's outrageousness invited criticism. It justified the purges, glorified Stalin, confused democracy with tyranny. With the ultimate victory of the Allies in sight, the differences between them were brought out into the open. A major anti-Stalinist letter of protest was circulated and published in the *New Leader.* John Dewey and Susanne LaFollette (who had been secretary to the Dewey Commission, which issued a negative report on the Moscow purge trials before the war) published a detailed critique of the film in the *New York Times.* High officials in the State Department were reported to be disturbed by the fact that a former employee of Moscow's International Bureau of Revolutionary Literature had been hired as an adviser to the film.

A fissure, revealed by this case, developed between the war propaganda needs of the U.S. and leftist ideology. For the left, the war was an integral part of the struggle for a revolutionary transformation of the world order. For the American government and most of the public (and the British government and public), the world had to be ordered in pursuit of national interests and fundamental principles of human decency. With victory near, the significance of these differences grew. Internationally this meant a growing tension between the allies, culminating in the Cold War. Nationally, this meant the banishment of the left from American politics, culminating in the anticommunist purge.

III

The purge has been well analyzed and documented.[7] In terms of the later development of American politics, its primary contributions, in my opinion, were to decrease the ideological politics of the left and lay the foundation for the emergence of an empowered ideological right in America. These developments are much more profound than is often observed.

The decline of the ideological politics of the left was a result of both repression and the moralization of political positions. Neither would have been as consequential as they were if there had been significant popular support for the left. Quite simply, the anticommunist purge proceeded as it did against government workers, trade unionists, academics, and movie stars, among others, because only they, and those few with major concerns with constitutional liberties, cared to defend these liberties. Americans believed in a communist menace, and found good reasons to support the developing political repression. They supported the various government and private agencies of repression, from the congressional committees—the House Committee on Un-American Activities, the Senate Internal Security Subcommittee, and the McCarthy Committee—to the FBI and the Red Squads of various city governments, to the entrepreneurial private firm, American Business Consultants, which specialized in blacklisting for television and radio, publishing information on security threats and clearances. Even those who had doubts about the severity of the internal communist menace or the one-sided accounts of the origins of the Cold War found good reasons to acquiesce in political repression. Self-interest, of course, was primary among such reasons. Silence about and cooperation with the anticommunist repression were required for employment in government, the universities, and in the entertainment industry, and often made the difference between a trade union that flourished and one subject to intimidating government scrutiny. But self-interest is rationalized in a variety of ways, and sometimes with general import. Further, silence and cooperation, even by those who were critical of the anticommunist hysteria, could be and was principled.

Take the case of a Communist university lecturer. An argument can be made that fealty to the communist party fundamentally contradicts commitment to the ideal of free scholarly exchange which normatively constitutes the liberal university.[8] As a party member, the lecturer is not simply the member of some sort of club, he is committed to an absolute truth which is derived from a particular philosophy and enforced by a political apparatus. Other philosophies are ideological and wrong, to be combatted by any means necessary. The free exchange of ideas is viewed as a bourgeois prejudice, an ideology to be used by the apparatus when convenient, but not respected as the first principle of association, as it must be in an autonomous university. Thus, exclusion of the party university lecturer from the university may be in order. But on the other hand, in that an imminent Communist takeover of American universities was not likely in the postwar period, such argumentation appears to be disingenuous. Then again, is the issue practical or principled? If practical, it would seem that Communists can be university members as long as they do not have any chance of affecting university life, i.e., if they are a small minority. But if the issue is viewed as a matter of principle, then exclusion of Communists may be viewed as being in order, especially at a time when Stalinism was very much a force in the international cultural world.

Oddly enough, for most American academics, discussion of such matters was viewed as a pleasant diversion from the mundane matters of daily college life.[9] But for at least one university, these issues were a pressing combination of the practical and the theoretical. The graduate faculty of the New School for Social Research was founded as the University in Exile. Its faculty was made up of exiles from Nazi Europe, primarily Germany. For them, the politicization of the university by totalitarian party members was not just a theoretical possibility but a recent personal memory. Thus they added a statute to the university's bylaws, excluding from university employment all those belonging to political organizations which do not respect academic freedom. In this way, the New School cooperated with the anticommunist hysteria, leading to very critical judgments of the university by its sympathetic historians.[10] The New School's actions undermined its fundamental founding principle of being open to all points of view, which had its roots in the post–World War I era, when superpatriotism and the first anti-Red wave limited academic freedom.

Such moral dilemmas characterized the McCarthy era. For some, the clear repressive force was the national anticommunist hysteria. They perceived the development of systematic repression as an instance of American tyranny, or at least as a very significant prelude to tyranny.[11] Following this logic, cooperation with the various investigative committees and the enforcement of new security laws was unethical, antidemocratic, and antiliberal. For others, to the contrary, the major threat to liberalism and democracy was the surviving totalitarian power, the Soviet Union. They focused upon the absolute unfreedom of the Soviet order, its domination of Eastern Europe, and its threat to Western Europe and beyond. They knew about the uncritical American justifications of Stalin's crimes and the celebrations of his democratic achievements. Thus, they labeled Stalinism rather than McCarthyism as the clear and present danger.[12] Following this logic, the anticommunist purge was understood as a necessary evil, perhaps condemned for its excesses but not for its fundamental aims.[13]

Debates about such issues constitute the continuing cultural tradition of the Old Left in America. These debates are heatedly polemical, blending self-justification with high philosophical reflection. They are ideological, and drenched with the horrors of what that means in this century. They are also remarkably naive and nostalgic. The most naive and kitschy version of these polemics can be found in the controversies between Lillian Hellman and Mary McCarthy. But despite their interesting cultural character, these debates had and have very little to do with a real leftist American political movement. Ideological arguments about Stalin and Trotsky, the Popular Front and anti-Stalinism, and about the true class character of the Soviet Union, were divorced from the movements for social change and justice that were becoming part of the politics of the postwar period. Those who sought fundamental social change had to transcend the hermetic ideological discourse. They had, in Tom Hayden's formulation, to "speak American." It was with the rejection of the old leftist ideological discourses that the New Left was born.[14]

IV

The American New Left presented neither a new anti-Stalinist program nor a new version of the Popular Front. It was born in non-ideological struggles—first in the civil rights movement and later in the student movement. In its formative years, it gained its strength from its close connection with the American experience. This is most evident in the social activism of Martin Luther King, Jr.,[15] and the social theory of C. Wright Mills.[16] King confronted the "American dilemma" with the high ethical principles of the American political tradition. Mills continually appraised central American social and political practices, utilizing a Jeffersonian sense of what they ought to be. King personified the civil rights movement, the first phase of the New Left. Mills gave many student activists a means by which the struggle for African-American civil rights could be linked to the broader struggle for social justice, while avoiding the sterility of old leftist polemics and controversies. The old left debates continued between the anti-anticommunists and the anticommunists and these were given new life by the controversies of the Vietnam War. The old anti-anticommunist liberals blamed the old anticommunist liberals for their myopic obsession with the communist threat which led us into the Southeast Asian debacle. The New Left, though, was born by turning away from the controversies.

The split between the Old and New Left was most evident in the early years (1962-63) of the Students for a Democratic Society (SDS). The SDS was the youth wing of the League for Industrial Democracy, an anti-Stalinist socialist organization. For the parent organization, a creature of the Old Left, its anti-Stalinism was of definitive importance. For the students of the sixties, it was not. In the thirties, the student organization of the league was severely compromised by its youth organization's merger with the communist-dominated American Student Union. After that time, the parent organization was strongly anticommunist. For the students of the sixties, such anticommunism (which may have accounted for the organization's survival during the McCarthy era) was an anachronism. They wanted to build a new sort of radical social movement in America, bringing the civil rights struggle north. In their working document of principles, The Port Huron Statement, they openly questioned key elements of old left-wing anti-Stalinist, socialist orthodoxy. They criticized the labor movement for being "too rich and sluggish," indicating a "crisis of vision." They questioned the assumption of the inherently expansionist character of the Soviet

Union, and even went so far as to argue that "the savage repression of the Hungarian Revolution was a defensive action rooted in the Soviet fear its empire would collapse." Tom Hayden, the principle author of the statement, went on to observe, "While the older radicals are indispensable for information and advice . . . and while our sympathies parallel theirs on nearly every other domestic issue, they tragically coalesce with the less informed, conservative and even reactionary forces in performing a static analysis, in making Russia a 'closed question.' "[17]

For the New Left, communism was not a direct domestic question. The American Communist party had been all but eradicated, through a combination of repression and self-destruction. The Soviet threat seemed to be far less pressing than right- and left-wing anticommunists claimed. The postwar division of the world was taken as a given. Even if both sides of the "iron curtain" were not equally to blame for the geopolitical map, they must be held equally responsible for avoiding the dire consequences of the escalation of geopolitical tensions.

More than communism, domestic anticommunism was important. It was understood as a smokescreen for avoiding the pressing problems of domestic injustice. The civil rights movement addressed these in the South in a nonideological fashion. Using African-American churches in the South as its institutional and normative base, the movement called for social justice on the grounds of American political traditions and principles. The students hoped to transform American academic life so that the universities or at least students in the universities could extend the struggle for social justice. They looked not to the working class, the purported revolutionary subject of Marxist theory, but to themselves, members of the new generation "bred in at least modest comfort, housed now in the universities, looking uncomfortably to the world we inherit."[18]

When Michael Harrington, a promising young leader of the league but not yet the nationally famous author of *The Other America*,[19] came to speak to the Port Huron Conference, he was deeply antagonistic. He remembers the question of historical agency as being a key to his concerns. He was "probably very critical about the idea that students were the vanguard."[20] The insufficiency of the document's anticommunism was scandalous to him, and the antagonism to the labor movement was simply unacceptable. Richard Flacks remembers that Donald Slaiman of the AFL-CIO, who accompanied Harrington to the conference, made the latter point quite clear. Slaiman shouted, "The American labor movement has won more for its members than any labor movement in the world! You people have some nerve attacking the labor movement! You people will stand for any left-wing Stalinoid kind of thing."[21] In that the League for Industrial Democracy was closely aligned with the anti-Stalinist labor movement, this was a fundamental condemnation which ultimately led to the formal split between SDS and the League, and was a foreshadowing of the major conflicts between labor unions and their members and the student movement during the sixties.

The later conflicts had a quality of ideological excess. The anti-communist labor movement defended the free world, the student movement declared war on "Amerika," "bringing the war home." The flamboyance of the later period has overshadowed the more profound, in my judgment, political nature of the earlier conflict. The conflict was between old political sectarians and those who wanted to resist sectarianism as a matter of principle. Tom Hayden recalls:

> Those of us entering SDS from non-political backgrounds found [the sectarian] atmosphere amusing, obscure and irrelevant, like fervent religious sects poring over cate-chisms or the Torah. I could not understand how seemingly serious people could get so enmeshed in such endlessly divisive hair-splitting debates. Surely there was no lesson in their experience for us.[22]

The unintentional ambiguity in Hayden's recollection is signifi-cant. He, of course, wants to say that the new student activists sought to avoid the doctrinal conflicts which characterized the polit-ical life of both the communist and anticommunist Old Left. He personally looked elsewhere for an understanding of America's so-ciopolitical situation (to C. Wright Mills) and for a conception of the ethics of political action (to Albert Camus). But the New Left as a movement too quickly turned away from the negative Old Left lessons of sectarianism, and by the end of the sixties had become just as doctrinnaire, and developed the same kind of sectarian splits. There were those who sought to work within the system, supporting Eugene McCarthy for president in 1968. They "stayed clean with Gene." Those who dropped out turned to youth and drug culture. They "turned on, tuned off, and dropped out." And those who chose rather to blow things up (they didn't need a weath-erman to know "which way the wind was blowing") became the Weathermen terrorists. The Trotskyism, Maoism, and good old-fashioned Stalinism of the sixties marked the end of the New Left in a fashion quite similar to the final years of the Old Left. First the destructive disciplined (Leninist) vanguard was the Communist party, later it was the Progressive Labor party (an ultraleftist group which infiltrated and took over SDS), but the end result was the same, a left politics in the name of "the people" without popular support.

V

The ascendance of vanguards and the increasing use of exotic ideologies were not natural or necessary outgrowths of the New Left's starting points. Quite the contrary, they were a result of the movement's amnesia and defeat. The movement began with very concrete social concerns: civil rights, avoiding nuclear warfare, and the amelioration of severe social inequalities in the North, most evident in profound urban decay. The means of addressing the issues drew upon generally accepted American cultural values—equality before the law, equal economic and social opportunity, and local voluntary associations and self-governance (participatory democracy). The New Left began by comparing the distance between American promise and American realities and calling for radical solutions. First in nonviolent resistance in the South, then in community organizing in the northern cities, and then in the antiwar movement, the New Left developed decentralized politics which connected with the lives of ordinary people. The Vietnam War, and the celebrity status it bestowed on the SDS, disrupted this pattern. The very goals the movement had for society became impossible for itself. The Port Huron statement called for a democracy in which "the individual share[s] in those social decisions determining the quality and direction of his life."[23] But when the antiwar movement became the topic of mass media attention, New Left spokesmen, particularly in SDS, started making decisions independent of its membership. The choice seemed to be the emergence of a relatively unacceptable leadership structure or political ineffectiveness.[24] A mass movement developed which could not be accommodated by the informal structures in place.

This was most evident when both the war in Vietnam and the antiwar movements escalated. In those circumstances, a small, relatively peripheral, radical student movement suddenly was brought onto the central stage of American politics. The New Leftists constituted and occupied an alternative center of power, culture and authority with democratic consequences. The process of political and cultural conflicts emerged not only from the issues of the day but from tensions emerging from the problematic of democracy itself.

The original program of the New Leftists, revealed in the Port Huron Statement, was relatively modest. There was a grand and somewhat romantic understanding and vision of America, but this was coupled with a realistic understanding of American politics and of the place and role radical youth could play in politics. They understood themselves as intellectuals based in the universities, developing a critical understanding of American society, supporting African-Americans in the South and poor people in the North in mounting social movements of protest for fundamental change. They hoped to facilitate social change through grass-roots activism—from voter registration drives in the South to community organization in urban slums—and through activism in the Democratic party; they wanted the Democratic party to become the party for social change. The enfranchisement of African-Americans and poor whites in the North and South, and the expulsion of the racist Southern Democrats (the so-called Dixiecrats) would, they envisioned, help to bring this about. Their program and its projected means of implementation were realistic and within the tradition of American political culture. Whether it is achievable is still one of the pressing questions of American political life twenty-five years after its conception.[25] Yet the program was not to be tested in the sixties, thanks to the war in Vietnam. The war overwhelmed the national and international official politics of the era. It also, most crucially from the point of view of this inquiry, compromised the politics of alternative movements for social change. The SDS's relatively minor concern that anticommunism should not define its program nor overshadow commitments to social justice, ironically became the tag by which the American public knew of its existence—the radical antiwar student movement of draft-card burners. Following a Washington antiwar demonstration, the SDS and the young New Left generally became an object of mass media attention. A little-understood but escalating war (or "police action") was meeting radical resistance. Major news dailies and weeklies and television news focused a great deal of attention on a small group of political activists opposed to the escalation. A new structure of mass political culture was being constituted.

As we observed in Chapter 3, when discussing the theory of Edward Shils, central values of a society stand both as a source of authoritative legitimation of those in power and a source for judging the inadequacies of the empowered. Such judgment is a realistic ground for effective social change in the society. We also observed how the distance between center and periphery, the inequalities among citizens, led to the development of mass media in American culture and politics. The practical implications of this has been the growth of mass structures of culture and party politics. Here we observe, in the case of SDS and other New Left movements, that mass structures have also shaped movements for social change.

The mass media, particularly television, fictively portrayed New Leftists and the counterculturalists as irrational, criminal, and sinister in nightly comedies and action shows and on daytime soap operas. Millions of people understood the changes of the sixties through these fictive portrayals. Still, such distortion was the least of the SDS's TV problems. Television and radio and newspapers challenged the members of SDS to confront the firmness of their own fundamental democratic commitments. A new iron law of oligarchy was in place. Robert Michels observed that political parties, even social democratic ones, require organization in order to reach their goals, and "where there is organization there is oligarchy." Thus, in order for a democratic party to reach its goals, it must be antidemocratic.[26] The experience of the New Left suggests that at least in a mass society, even a democratic (anti-mass) movement must use the mass media to reach its goals, but in the process it strengthens mass structures.

The SDS sought fundamental change in American society. Its early leadership of the antiwar movement brought national attention. Leaders of the group could suddenly speak to the nation. But in the process, not only was oligarchy constituted but leaders with access to the media rapidly developed an independent power as media figures based on their access. They could effectively call for national demonstrations, but the fundamental principle of the group—that Americans should actually take part in the decision-making which affects their lives—was no longer even true of the antiwar movement itself.

Among the original SDS members, the development of a media-based authority structure within its ranks led to strong anti-authoritarian strategies: rotation of leadership and public self-criticism, primary among them. But in that the original group was overwhelmed in numbers by people who joined it after its mass--mediated popularization, these strategies proved ineffective. Further, the group itself became less important than the sort of relationship it developed with the media. Throughout the country, antiwar leaders learned that provocative statements and dramatic actions would attract media attention and mobilize activists. The culmination of this cynical logic, its logical conclusion and absurdity, was the formation of the Youth International Party (the Yippies) of Abbie Hoffman and Jerry Rubin. They very significantly and negatively affected American politics and culture by becoming stars of the New Left. They knew that their mass constituency, disaffected young people strongly opposed to the war, was raised on television culture with its cynical consumer appeals and surrealistic portrayals of upper-middle-class life. So they appealed to the young using the strategies of TV marketing. Abbie Hoffman declared: "I fight through the jungle of TV."[27] And Jerry Rubin characterized the world of the younger in contrast to the older generation:

> Those who grew up before the 1950s live today in a mental world of Nazism, concentration camps, economic depression and communist dreams Stalinized. A pre-1950s child who can still dream is very rare. Kids who grew up in the post-1950s world live in the world of supermarkets, color TV commercials, guerilla war, international media, psychedelics, rock and roll and moon walks. For us nothing is impossible. We can do anything.[28]

Thus the continuity of historical experience is broken metaphorically, as if different experiences were related to each other like TV channels. The Yippy message seemed to be little more than an admonition to turn off the experience of the older generation and turn on the experience of the younger—to change the channel. It was not serious, just a cynical media hype which amazingly mobilized a significant political demonstration in Chicago and is remembered as a central force in the politics of a turbulent decade.

The Yippy experience is an instance of a politics of media performance. It was practiced all over. H. Rap Brown, the black-power advocate and leader of SNCC (the Student Nonviolent Coordinating Committee) ironically but menacingly declared, "Violence is as American as cherry pie." Tom Hayden in Chicago called for blood to "flow all over this city." In the language of the eighties, these were instances of New Left sound bites. In condensed cynical form, they gave expression to a political position. Reason was not required. Hoffman explained to a reasonable interviewer, "You need 300 pages, you know, beginning with a capital letter and ending with a period. Young kids don't need that, they don't even want it."[29]

But Hoffman did not have it quite right. Some of the young people, the critical students of the sixties, wanted "it" quite a bit. Most prominent among them, of course, were the activists of the early sixties. They were intellectuals, who seriously attempted to develop a nonideological critical understanding of American society. Two SDS leaders, Todd Gitlin and Richard Flacks, are now leading critical sociologists of culture and politics. As activists, they were critical of the Yippy turn. Later they continued the New Left intellectual project very much in the tradition of C. Wright Mills.[30] Indeed, a new generation of academics, deeply influenced by their political experiences in the sixties, have opened up new fields in political economy, sociology of the state, the study of collective action, literary theory, and dialectical anthropology, among others. Even Russell Jacoby (another old New Leftist) recognizes this, though he is surely right that the critical activist of the sixties did not find a clear public voice as earlier critical intellectuals had. When the New Left sought a broader audience, as we have seen, it turned to media high jinks instead, using the media's hall of mirrors to construct a mass social protest; or when it was clear to the more sober-minded that countercultural irrationalities would not directly and positively change American domestic and foreign policy, it turned to ideological illusions.

VI

Notions of vanguard politics in American society in the sixties were a kind of leftist nostalgia, a retrospective politics in the guise of progress, political kitsch. But people turned to such politics seriously. How could they ever believe they would succeed? Why did this obvious absurdity ever develop? Trotskyism, Maoism, even Stalinism, again in America? One way of answering these questions is to explain them away, to point out that ideologies are generally not rational (people who take this position will often maintain this by definition) and to maintain that youth politics also generally are not rational, being manifestations of oedipal complexes rather than rational critiques of the military-industrial complex. But such assertions avoid rather than confront the issues. Ideologies must be understood as they are, or are not, persuasively linked to autonomous social, political, and cultural movements. Condemning them as irrational, emotional, or unscientific is beside the point, as Clifford Geertz and Paul Ricoeur have forcefully demonstrated.[31] With regard to oedipal conflicts, they may or may not be universal, but surely their political content at a specific moment in time and a specific place is more important than the generality of youthful revolt. Revolutionaries are often young, but not all youths are revolutionaries.

Taking the aforementioned questions more seriously leads us to the structure of mass society. Without a democratic link to an active public, a link which characterized the early civil rights movement and SDS, and rejecting the cynical countercultural versions of media politics, disoriented New Leftists sought one sort of ideology or another to overcome the isolation of mass society and a sense of political ineffectiveness. To paraphrase Marx, in the first half of the twentieth century modern ideologies, particularly Marxism-Leninism and Nazism, culminated in tragedy; in the second half, specifically in the sixties, they appeared in the United States as a leftist farce.

Marx in the nineteenth century and even Lenin (as a practitioner) and Lukács (as a theoretician) in the early twentieth,[32] could convince themselves of the redemptive truth of their own political judgments. They committed themselves to a view of historical progress and found the (class) agent that would enable them actively to take part in its teleology. Further, the Soviet experience for much of this century, with its effective propaganda and geopolitical successes, could seem to many in the so-called Third World as an alternative to colonialism and neocolonialism, a model of economic and industrial development with social justice. Even for those devastated by the Nazi horrors in East Central Europe, Marxist ideology could be adopted as a means of avoiding European barbarism.[33] We must remind ourselves of this in the age of Glasnost, now that the cold war is over, and the West has won.

Marxist ideology (and reactionary Nazi and fascist ideologies opposed to it) empowered intellectuals to reach out to the populace and act politically. It made sense of popular misery and gave both the general population and its theoretically minded leaders a role to play in the making of human progress. The proof of the validity of the theory was its successful implementation, the so-called praxis. Even if the workers of the world did not unite, the ideology had broad appeal. Its success in conflating reason with force, i.e., in becoming an official state-enforced truth for the majority of the world's population, brought on some of the most significant horrors in human history. It should be clear that the radical ideologies in America in the sixties presented no such dangers (at least directly).[34]

When the New Left activists turned to the exotica of Marxist ideology and sectarianism in the sixties, they did so for the exact opposite reasons of earlier Marxists. Earlier, people turned to Marxist ideology as a means to facilitate a connection between the "masses" and radical intellectuals, and they (sometimes very unfortunately) met with successes. In the sixties, Marxist ideology's first appeal was an explanation for the chasm between radical intellectuals and the "people." Marxism could illuminate the lack of success of the radical social movement in reaching the American public. Thus the neo-Marxist pessimists of the Frankfurt school, and particularly Herbert Marcuse, had great appeal.[35] The ideological turn was a turn of democratic despair. The two faces of the American political order, as mass society and democracy, were key issues. The normative promise of democracy and democratic social criticism collided with the facts of mass structures, and for some persons ideology was the only means of escape.

Consider the essential tragedy of the New Left's democratic logic. As we have noted, student activists started the decade with a clear democratic commitment, a sense that the major contradiction of the American democratic experience, its racism, must be addressed. In engaging this issue, the students were not only taking part in a broad social (civil rights) movement, they were helping to constitute a new dominant consensus in American society. Citizens at all levels of the American polity (federal, state, and local), and leaders in all branches of government (judicial, legislative, and executive), contributed to this new consensus. History was even revealing happy ironies; by 1964 the racist J. Edgar Hoover was supporting the new consensus by directing (even if reluctantly) the FBI's investigation of the criminal official and unofficial activities enforcing Southern segregation (this at a time when there were still no black FBI agents). The New Left's activities then were clearly linked to broadly shared democratic norms in the society.

But of course these norms met with serious resistance, both gross and subtle. Eugene (Bull) Connor, the police chief of Birmingham, Alabama, who set dogs and hoses on African-American children, epitomized the grossest sort of resistance: the official system of segregation and its brutal system of repression; yet the philosophy of business as usual in political parties, government agencies, and private enterprises, also systematically excluded African-Americans from full participation in American political, economic, and cultural life.

When the successes of the civil rights movement accumulated but the lot in life of the great bulk of African-Americans and other oppressed groups did not significantly improve, because of the more systematic discrimination practices, the young radicals intensified their social criticism and activism. After the Port Huron Statement, the next major theoretical initiative (primarily written by Richard Flacks), published as *America and the New Era,* called for a new insurgency—radical grass-roots organizing which culminated in the Economic Research and Action Project.[36] This project organized community action groups to demand economic, social, and political inclusion. The articulated radical critiques of American daily life were used to organize the poor in demanding their right to an improvement in their life situations. The demands the group made were not greeted with enthusiastic support by those commanding local power structures in City Hall and the business community. But in that this was the time when Lyndon Johnson declared his War on Poverty, it should be noted that the New Left activists, along with the powers that be, were following the same democratic logic. Their projects shared with the government programs the same democratic valuative grounding. Put simply, slavery and systemic discrimination were understood as being antidemocratic and unconstitutional, and were seen as having disadvantaged African-Americans in the past. Therefore a concerted effort had to be made to right not only the legal barriers to racial equality but also the social, political, and economic consequences of past officially sanctioned discriminations. Even further, sentimental notions about America as a land of plenty and opportunity demanded that the systemic reproduction of poverty in America had to be put to an end. Michael Harrington's *The Other America* and the attention the Kennedy administration gave to it put this concern for social justice on the federal government's agenda. Democratic aversions to gross inequalities, to extreme privilege and extreme wealth, were broadly held central values. Through these values, the New Left had a means to reach a broad public.

Nonetheless, the international implications of these values were a source of diametrically opposed interpretations. Fighting for democracy meant, for the New Left, disengaging from combat with the international Communist menace. For those in power (and through an odd course of constructing public opinion, the general population), the good fight had to continue. Thus, with the Vietnam War the young radicals lost their link with the public. To be sure, the American people when given a choice seemed always to vote against engagement in the war in Southeast Asia, most clearly in 1964 in choosing Johnson over Goldwater, and after the ambiguities of the conflict became well known and the vehemence of student opposition was strongly articulated, broader and broader segments of the public and the political leadership turned against the war. But the New Leftists went much further than their fellow citizens. The war exposed the underside of the Pax Americana. It revealed that the United States was essentially capitalist and imperialist, not free and democratic. Formerly recognized shared democratic commitments now seemed to be little more than hypocrisies. When an American officer in Vietnam declared that a village had to be destroyed to be liberated, he seemed to epitomize American political culture. American democracy became, in the symbolics of the extreme left, Amerika the political monster. Ideology, in the name of true peace, freedom, and democracy, was called upon to explain this state of affairs. A leftist cynicism emerged.

Ideology was used to explain why all American governmental practices were a sham (they were merely bourgeois democratic practices), why the American public, its working class, oppressed minorities, and rural poor seemed not to question the legitimacy of the practices (they suffered from false consciousness), and why some other system, be it in Vietnam, Cuba, China, the Soviet Union, or the realm of the imagination, was superior despite appearances of repression. The ideology, usually of a Marxist variety, allowed for the illusion of continued democratic commitment even in the face of popular disdain and antagonism. New Leftists acted in the name of the people or the working class or the progressive future, as the people, working class, and progressive (democratic) future were imagined in their ideologies. Since it was clear that American working people were unwilling to take on the role of the universal class (having become, in Lenin's terms, "the aristocracy of labor"), ideologists became enchanted with the Third World and Chairman Mao, this during the disastrous Cultural Revolution. And if not the Third World, then the oppressed lumpenproletariat of American blacks, Chicanos, American Indians were valorized. These groups, though, were not represented by elected leaders or major organized movements (from King's Southern Christian Leadership Conference to the NAACP), but by groups, the Black Panther party most prominent among them, which shared revolutionary fantasies. Dreams of revolutionary violence which would polarize the community and lead to societal transformation replaced community organizing and participatory democracy as the way to reach the public. Indeed, participatory democracy, which was originally presented as SDS's way of deepening American democratic practices, was now seen as the ideal replacement for American democratic institutions.

Obviously the problematics of democratic governance were no longer given much thought. Ideologically derived knowledge of what would truly be good for the people led to a cynical lack of concern for what was on people's minds. As a result, at the end of the sixties the fundamental problem for democratic political culture and action in a mass society—finding an audience and a means to act in concert in nonmanipulated ways—was addressed by the New Left in two ways. One was to develop a mass counterculture, as the Yippies did. The other was to turn away from the problem, with ideological explanations for political failures and ideological fantasies of future victories. Not surprisingly, eventually the cynical cultural hype became unfashionable. The Me Generation replaced the rhetoric of cultural transformation, and the ideologists dropped into adult life or were marginalized into silly sects, one making a full ideological turn to crypto-fascism (Lyndon LaRouche's American Labor party), another becoming a model for later terrorists (the Weathermen), and still others, with stronger political traditions, turning to the Communist party or the Trotskyist Socialist Workers party, which still continued on. A good number, of course, either never abandoned the original radical democratic politics or rediscovered them (Tom Hayden) and have been active in social movement politics for the last twenty years.

A positive outgrowth of the New Left, from the point of view of intellectual history, was the development of scholarship in the Marxist tradition in America, drawing upon the sophisticated, unorthodox Marxisms of Horkheimer and Adorno, Benjamin, Lukács, Gramsci, and others. But as Jacoby has pointed out, the effect of this has been confined to the universities. In the final analysis, the New Left's ideological and mass cultural turns, like the Old Left's ideological and moralistic obsessions, began with a roar, and ended with a series of whimpers. But the cynical leftist whimpers fostered the development of a partisan cynicism of the right-wing powers and the institutionalization of right-wing ideology, key components of present-day cynical practices. As we broadly observed in Chapter 2, cynicism has moved from critique to mocking to institutional apology. Now, we turn to the right-wing specifics.

SEVEN

Ideology on the American Right—A Clear and Present Danger

The connection between mass society on the one hand and politics and ideology on the American left on the other is obvious, inconsequential, and comical. The connection on the right is obscure, dangerous, and tragic. Comedy sometimes masks dangers, particularly in the form of institutionalized cynicism. Here I hope to explain the present danger.

First, perceive the masked danger as comedy. Spiro T. Agnew lashed out not only at students and antiwar protesters. Nixon's obscure choice for vice president went after the press with a particular venom, those who told the truth about the Vietnam War, "the liberal elitist press," "the nattering nabobs of negativism." He did this in the name of the interests of the so-called "silent majority." Because Agnew left office in disgrace, forced to resign as a petty criminal, and because of the Watergate scandal, which seemed fundamentally to undermine Nixon's attacks on the Constitution, Agnew is remembered as a buffoon of little consequence. Yet his cynical attacks furthered the development of an increasingly effective right-wing ideology in America.[1]

Unlike the American left, the New Right's politics became ideological when it was most successful in the seventies and eighties. The right's ideological successes are linked with the left's ideological failures. Anticommunism has been the rightist twentieth-century popular ideological starting point, from which it has been developed. All leftist ideologies are labeled communist. The presence of these ideologies instigate and stimulate the rightist call to action. The ineffectiveness of the left supports the ascendancy of the right.

In order to appreciate such interactions, Werner Sombart's illogical question, "Why is there no socialism in the United States?" must be reformulated. The more logical question is, "Why have socialist or leftist politics and their ideologies failed in gaining significant public support in America while right-wing parties and their ideologies have succeeded in gaining support?"

To begin answering this question requires extensive and intensive historical and sociological investigation. Grand and purportedly complete attempts have been made; most prominent and influential in the postwar era was Louis Hartz's *The Liberal Tradition in America*.[2] It was Hartz's central thesis that because the United States has always been a modern, albeit capitalist, order, it has been immune to all cultural and political appeals other than ones that fit into its "Lockean tradition." Yet, the cultural determinism in his formulation is suspect on two counts. First, because the American political tradition is not simply Lockean. Even in its origins, it drew as well upon communitarian republican and puritan principles,[3] and much has been added since.[4]

The Lockean thesis also fails for more general reasons. The very idea of political culture, or national character as political destiny, is untenable. Thus, despite prevailing notions of political culture and character, the Germans, before unification in the nineteenth century, were known to be inefficient, and in the post–World War II period the political resistance of Polish oppositionists has been remarkably realistic and practical. Political culture is a resource facilitating political action. It may delimit possible courses of action, but it does not determine them. The very odd but popular configurations of the American ideological right indicate this. Its blend of "American Lockeanism," religious fundamentalism, and radical political styles adapted from the New Left, shows cultural malleability as well as cultural continuity.

We will see that the recent successes of the right are probably the most telling explanations for the recent failures of the left. But such straightforward political explanations are not adequate. Political struggle is embedded in daily life, as a part of the history and function of specific social institutions within a social order. Thus, historical investigations of ideological conflict within specific social institutions reveal the resistance of Americans to socialist appeals. For example, the politics of race and ethnicity overwhelmed the politics of class (contrary to Marxist ideology) in the making of American school systems.[5] The chasm between leftist ideology and institutional practice, along with the ascendancy of right-wing ideology, are the keys to understanding leftist ideological failures, concomitant with both political success and failure.

As we have observed, before and during World War II the left had some political success; immediately after the war, it was a dismal failure; during the sixties, when it de-ideologized, there was success; and with the ascendancy of ideology in the late sixties, failure returned. Common to this history is a public resistance to leftist ideology. It is quite simply beside the point. Leftist cynicism does not work in America.

The successes of leftist appeals in the thirties and forties were not ideological. The success of the Popular Front organizations came about not because they were communist but despite the fact. Extreme anticommunists would have us believe that the communists successfully manipulated unsuspecting people, who then served the party's cause. But antifascism, a concern for distributive justice at a time of economic depression, support of worker self-defense in trade unions, antagonism to extreme wealth, and sympathy for the plight of common people motivated participation in the Popular Front. These were not controversial issues, although even then communist instigation and manipulation were controversial issues. Nonetheless, Roosevelt, the aristocratic president of the United States, regularly supported these causes. This led to wild charges from the right-wing fringe concerning the aristocrat's pink character, with accusations of his class betrayal. But actually, along with the Popular Front organizations, he was articulating the general sentiments of a plurality of the public.

The communists hoped to capitalize on the populist sentiments but never did. Likewise, Communist party policy and American opinion on the war had much in common, but, again, ideological appeals did not bring the public into the communist fold. Appeals to class consciousness, a class interpretation of history, and national and international politics involving a vanguard party subservient to a foreign power, were not at all attractive to Americans; quite the contrary. There was no attraction during the time of the Great Depression, and even less so in the postwar affluence.

I

Rightist ideology on the other hand does have deep roots in the American experience, and has had profound effects upon our political culture. The culture has been resistant to leftist ideology both when the political project of the left has been highly popular and unpopular. On the right, the opposite is the case. Both when rightist ideology is popular and unpopular it has, in fundamental ways, shaped American institutions and practices.

American right-wing ideology has a variety of sources: nativism, racism, anti-intellectualism, political and economic individualism, Christian fundamentalism, and of course anticommunism. All these commitments are concretely rooted in American experience, with broad appeal. As with the early New Left, the right's principles draw upon generally shared political experiences of a broad spectrum of the American population; unlike the left, both new and old, the right's ideology has a deeply American cogency. Herein lies the danger to American politics.

To appreciate the dangers, we must distinguish between conservative values and principles on the one hand, and right-wing ideology and cynicism on the other. These are not the same, and from a theoretical point of view can even be understood as opposites. Nonetheless, tragically, from the point of view of present-day politics, they have been mutually supportive. The general acceptance of key conservative values predisposes Americans to periodic right-wing ideological excursions; in the twentieth century, such were the Red Scare of 1919–20, the McCarthyism of the post–World War II period, and the so-called Reagan revolution. Each of them drew upon centrally accepted American principles and were brought to a logical (i.e., ideological) conclusion. In the process, central democratic norms—some of them quite conservative—were compromised.

Like all ideologies, American right-wing ideology is based on a set of core ideas viewed as being eternally true. Instead of all history being the history of class struggle, for the American right history is the struggle between individualism and collectivism. This struggle has both sacred and profane ramifications and justifications. Deductions from these, and the applications of the deductions, constitute "correct conservative politics." Barry Goldwater clearly expressed this ideological position when he wrote the following:

> The laws of God, and of nature, have no date-line. The principles on which the conservative political position is based have been established by a process that has nothing to do with the social, economic, and political landscape that changes from decade to decade and from century to century. These principles are derived from the nature of man, and from the truths that God has revealed about his Creation. Circumstances do change. So do the problems that are shaped by circumstances. But the principles that govern the solution of these problems do not. . . The challenge is not to find new or different truths, but how to apply established truths to the problems of the contemporary world.[6]

Richard Hofstadter, probably America's greatest historian of our political culture, called this ideological position pseudo-conservative politics. He strongly contrasted it with genuine conservatism. He observed:

> Most conservatives are mainly concerned with maintaining a tissue of institutions for whose stability and effectiveness they believe the country's business and political elites hold responsibility. Goldwater thinks of conservatism as a system of eternal and unchanging ideas and ideals, whose claims upon us must be constantly asserted and honored in full. The difference between conservatism as a set of doctrines whose validity is to be established by polemics, and conservatism as a set of rules whose validity is to be established by their usability in government, is not a difference of nuance, but of fundamental substance.[7]

Goldwater's position, clearly, had its roots in American notions of rugged individualism and Christian fundamentalism. Yet in that it is derived from asserted eternal truths (an ideological position) rather than accumulated practical wisdoms and customs (a traditional conservative position best exemplified in recent years in the writings of the English political philosopher Michael Oakeshott), Hofstadter properly notes that Goldwater's is a pseudo-conservative politics. The issue is the persistence of such ideological politics and its relationship with conservative and other political traditions in American society.

Right-wing ideological politics persists as a politics of collective identity and status insecurity. It is a paranoid style of politics, in Hofstadter's words. Viewed less negatively, it is a politics of collective self-defense and national and civilizational conservation and assertion. It has both crude and refined exponents, benign and extremely pernicious manifestations. It has a long tradition, but derives its distinctive modern ideological identity from the twentieth century.

In the early years of the republic, conservative partisan attacks (resembling ideological attacks) upon Jefferson and his Democratic-Republicans were common. He was undermining the moral and religious (Christian) basis of American life with his rationalism, importing subversive European Enlightenment ideas at the service of a foreign power, i.e., France. In the nineteenth century, such attacks were diverse, directed against Popism and the new Catholic immigrants, the Chinese, blacks, Jews, Mormons, and so forth, who were supposedly in the service of European monarchs, the international gold rings, and the Masons. All this and more was said to be undermining American virtue and customs. In the twentieth century, with the Bolshevik Revolution, the diverse fears and anxieties that the earlier reactionary attacks expressed were drawn together around a unifying object, international communism.

It should be remembered that the concerns of the nineteenth and twentieth-century reactionaries were very real and deeply felt. Often the concerns were expressed in an exaggerated and grotesque fashion. The nineteenth-century paranoids could imagine that each Catholic immigrant was a secret agent of the pope. The twentieth-century paranoids, from Attorney General Palmer to Senator McCarthy, imagined every liberal and every advocate of social justice to be a communist agent or sympathizer. Despite exaggeration, in both the nineteenth and twentieth centuries, American democracy was challenged.

During the time of the constitutional debates, it was evident to the most clearly committed democrats of the age, the so-called anti-Federalists, that cultural and ethnic homogeneity were requisite for republican liberty. These democrats were against the centralization of government which the Constitution represented, because it would bring too diverse a population into a single political system; even so, this respected common wisdom, drawn from a long tradition of political inquiry, most prominently including Montesquieu, was refuted by Madison in the Federalist Papers.[8]

Likewise, only now, when the victory over communism appears to be won, can we securely minimize the threat. With the gross injustices of industrial capitalism, especially in its late nineteenth- and early twentieth-century forms, and with the grand promise of socialism, especially in its militant communist variety, the communist challenge to capitalism, to liberal democracy, and to conventional morality and religion appeared to be very real. The ideological boasts and claims of a broad variety of relatively isolated radicals could be taken seriously. Every popular discontent, especially when it was expressed by immigrant workers who did not always speak English, could be viewed as a fundamental threat to the American way of life. Add to this the tyranny of Stalinism, the successes of the Popular Front, and Soviet expansionism in the post–World War II period, and one has fertile ground for a twentieth-century reactionary or counterrevolutionary ideology.

The ideology gained steam in the postwar period. Anticommunism is only its starting point. It was used to integrate, intelligently and not so intelligently, inherited conservative and right-wing positions. Besides Goldwater, there were Richard Nixon, Joseph McCarthy, George Wallace, and Ronald Reagan who, as major national figures, drew upon right-wing ideology to advance their political careers. Each used the stark Manichean imagery of an anti-communist crusade to strengthen his political position, but each did so for very different purposes. McCarthy created for himself a kind of right-wing cult of personality, which took advantage of the anti-communist hysteria, raised the hysteria to a frenzy, but so forcefully attacked even political allies (most strikingly the Army) that McCarthy self-destructed. His was a game of self-promotion. In contrast, Nixon used his anticommunism wisely. Through the Hiss case, he craftily manipulated the nation's paranoia to construct a political career which took him from the House of Representatives to the Senate to the vice presidency and presidency, until his own personal paranoia led to his disgrace. George Wallace fought a rearguard action, blending anticommunism with anti-intellectualism, to express a last-ditch racist populism, only to end his career as a nonracist populist governor of Alabama, with significant black support. And Ronald Reagan, probably the most ideological president in American history, used anti-communism to clarify his most demanding role—the "leader of the free world." Reagan, with a sure sense of the dramatic and a very weak sense of social reality, brought his enthusiastic audience along the American right-wing journey. He was a one-man right-wing (counter)revolutionary vanguard. He identified both his career and American fate with the ideology of the right-wing script.[9] The only thing standing in his way was the apparent collapse of Soviet totalitarianism. The geopolitical situation, more than inherent anti-ideological American propensities, quieted the American ideological fervor.

Nonetheless, the American right wing has deeply penetrated American politics. This is Ronald Reagan's lasting accomplishment. The Reagan revolution has infused American political and social life with the counterrevolutionary ideology of the American right wing.

The irony is that the counterrevolution was staged against a fantasy of revolution, at most. To be sure, the New Deal did introduce into American life a weak version of a welfare state (very weak in comparison with just about any other industrial capitalist economy). But the leftist ideology, as we have observed, was quite ineffectual in American society. Only within very narrow circles of intellectual, academic, and cultural affairs was it really prominent. Leftist and rightist ideologues greatly inflated leftist influence. For the left, the object was self-empowerment. The right needed its clear and present danger.

Again, the fantasy had some basis in reality. The postwar period was a dangerous time. The war alliance was unstable. Stalin as a Great Russian imperialist, a revolutionary ideologue, and a megalomaniac did pose a threat to Western Europe and did swallow up East Europe. Right-wing ideologues saw a more immediate threat: liberal, secular, privileged intellectuals and statesmen, who not only misunderstood the fundamentals of American belief but were selling America out. On the grand political stage, McCarthy led the charge for the short repressive run. William F. Buckley, Jr., more persistently, laid the long-term intellectual bases in his *National Review*.[10] He entered the political arena with his attack on the liberal university, *God and Man at Yale*, which had the significant subtitle, *The Superstitions of "Academic Freedom."* He forcefully facilitated the transition from a sustained ideological anti-communism to anti-liberalism. Reflecting on his own experiences at Yale, he clarified what he saw to be and what has become the ideological battlefield:

> During the years 1946 to 1950, I was an undergraduate at Yale University. I arrived in New Haven fresh from a two-year stint in the Army, and I brought with me a firm belief in Christianity and a profound respect for American institutions and traditions. I had always been taught, and experience had fortified the teachings, that an active faith in God and a rigid adherence to Christian principles are the most powerful influences toward the good life. I also believed, with only a scanty knowledge of economics, that free enterprise and limited government had served this country well and would probably continue to do so in the future.
>
> These attitudes were basic to my general outlook. One concentrated the role of man in the universe; the other, in all its implications, the role of man in his society. I knew, of course, of the existence of many persons who had no faith in God and even less in the individual's capacity to work out his own destiny without recourse to the state. I therefore looked eagerly to Yale University for allies against secularism and collectivism.
>
> I am one of a small group of students who fought, during undergraduate days, in the columns of the newspaper, in the Political Union, in debates and seminars, against those who seek to subvert religion and individualism. The fight we waged continues even though little headway was made.[11]

The rest of his career, along with the careers of associated right-wingers, has been dedicated to making such headway. It was made, perhaps, not at Yale but in the country. Clearly the battle has escalated. It is no longer primarily concerned with Godless communism but with liberalism. At the turn of the century, it was un-American to be an anarchist; after World War I, one could no longer be an American if one were a "red," a Bolshevik or a socialist, according to the right-wing ideologues. It took a long time, but in the 1950s the assault on liberalism bore fruit. Through the fifties, sixties, and even the seventies, right-wing attacks on liberalism were viewed as fringe phenomena. By 1988, they were a key element of presidential politics, as we observed in Chapter 1.

But the escalation of rhetorical harshness and its general acceptance is not the most significant ideological challenge. Even the general acceptance of racist ideologues such as Jesse Helms into the political mainstream is not the primary political problem. (It may be the primary ethical problem.) Rather, the major problem is the institutionalization of ideological thinking. There is, to use the rhetoric of the right wing, a clear and present danger that democratic norms are being compromised by the ideologicization of American culture and a consequent development of cynicism.

II

The left-wing ideologues of such groups as the Communist party USA, the Trotskyist Socialist Workers party and the Progressive Labor party are quaint in their political strategy and organization. They are relics of the past, if not in theory certainly in practice. They still use political pamphlets and newspapers to reach the masses. Their idea of mass propaganda includes at most political posters, agit-prop theater and films. Even their ideas of a revolutionary vanguard and democratic centralism, Lenin's organizational innovations for the making of revolutions (once a brutal necessity with very ominous consequences), now have little more than an aesthetic attraction. These "revolutionary tactics" are grossly inappropriate ideological weapons in American society. The right does much better, with much more sophisticated means.

Earlier in this century, terror and ideology were conflated to form modern totalitarian tyrannies of left and right, realized by vanguardist party henchmen. Now the New Right seeks to dominate using the computer programmer, media consultants, mass mailings, and a remarkably constructed organization of material and ideological coherence. The New Right presents a new form of synthesized ideological politics. The mass mailings are its material base, the media performance its superstructure. Social theorists and ideologues, usually on the academic margins, purport to explain the concrete realities of the synthetic performances. They attempt to teach the unknowing how to listen to an electronically synthesized performance as if it were played on original instruments.

The new ideological politics, like the old, is a politics of movement, not parties. Richard Viguerie, one of the chief strategists of the New Right, explains:

> Conservatism had broken loose and was spilling out over the old party boundaries. Conservatives, at long last, were building independent constituencies and pressure groups to match the liberal coalition. The Republican Party was no longer a "reservation" where conservative concerns could be conveniently segregated. Pro-lifers, gun owners, religious groups, each of these now developed its own base. . . .
>
> The New Right . . . is basically this new style of non-party conservatism. It speaks to and for disillusioned Republicans as well as people who never trusted the Republican Party in the first place. Many people of Democratic ancestry and affiliations have felt right at home in the New Right.[12]

What is new about the New Right, from the point of view of American conservatism, is its basis in a well-articulated coalition of diverse social movements and interest groups. One-issue campaigns against abortion (the so-called pro-life movement), against the equal rights amendment (pro-family), against school busing (pro-community) and against affirmative action (pro-individual rights) joined the pro-gun lobby, the religious fundamentalists, and the anticommunists (those who sought to make America strong again), the libertarians and the neoconservatives (i.e., liberal or radical intellectuals who in the shadow of the sixties became conservatives in one way or another) to form the New Right. But the joining was not a simple matter of coalition building. It involved, rather, a new kind of sociopolitical form. Ideology was central, but not highly rationalized. Compromise was not part of the package, nor were party loyalty or discipline. In their place were computers and mass mailings as the chief tactics. As Viguerie explains his enterprise:

Direct mail has been our basic form of communication. The liberals have had control not only of all three branches of government, but of the major universities, the three major networks, the biggest newspapers, the news weeklies, and Hollywood. You can hardly over-state their influence on public opinion—or the difficulty conservatives have run up against in their attempts to gain serious hearing.

So our communication has had to begin at the grass roots level—by reaching individuals outside the chan-nels of organized public opinion. Fortunately, or rather providentially, a whole new technology has become available just in time—direct mail, backed by computer science, has allowed us to bypass all the media controlled by our adversaries. We have built an eight-to-ten-year lead over the liberals in the use of this technology, and we have most of the sexy issues now to boot.

As a result, we have become as independent of the mass media as we are of the old political parties. The old roles are reversed. Today they are coming to us. We have our own agenda, our own network.[13]

Here we have the strange brew of the New Right: a postindus-trial, high-tech, communicative form expressing premodern politi-cal content; computer software, supporting a fundamentalist in-terpretation of the Bible, applied to a paranoid politics. The enemy controls all standard bases of power, according to the New Right script, both governmental and nongovernmental. But the forces of light can battle those of darkness, the liberals, thanks to a gift from God himself, a new technology. Thus there is hope for the conser-vative agenda. True Americanism may again prevail, having reversed the tide.

The distinctive message of the New Right is constructed by those who control the new technology of politics. Though the medium is not the message (it could be used for leftist purposes as well as right-ist), the new medium is very much a source of message building. The virtuoso of direct mailings composes the political message. The single-issue movements are brought together by those who articu-late the new technology. Computerized lists of those likely to support one cause or another are developed. Appeals are presented to those on the list in a dramatic and highly emotional fashion. There is a clear and present danger concerning the "murder of the unborn," the "Panama Canal giveaway," the Soviet military threat and window of vulnerability, etc. The recipients of the appeals are asked to contribute a modest sum to address the pressing problem. Of the sum contributed, a portion is used for the pressing problem, perhaps defeating a particular bill before Congress, but the bulk of it is used to subsidize the direct mailing organization, extending its lists, paying for its overhead, so that it may address future issues. The mailers decide to back a set of issues in a particular way. In a sense they create the New Right constituency's direction by using their resources as they wish to balance the various issues on its agenda. We have a coalition politics without the difficult process of coalition building. There is then a potential for a friction-free ideological politics.

In old-fashioned extremist politics, totalitarian politics, the relationship between members and leaders and between stances on issues and a scientized philosophy of history were highly rationalized. A key idea explained the secret workings of human history (e.g., history is determined by class struggle or the political biology of race). With the key idea, all the apparent complexities and problems of the modern world are explained deductively: past, present, and future. Between the past and future are the brutal practices of the ideological movement. Leaders explain to the followers what the ideology demands of present-day activists to insure the inevitable future. A pseudo-science explains the world and motivates and rationalizes the roles of political activists. In such practice, the modern enlightenment dreams of a science of politics, dreams shared by democrats working out of both the French and the American political traditions, show their dark side.[14]

The new right-wing ideology, especially as it has developed during the Reagan years, turns away from dreams and horrors. Its practice is in a sense a postmodern ideological politics. Sentiment and prejudice connect stances on particular issues. These are vaguely connected to fundamental master problems: specifically, the battles between moral individualism and immoral collectivism. The connection is made most explicit in the computers of campaign strategists and mailers, not through a highly rationalized program in the older ideological mold. The contributors to the various one-issue campaigns can be perfectly ignorant of the deep ideological script, and it still works. They must simply have a feeling that they are part of a social renewal, centered on the issue which most concerns them. The hard material structure of the synthesis is the computer; the identification of unity by the citizenry is achieved through high-level public relations. Reagan, as the Great Communicator, brought together those with a disparate set of commitments.

He convinced them that he shared their interests and concerns, and they united around his person. Details were of little concern to Ronald Reagan. If they had been, the stark contradictions in his commitments would have become all too evident. The New Rightists built their movement around the anonymity of the computer. They sustained it and reached the masses through the ideological clarity and amiable personality of Ronald Reagan.

George Bush obviously understood this. His was an election campaign of ideological clarity, and he opened his administration with extraordinary attention focused upon the presentation of an amiable self to the viewing public. The PR personality was different, but it served the same purpose—political empowerment.

This is a cynical ideological politics of the television medium. It is often observed that Reagan was the first American president to fully take advantage of television's political possibilities. As Franklin D. Roosevelt was our first radio president, Reagan was our first TV president. But the political and ideological implications of this fact are still to be adequately understood. Again, the medium is not the message, but it does open up new, highly irrational possibilities.

The central one-issue campaigns of the New Right do come together in a certain unreflective way. The anti-abortion movement concerns itself with the sanctity of human life. The reactionary women's movement, i.e., the anti-equal-rights-amendment movement, with Phyllis Schlafly as the most prominent leader, focuses on the sanctity of the traditional family. Committed to nurturing the souls of the reborn, born, and unborn, this reactionary movement (reactionary in the sense of being against feminism) supports the pro-life movement. And since healthy families flourish within strong neighborhoods, i.e., local communities, the pro-life and pro-family movements have a natural affinity for the anti-busing movement. A saved soul, nurtured in a cohesive family and strong neighborhood schools, certainly with prayer in them, helps to make for moral individuals, who certainly should not face discrimination for this proper upbringing. Thus, those who support the pro-life, pro-family, anti-busing and moral majority (specifically concerning prayers in the schools) causes are naturally opposed to affirmative action. This is how the ideological script works and, it not only goes unexamined, it is barely articulated with the logical connections made explicit. For there are other more complex reasons to support these and other movements, and there are serious tensions among these reasons. A strong commitment to individualism concerning both merit and choice leads to opposition to affirmative action and support of the individual woman's right to abortion. A concern for the viability of even the traditional family can include an understanding that unwanted pregnancies lead to serious financial and emotional disruptions. Support for strong communities, even among oppressed groups such as African-Americans, is understood to require positive role models achieved through affirmative action.[15] In short, the single issues do not logically or actually in practice cohere.

Thanks to TV performance, they need not. Images replaced rationalized explanation to hold the movement together. The segmented sound bites and visuals of television reporting and advertising create an overall sentiment which unites the supporters of New Right political leaders. Neither the audience nor the performers need concern themselves with the practical or logical connections between the issues. Ronald Reagan promised to make America strong and proud again, and to balance the budget, and to cut taxes. He and his supporters, thanks to the politics of TV images, never publicly faced the implications of these commitments. Likewise, George Bush, the macho candidate, had Americans read his lips. In the manner of a Clint Eastwood performance, he promised no new taxes. But he also promised a kinder and gentler America. The images were persuasive, even if the rational message was muddled.

True believers, a cynical process of mediation, and a half-believing, half-cynical political audience, combine to make up the New Right movement. The true believers keep the media manipulation and the computerized mailing operations going, and when they present good performers such as Reagan, they most effectively gain support for the movement from the general population. In the jargon of the Old Left, they reach the masses. The political problem of mass society is addressed. Since the machinations of manipulation are quite visible, they are either supported directly by the believing and half-believing leaders (apparently such as Bush) and followers, or they are simply accepted as inevitable by the cynical press or public, as we observed in Chapter 1. That this whole process deeply affects society is manifest in everyday social life. The New Left ended its history in ideological confusion. The New Right continues its history with successful presidential politics and the transformation of daily life. This is most evident in the case of education, but the transformation is far from a clear demonstration of ideological success.

The case of education is of central importance. It is the institution where the problematic of a democratic culture must be addressed. If democracy is to be successful, as the rule of the people, there must be an informed, intellectually critical citizenry. But the citizenry must have the means to develop its intellectual capacities and the ability to absorb information. It must have a sound public educational system.

This, obviously, we don't have.

EIGHT

The Crisis in Education

Ideology and cynicism threaten not only American democracy but also American education. Yet it is not the ideology of Nietzsche or Marx or Marcuse, as Allan Bloom asserts, that threatens American education. Rather, today, it is the cynical ideology that connects Bloom with E. D. Hirsch, Jr., William Bennett, William F. Buckley, Jr., and especially Ronald Reagan. Their ideology (not their conservatism), when institutionalized, fosters the development of a deeply rooted cynicism and undermines education. In this way, their position is the opposite of a conservative approach to education.

The modern conservative worries about the extra-intellectual preoccupations of the modern educational project. Some conservative worries, but by no means all, are shared by the right-wing ideologues. Like the ideologue, the conservative wonders how educational institutions can be organized to realize social justice, equality of opportunity for the handicapped, and food for the hungry, and still have time for teaching and learning. Like the ideologues, too, they worry about the diminution of authority (religious and secular) and discipline in the schools (though the conservative and right-wing ideologues may interpret this quite differently). Unlike the ideologues, the conservatives, further, may be concerned with the emphasis on job training and social mobility to the neglect of education as a significant end in itself. The ideologues use conservative and, for that matter, liberal concerns to get on with their ideological projects. The conservative position constitutes an intellectually honorable tradition. The ideological position constitutes what Richard Hofstadter called the American anti-intellectual tradition.[1] They have in common a distaste for liberalism.

The conservative critique of educational liberalism centers on the need to make distinctions.[2] Fundamental among these are the distinctions between the capacities and obligations of children and of adults; and between those of students and of teachers. Also crucial are the distinctions between the sphere of education and other social spheres—particularly political and economic affairs. The conservative knows that false identities and equalities compromise education. Children must learn to take part in the adult world. It is the responsibility of adults to teach children what is important in the world and how to properly get on in it. Skills for adult participation must be taught, and adults must judge how and when they are taught. Adult judgment and discipline must shape the educational enterprise, not the desires and inclinations of children. Hierarchy is crucial for successful education. Adults must take responsibility for the order of things and teach children to take part in the social order, since they inherit it. To treat children as adults, or adults as children, compromises education and social life in general.

From this starting point follows a distinctive view of the proper place of education in society and the proper working of the educational enterprise. Basic academics is the work of education, and is that which distinguishes educational institutions from the rest of society's institutions. There is an emphasis on cultural fundamentals: literacy, basic computational skills, and knowledge of cultural inheritance embodying basic religious and ethical societal ideals. An ordered classroom in which these fundamentals are taught is understood to support ordered minds prepared to take part in a well-ordered society. It is understood that the pressing problems of the day (e.g., social injustice) should not be addressed in the classroom, nor should social problems be treated as problems of adult education, i.e., political life should not be treated as a classroom subject (educating the adult masses has nothing to do with the conservative educational approach).[3]

Though Ronald Reagan's educational programs were clearly related to such a conservative approach, by turning education into an ideological arena conservative educational values were lost. It must be observed that Reagan as a man with little understanding or regard for education, did not put it on his primary political agenda.[4] As a right-wing ideologue, his primary domestic concern was to diminish government interference in people's lives in order to open up opportunities for individual economic initiative. In keeping with his major objectives, his campaign promise for education was to dismantle the Department of Education, which Reagan's close political adviser Edwin Meese had called "a great bureaucratic joke."[5]

Apart from dismantlement, Reagan's educational program was to support school prayer and local control of schools, slow down desegregation plans (in the main it was too late), and support school voucher schemes, as kinds of educational privatizations. Each of

Reagan's programmatic commitments had more to do with his over-all political ideology than with education. Following a fundamentalist program, Reagan as ideologue wanted Christianity back in the schools. Support of local control and opposition to school busing and other desegregation efforts certainly had something to do with the conservative understanding that educational enterprises should be isolated from extra-educational issues, and with a conservative sense that distinct localities knew best and should be responsible for the education of their children. The ideological concern becomes clear with the protection of racial and class privileges, and opposition to political attempts to minimize political supports of those privileges. It may be understood that government attempts to minimize inequality are inappropriate from a conservative point of view, but the previous practices of local and state governments in using the government to support segregated housing and schools were just as inappropriate, especially in the South but in the North as well. By not facing up to the legacies of this past inappropriateness, Reagan revealed his right-wing ideology. It was especially evident in his attempt to support educational privatization and government aid to private, segregated schools.

Reagan's purposeful and (ideologically) principled neglect of education took ironic turns. His first educational tasks were to dismantle the Department of Education and reduce drastically the federal budgetary commitment to education. He called on Terrell Bell, a solid conservative educator, to fulfill those goals. Bell faced a sort of ideological surrealism during his governmental service. In his initial job interview with Edwin Meese, Pendleton James, and Martin Anderson, Meese and Anderson ridiculed what they took to be Carter administration educational policies, most of which were Nixon administration policies that had been coordinated by Bell. In anger Bell corrected them and left the meeting. To his shock, four days later Reagan called him for a meeting. Bell then explained his commitment to federal aid to education, although he indicated he could support a reduction of the department to agency status. On those grounds, Reagan nominated Bell.

At Cabinet meetings, education was not discussed (the original focus was on budgeting matters, and education's only relevance was as an opportunity for cutbacks). Even with no direct access to the president, Bell proceeded to fulfill his agreement with Reagan and formulated a bill that would downgrade the Department of Education to an agency. To Bell's mind, the bill maintained all significant federal education programs. To his ambivalent dismay, when congressional support for the bill proved to be practically non-existent, Reagan did not push it. This was a victory for the federal role in education but significantly weakened Bell as an education advocate. Nonetheless, Bell found a way to strengthen his position and put education on the national agenda, despite Reagan's lack of interest. First, he proposed the creation of a presidential commission to study what he perceived to be a disastrous decline in educational standards. Then, when there was no interest in passing this within the White House, he founded his own commission, which in 1983 issued its now famous report, "A Nation At Risk: The Imperative for Educational Reform." The report stimulated a lengthy and serious national debate on the nation's educational system, turning educational quality into a hot political and intellectual issue. Thus Bush during his presidential campaign indicated that he wanted to be known as the "Education President." Allan Bloom and E. D. Hirsch's best sellers are part of this debate. The commission report was so powerful and well written that it demanded presidential action. One of its sentences drew particularly wide attention and could not be ignored: "If an unfriendly foreign power had attempted to impose on America the mediocre educational performance that exists today, we might well have viewed it as an act of war."[6] Reagan's immediate response was to read a statement in support of the report and to add an ideological non sequitur pressing for tuition tax-credits and prayer in schools.

During the course of the 1984 campaign, though, Reagan used the education issue. He supported federal aid for students in poor communities and for the handicapped and reaffirmed a commitment for college loans. These commitments indicated an understanding that support for educational improvement must involve some federal expense. Yet, when Reagan accounted for the crisis in education, he used a gross correlation to support ideological conviction. Educational standards in the postwar period, as measured by "objective criteria" such as college entrance examinations, were negatively correlated with federal spending. Here we observe Reagan's ideologized leap: federal intrusion into local affairs explains educational decline. Parents know better than federal bureaucrats and educational professionals. They understand the importance of religion, the evils of government, and that throwing dollars at social problems does not solve anything. Using such anti-intellectual rhetoric, Reagan made education a political issue.

After the 1984 election, Reagan fulfilled his campaign promises in a grotesque way. Understanding that federal support of education had contributed to educational decline, he proposed drastic cuts in the Department of Education's budget. Terrell Bell then resigned. Reagan appointed a committed right-wing ideologue, William Bennett, to replace him. There rapidly followed calls for discipline, prayer in school, the core curriculum, back to basics, and budget cutbacks, and attacks upon students for squandering their loans, upon professors for teaching other than traditional topics, and upon university administrators for poor management practices.

To his credit, Bennett did help to focus attention on educational issues, but he did it as a cynical ideological showman. He instigated a generalized confused concern more than a reasonable approach to a serious problem. Again the United States committed itself to educational reform, but the reform very well may turn out to be worse than the problem it presumably addresses. Ideologically inspired hysteria will likely yield cynicism, and the educational status quo will remain.

I

The American educational system is not without powerful strengths. In our major universities and research centers, a disproportionate percentage of the world's Nobel laureates teach and do their research. A heterogeneous population with diverse experiences takes part in the great accomplishments of modern and ancient arts and sciences. In the public elementary and secondary schools (supplemented by private and religious schools), perhaps the most heterogeneous of populations from all over the world, speaking all the world's languages, from diverse classes and racial, ethnic, and geographic backgrounds, receive a basic education; furthermore, they receive it as a right and not a privilege. For many in this system there is significant upward social mobility. More complex educational challenges are hard to imagine, and the American educational system has addressed these challenges over a long period of time, supporting both cultural excellence and democratic values.[7]

Yet, observation of the accomplishment should not obscure the serious problems. For most, education does not provide the basis of social mobility. It reinforces ascribed social status: of the underclass, the lower and middle classes, and the upper class. Further, knowledge of the arts and sciences and the history of our society and its place in the world is woefully unsubstantial. Even basic literacy is a major problem for a great bulk of the American population. The present state of American education does suggest we are a nation at risk. And right-wing ideology, the structure of mass society, and cynicism significantly block a reasonable and effective educational reform effort.

II

Ideology disorients. It confuses issues, and falsely promises easy resolutions to complex problems. American education is a complex business. In the hands of Reagan and his successors it becomes simply a domain for common sense, discipline, the 3 R's, prayer in schools, and parental choice, i.e., manifestations of the New Right's agenda—Christianity and rugged individualism. When William Bennett highlighted educational achievements, he included Joe Clark, an authoritarian principal in Paterson, New Jersey, who walked around his high school with a paddle and solved the discipline problem by expulsion (even against the wishes of the local school board). This is not achievement but resignation. It may be necessary to declare that the most decimated of the young are beyond help, but Clark and Bennett on national television, in national magazines, and in major newspapers cynically celebrated this sad state of affairs as reform. Such theatrics and a very modest increase in objective testing results were presented as proof that the reform was working. Law and order during the Nixon era was a racist code phrase. During the Reagan regime, discipline in the schools became a know-nothing response to the complicated crisis in American education.

The simpleminded means used to perceive the educational problem yielded simpleminded proposals for resolution and simpleminded measures of improvement. The performance on various intelligence tests were at the center of this simplemindedness. Those who think and care little about education readily misappropriate the findings of these tests. At best, when such tests are working, they are sound predictors of educational achievement, not the achievement itself. The tests work, but it is not completely clear why. After all, we do not really know what intelligence is, how knowledge, creativity, memory, and perception contribute to general intelligence, and even whether there is such a thing as general intelligence. Among psychologists the standard operational definition of intelligence is that which intelligence tests measure. Using general objective tests to measure a national educational crisis and its resolution is clearly a misuse of these tests. They were not constructed to measure such problems, and they significantly mislead when they are so applied.

III

America's educational system is radically decentralized. Even with the creation of a Department of Education, American education is still overwhelmingly a local matter. Both Bennett and Bell understood this, and knew full well that their influence on education in the age of federal fiscal austerity depended on shifting public discussion about education to the level of local decisions. In the seventies there were tax revolts, with local school budgets being rejected nationwide. In the eighties, "suddenly" the consequences of national neglect worried many, including Bell, as we have observed. But in a decentralized system, ultimately the worry has to be addressed locally. School boards must propose educational reforms, and taxpayers must willingly support them. The hoopla in the national media must be translated into discrete, often quite undramatic local actions.

At the local level, even in the most secure and safe communities, those relatively undisturbed by the most severe racial and class conflict, and without serious drug problems, addressing the crisis in education is still an extremely complex task. (Of course adverse socioeconomic factors make it even more so.) It starts as a simple political contest. Predictably, local politics is about local taxes and schools, with two primary groups identifiable within the community: those who support high-quality schooling and are willing to pay for it, and those who are concerned with tax rates and believe or hope that the schools are wasteful. To some extent the two groups control each other. The "educationists" must be concerned to control waste for fear that the "taxpayers" will reveal it and prevail among the undecided in cutting back the budget. The "taxpayers," on the other hand, must be cautious not to clearly undermine educational quality, for fear that the "educationists" would then prevail. The taxpayers, typically, are those without children, or those whose children have already grown or are attending private schools. They are on fixed or relatively modest incomes and they themselves are more likely to be poorly educated. The educationists are better educated, more likely to have children in schools and have better incomes. The balance between taxpayers and educationists defines the character of a community's schools. When the educationists predominate, the schools generally are better, but school taxes are relatively high. When the taxpayers prevail, there is less tax burden but the schools are more likely to be mediocre.

Not only is the character of a school district so defined, but the discrete decisions by specific local communities add up to the state of education in the nation. Not surprisingly, after the national taxpayer revolts of the seventies, when taxes for education were the most easily resisted by the citizenry (it is much easier for citizens to directly and effectively hold back school taxes than state or federal taxes), there was a decline in support for education, both financial and nonfinancial support. The national debate following the publication of "A Nation At Risk," then, would result in reform if it shifted the political balance between taxpayers and educationists in enough local communities.

Here is where the complications begin. Even if there is a will to improve local schools, the question is how. Ideologues, professional administrators, and teachers' unions all have an opinion, expert or otherwise, and the nonprofessional public most likely is confused.

Given the ideological atmosphere, the public starts in a confused state. The simple solutions to complex problems that ideology provides are applied to local difficulties. Some of the solutions are only emotionally satisfying, but some, as in the case of education, can yield spurious positive results. Emotionally pleasing for the confused are more rigorous discipline and calls for the teaching of fundamental (Christian) morality, specifically through prayer in schools. Orderly, disciplined classrooms certainly are a necessary condition for getting on with education, but the relationship between discipline and education is not only positive. Too much order stifles independent thought, allowing education only by rote and through fear. Morality, on the other hand, is certainly an end in itself. But in the educational sphere in a pluralistic society, morality's role in education is bound to be controversial. The assertion that there is a relationship between a specific morality and educational performance is just one of the beliefs that make up the controversy. Other members of the public, usually more secularly oriented, hold equally valid alternative beliefs, questioning the instrumental effectiveness and political wisdom of teaching morality in school. There are those who are sensitive to both positions, such as Governor Mario Cuomo of New York, who try to get around the problem by advocating a kind of generic value system which would satisfy the moralists and the secularists. Such moderates tell us that at least a certain ethical level of courtesy and mutual respect is a necessary condition for education to occur. But as with discipline, when manners become an obsession, they can just as well block as support education. For example, deference to even legitimate authorities must be combined with independence of mind for education to be successful. We may say that discipline and morality are important issues but are not clearly linked with the crisis in education, or that at the very least agreement on these matters is unlikely.

Much more potentially pressing are the apparently conservative reforms of the back-to-basics movement. They have achieved results. The back-to-basics advocates point out that when modern child-centered teaching techniques such as open classrooms, teaching creativity, and self-actualization were used, test scores declined. Now, with the reemphasis on basic computational, reading, and writing skills, the scores are going up. These results are especially evident at the local level. Anxious parents called teachers, administrators, and school boards to task for the decline in "educational output." They wanted their local educators to be accountable for results. And now, going back to basics, the results are forthcoming. The scores are up in many districts with concerned parents. From the elementary-school Iowa tests to the college entrance exams, the schools are showing how well they are doing in comparison to their own past performances and in comparison with neighboring school districts. Such results are so important that they affect property values. Homes in districts with low scores are worth significantly less than homes in districts with high scores. There is an apparent convergence of interest between the educationally minded and the economically minded.

But these things are not what they seem. This is obvious from the viewpoint of the economy, and tragic from the viewpoint of education. The economic problem is not one of general worth. For those on a fixed or modest income, even if they are homeowners, the economic problem is one of cash flow. They simply do not have enough money in hand to meet their expenses. Increased property value does not solve this problem, so the economic justification for paying more school taxes to improve the schools does not address their immediate concerns; lower taxes do meet those concerns. Such taxpayers understand their interests, and can act rationally according to these interests.

Yet, people in such an economic bind can and do act altruistically. They can remember the importance of education for themselves and their children and try to support the schools, along with the "educationalists." The national debates affect such altruism, but these "altruists" and the educationalists are not necessarily getting what they are paying for. This is because of a fundamental and cynical flaw in the educational reforms and the means of measuring their success.

To a frightening degree, what is taught in schools under the influence of the present reform movement is not basic education but techniques in test-taking, and only the able benefit. Two very primitive means are used to increase test scores. The most crude (and cynical) is simply to expel or not promote the so-called unteachable. They then do not weigh down the aggregate school scores, and miraculously the scores improve. This is the favorite approach of the inner-city schools. We might call it the Joe Clark technique of educational cynicism. The less crude approach, more prevalent but also cynical, is to develop teaching programs which have as their end improved test scores rather than education. Children are taught reading skills with multiple-choice reading comprehension examinations in mind. They are taught mathematics with multiple-choice tests as the end, and likewise for science, literature, history, and the arts. A clear indication that it is test success and not learned abilities and knowledge that is the goal is the prevalent practice testing that usually precedes the administration of the "real tests."

Schools spend a lot of time in coaching their students before they take big exams. Teachers know their jobs are on the line. If their students do well on the "real tests" (that "count"), the teachers will be deemed successful. If their students do poorly, they could be out of work. A part of the back-to-basics movement is to make teachers so accountable. The same goes for school administrators, from the school principals to the members of the boards of education. The pressure is on, but it is not clear it has much to do with real education. Students know it does not. It is about grades, as in good grades, good college, good job. In this configuration, there is little room for the love of learning, knowledge, and creativity. The irony is, as well, that the configuration is not true. Educators in universities and employers in the so-called real world know that illiteracy is rampant, even among those with good grades. As one generation of students passes uneducated or at least undereducated because of societal neglect (in the seventies, those now concerned about education were engaged in the tax revolt), another generation is passing through our schools undereducated because of a societal self-deceit. People think they are addressing the educational crisis, when they are in fact deepening it. Cynicism and the structure of mass society are getting in the way of democratic education.

IV

Going beyond simple sociological demographics, we must understand who the educationists are in these local school districts. They are from broadly diverse segments of the population. Of greater importance than their class, racial, or ethnic characteristics are their educational achievements. Some certainly are from the educated elite, who are not only well schooled but care deeply and are knowledgeable about education and the worlds of the arts and sciences. There are those who have higher education from all sorts of colleges and universities and who have used their education as a means to an end, sometimes only as a credential which made it possible for them to be considered for a job. Some others have received a basic primary and secondary education for the same reasons, or have used it as the basis for their own appreciation of learning. Still others, all too numerous, are themselves fundamentally uneducated (regardless of the amount of schooling they have received) and want something better for their children.

This schema, of course, is crudely drawn. Yet it can highlight one central point. The quality of the local school-politics depends on the relative makeup of the educationist population. When there are those in the community who care about and are knowledgeable about education as an end in itself, and these people are effective in influencing their fellow citizens, real democratic educational reform is possible. But when there are no such people, or they are without influence, reform is dependent upon the intervention of experts. If the community does not have the capability or desire to critically judge the work of the experts, reform will likely follow the tragic script, and testing rather than education will be the end of education. The experts, local school administrators, union leaders, and teachers will have to show concrete results of their work and this is most powerfully presented in the form of test results.

Though I know, of course, that there is a positive correlation between good test results and learning, I am concerned with the cynical misdirection of learning throughout the American educational system. For very good political and sociological reasons, the tests have become ends in themselves. These tests address the problems of local politics (as we have seen) and the problems of a massified social structure in a very undemocratic fashion.

There is a fundamental asymmetry between those who offer education and those who receive it. The asymmetry involves unequal training and capacity, to some degree, but also a culture of dis-respect for education, Hofstadter's anti-intellectual tradition. On the one hand, teachers and educational administrators are called on to educate the young; on the other, there is a general sense that edu-cation is only a means to an end, not very valuable in itself. Money and power are the ends. Thus educators, poorly paid and relatively powerless in the real world of politics and economics, are not really respected even in their fields of expertise. The best and the brightest do not become teachers. People know that if teachers were smarter they would not have chosen such an unimportant field; they would make their own way in the real world. Those talented eggheads and dreamers who do understand this and become teachers anyway are especially to be mistrusted, motivated as they are by alien ideas, thinking they are better than the rest. A Lee Iacocca seems like a reg-ular guy despite his extreme wealth and substantial power, while any Harvard professor, or anyone with an association with Harvard (such as Michael Dukakis), seems to smack of elitism and has an un-popular mark against him or her as a result.

Educators, then, are viewed as either elitists or fools, not to be trusted in either case, though they are needed. How are they to be controlled? How is society, or at least a community, to be sure they are competent? How is the community to be sure that dangerous ideas and values are not propagated in the schools? The answer to each of these question comes (at least in part) in the form of one ob-jective testing measure or another: competency tests for teachers, basic aptitude and achievement tests for students. Such tests also serve as the answers to another set of questions having to do with the more fundamental problem of the uneven capacity of citizens to judge educational quality. Objective tests tell undereducated par-ents whether or not the teachers and administrators they hire are competent, and whether or not their children have learned some-thing in the schools. They further facilitate the coordination of elementary and secondary local education with a national system of higher education, and this system with a national economy and job market. For example, the fast lane in law goes from college entrance exams to the law boards to the bar exam to the Wall Street firm, from anywhere in the country, at least theoretically. But because the test-ing often is too intimately related to the schooling and too distantly related to real learning, the theoretical test links are systematically broken. The difference between real education and test preparation and performance becomes strikingly evident.

V

Nowadays children learn to read in fragmented ways from workbooks and textbooks. These nonbooks break down reading into discrete sets of learning tasks. Texts and workbooks in phonics, skillpacks, English, and reading are used to teach fundamental skills systematically. The student learns these fundamentals one at a time, the elements of grammar apart from punctuation, phonics apart from reading comprehension, vocabulary apart from spelling. The poetry of the word is not to be found. The student "goes through" say ten pages of one element or another, takes a test assuring that the skill has been mastered, and goes on to the next skill. Theoretically the building blocks of reading are pieced together and eventually synthesized. This is a mastery behavioral approach to reading. Various sorts of holistic approaches oppose it. They want students to go "bottom up" (in the jargon), "top down," "middle middle," i.e., they emphasize the reading experience as an integrated whole. Whether the more behavioral or more holistic approaches more effectively teach reading is beside the point for the present purposes. Though I do believe that reading instruction that starts with the inculcation of the love of reading, with an awe for the treasures books offer, is likely to be the most successful, and I do suppose that today those who use holistic approaches are more likely to appreciate this, the major problem is not that the wrong approach is being used. Rather it is that the behavioral approach is used and misused because it more likely yields high test-scores, because the tests tend to measure the behavioral components of learning. Since the synthesis of components is not easily measured, reading education is not synthesized. Put succinctly, students are taught to read reading-comprehension paragraphs rather than literature. Literature is reserved for the overachievers, the talented and gifted whose high scores are taken for granted. Actually, the talented and gifted are identified as those with high scores. It is argued that other students are not yet ready, but in the end those other students may never actually get an education. Frequently, talented students turned off by the testing process, i.e., those who may have a love of learning but not a love of testing, are excluded. Further, class structure is being reproduced here. The privileged are coached to accept testing and to test well. The underclass views this as an odd and foreign practice. This very well may be at the root of the well-known ethnocentric qualities of the tests.

VI

We observe here an educational system reeking with cynicism, fueled by right-wing ideology, emanating from massified social structures. The ideology views both the problems and solutions in simplistic terms. Liberal educational philosophies and government interference lead to educational decline; basics, discipline, and morality yield reform. The reform, as measured by test results, makes education seem possible for and to the miseducated without seriously confronting the values and challenges of education. There is the false appearance of educational improvement; meanwhile, illiteracy spreads. Mathematical reasoning is a lost art among broad segments of our population. And human experience and accomplishment in American, Western, and other cultures are dimly known.

Over thirty years ago, Hannah Arendt wrote an essay with the same title as this chapter.[8] Her concern was with the progressive approach to education and politics, particularly John Dewey's. She worried that children were too quickly being treated as adults (specifically in American schools) and that adults were too readily being treated as children in the public domain (particularly by totalitarian movements and parties). We observe today a variation on her theme. Now it is not progressive ideology but right-wing ideology that threatens the educational enterprise. Then and now it is not progressivism or conservatism which is the major problem. Rather, it is simplistic ideologies and slogans. Canned approaches to education do not work. Education, as Arendt strongly argued, requires a love of knowledge, a love of children, and a caring for the world we pass on to them, by the community, political leaders, parents, teachers, and administrators. If we do not meet these requirements, any reform based on any formula, whether drawn from progressive or conservative principles, is bound to failure.

N I N E

The New Treason of the Intellectuals: A Critique of Ideological Critique

If the crisis in education has no simple progressive solutions, as Arendt cogently maintained thirty years ago, and no easy conservative solution now, as I have argued, how might we proceed? Clearly, despair is a temptation. And if we are not making progress, as the New Rightists argue we have on the education front, what about the apparently unresolvable problems of the underclass, urban blight, drugs, and crime? The dimensions of the problems overwhelm us. Absolute dogmatic faith in pseudo-conservatism or pseudo-leftism, in the magical powers of entrepreneurship or the working class, at this time and place are probably little more than elaborate political forms of collective cognitive dissonance, permitting comfortable political and personal practices.

The old-fashioned ideologues, the totalitarian Stalinists and National Socialists, knew that the world beyond their political programs and social movements was alien and antagonistic, and so with terrific force they brutally transformed the world. American ideologues clearly are not cut from this cloth. Theirs are happy ideologies, which purport that their truths are self-evident, ameliorating social problems without pain (keep in mind Reagan's idea of education reform: education improvement through lower federal spending on education). Given that real social problems have not disappeared, the ideologies persist only among those who focus exclusively on the ideology and ignore the social world, or more precisely, see the world only as their ideology depicts it. Ronald Reagan's detachment, epitomized by his dream-like approach to economic policy and nuclear armaments, allowed him to maintain his faith and publicly express his ideological convictions despite contrary counsel by sympathetic advisers and experts.[1] He just spoke sincerely, forcefully ignoring or not seeing the ugly facts. He seemed to think that if he ignored problems they ceased to exist, and the American public blindly followed. Thus, right-wing ideologues and their supporters of the eighties, like the Communists and their fellow travelers of the thirties, denied unpleasant realities.

In both cases, opinions, judgments, decisions, and statements of the ideologically inclined are more products of who and what they are ;han of their observation and reason. This sort of fact lends significant support for a relatively new kind of intellectual activity—ideological critique. A critique based on ideology seeks to reveal the material interests which purportedly stand behind ideas about politics, society, culture, economics, and more. It is a treacherous activity when it becomes part of the common culture, as it has in the United States today. It is a key cultural component of the cynical society. All ideas are treated as ideologies. Ideas and other cultural artifacts lose their independent significance. They are easily dismissed and lost. Apparently all that remains is ideational deception and power conflicts.

I

The first fully articulated ideological critique is *The German Ideology* by Marx and Engels.[2] In it, German philosophers, particularly the left-Hegelians, are dismissed as ideologues—i.e., people who peddle the false notions that ideas shape the world, rather than the world forming ideas. Marx maintains that these false notions serve the interest of the dominant class. The leading ideas of an epoch are the ideas of the ruling class. Or, as Marx more baroquely put it, "The ruling ideas are nothing more than the ideal expression of the dominant material relationships, the dominant material relationships grasped as ideas; hence of the relationships which make the one class the ruling one, therefore, the ideas of its dominance." Thus, not only is there no such thing as an independent history of ideas (such a history in the final analysis is a history of class dominance in ideational form), but ideas about politics, culture, and social practices are simply forms of class conflict. The critical theories should not worry about the substantive content of competing notions of democracy and culture but must reveal the class basis of these notions and link them to the class logic of history. This is an early variety of Marxist ideological critique, not very common in America. But it did open the door to cynicism as we know it.

Key figures in the Marxist tradition or in traditions stemming from it have opened the door more widely. They have legitimated cynicized reason as rational. Though people have always discounted the arguments of their adversaries as being self-interested, ideological critique confuses ad hominem attacks with scientific explanation. This confusion is now an important part of our culture.

It got here by a circuitous route. Lenin, Georg Lukács, Karl Mannheim, and Antonio Gramsci each supported the confusion. Lenin shifted the political ground. Whereas Marx contrasted ideology as a false philosophy of consciousness to his own true philosophy of historical (or dialectical) materialism, i.e., contrasted falsity to truth, Lenin contrasted ideologies, the ideology of the capitalists with the ideology of the working class. There is political abomination in this shift. Lenin as the professional revolutionary claimed for himself and for other vanguardists the capacity to discern that the actual ideas of the working class, e.g., ideas about trade unions, were capitalist ideologies, which the professional revolutionary had to struggle against.[3] Since the vanguardists are armed with the truth of history, the opposition to the working class in the name of the working class must proceed by any means necessary. This reasoning leads directly to the gulag, justified by party theoreticians, now described as party ideologists.

Lukács and Gramsci, probably the two most sophisticated thinkers in the tradition of Marxism (and Leninism) deduced the full implications of ideological critique. Lukács and his students of the so-called Budapest school developed a high-level critique of Western philosophy, centering on the problem of reification and an analysis of capitalist relations in philosophy and literature. When it came to practical politics, despite a commitment to the fundamental truth of party practice which led to a dutiful fluidity in public pronouncements, Lukács personally supported a broad popular-front position throughout his career.[4]

Gramsci's practical position was more novel, noble, and tragic, given his imprisonment and short life. He understood the fundamental support of capitalist relations as existing in consciousness through a hegemonic ideology. Popular common sense is made up of this ideology and others, some pre-dating capitalism, some pointing to its overturning. It was to be the major role of the Communist as ideological critic, then, to transform popular consciousness. Armed with the truth, the Communist becomes the teacher of the masses, allowing them to perceive their own position in history as the universal class. For Gramsci, as for Lukács, the truth of the party, of party ideology as the ideology of the working class, was used to reveal the political limitations of existing ideas. Gramsci allowed for a greater relative autonomy of these ideas, and clarified their importance. This, along with the fact that as an imprisoned Communist in the thirties he was one of a rare species—an innocent Communist[5]—probably explains the present popularity of his writing in academic circles.

But it took Karl Mannheim, a compatriot and colleague of Lukács, to popularize the idea of ideological critique well beyond orthodox Marxist circles. Mannheim, sometimes referred to as the bourgeois Marxist, developed a sociology of knowledge which is a kind of generalized system of ideological critique. According to Mannheim, the ideas of a time and place are products of the material conditions of that time and place in two ways: (1) as total ideologies, the general worldviews of particular classes are shaped by their practical experiences as they are embedded in an overall social structure; and (2) as particular ideologies, the ideas of particular classes justify their interests, within the context of social conflict. Mannheim maintained that all knowledge is in effect ideological, tied to the limited view of particular classes. Only the distanced ideas of unattached intellectuals can achieve some synthesis—a momentary common wisdom and good. As Lukács's theory elaborately justified the dictatorship of the Communist party, Mannheim's sociology of knowledge justified an expert-directed technocratic welfare state.[6] Mannheim and other sociologists of knowledge crucially do not subscribe to Marxist ideologies. The working class holds no special place in history. The only differences between the Communist party and others are its members' fanaticism and its brutality once in power.

Marxist theory, then, has been central to academic debate in the social sciences.[7] But on both sides, ideological critique has been accepted. For our purposes, this is the relevant point. A great deal of Marxist and non-Marxist social science takes as a major proposition that the practical significance of knowledge and culture, of the arts and sciences, is best understood by their social determinations. The theoretical danger in this is reductionism. The practical danger is cynicism.

When the arts and sciences are conceived as highly mediated or subtle ideologies, as they are by both Marxist and conventional social scientists, culture can be lost to the analyst. The beauties of line in the graphic arts and sound in music and poetry, the elegance and subtlety of mind in science, become but facades of interests, not embodiments of human reach and distinction. This is the sorry theoretical end game of the sociology of culture as an ideological critique. The result is a scholarly wasteland, especially evident in orthodox Marxist studies of literature, aesthetics, and science.[8] A highly technical theoretical apparatus is developed to explain away cultural experience. In the U.S., some of Jacoby's lost intellectuals have been overwhelmed by this enterprise. It is not only their use of dense language which discourages a general public, it is the triviality of their enterprise. Jean-Paul Sartre once noted that though Flaubert is a petit-bourgeois author, not all petit-bourgeois authors are Flaubert. At times it seems that some ideological critics want to prove Sartre wrong.

This theoretical end game supports professional philistinism. Scholars, often despite their own refined judgments, develop theoretical positions which in principle overlook the distinctive qualities of cultural work.[9] Ideological critique teaches that the quality of ideas is less important than their social origins. A simplistic democratic sentiment (but I do not think a deep self-reflective democratic commitment) suggests that to make distinctions between cultural artifacts is to support spurious distinctions among people. Qualitative judgment then drops out of all sorts of social inquiry, Marxist or otherwise.[10] The resulting academic sterility has effects beyond the halls of academe. It serves as a major justification of cynicism. It represents a new treason of the intellectuals, an abdication of fundamental responsibilities.

Ideas about politics and culture, about the true, the beautiful, and the good, are not taken seriously in American society. We know that talk about such things is "mere rhetoric," which fronts for raw conflicts of interest. Perhaps such talk is appropriate for Sunday school or a graduation ceremony, but not for everyday life. Of course there are people who believe in central principles, from Christian fundamentalism to secular humanism, from Main Street Republicanism to the ideas of Jesse Jackson's "Rainbow Coalition," from astrology to astronomy. But these principles have no common ground. The point is not that they are different. It is rather that they seem to have no cultural meeting point where differences can be overcome, reconciled, accommodated or compromised when they suggest conflict. People with different principles seem just to face each other and assert their power, using words to both justify and mask their positions. And the ideological critics say that this is all there is.

Cynicism has become a central interpretive frame in our mass society, undermining democracy. Democratic principle and cynical interpretation are tightly intertwined in normal social as well as political practice. In a massified order without a common culture, cynicism has become a general cultural form. Ideological critique provides its intellectual justification.

II

Ideological critique teaches that behind all culture is interest, and that ultimately the significance of culture is the interest it serves. Cynicism has become the cultural glue of the social order, which was previously served by shared values. Talcott Parsons, the pre-eminent American sociologist of the twentieth century, based his theory of social order and change on the idea of shared values. He conceived of orderly social evolution as a process of social differentiation and reintegration, achieved through value generalization. He thought that this evolutionary process made human societies more adaptable to environmental changes. His theory has been much criticized, not least because of the opacity of his language.[11]

More crucially, the idea of values holding society together has been hotly contested. Social order is as much a product of value conflicts as of consensus.[12] America has a power elite dominating society, not a normative order.[13] Domination and coercion are central to any given historical order.[14] And yet, the core of Parsons's viewpoint, free of the elaborate language of unnecessary abstraction, does present important insights into our present predicaments, not as a total or complete theory (as Parsons would have it), but as a framework for examining the problem of the integration of complex democratic or mass societies.

In complex societies, people do different things, ever more so with greater complexities. This is what Parsons means by "social differentiation." But once people start doing different things, they develop troubles in relating to each other; thus the need for "reintegration." The fact that people specialize in what they do means they do it better and adapt more easily to unforeseen contingencies; there is "adaptive upgrading." But such upgrading, differentiation, and reintegration are predicated upon shared general values. With shared values, the people doing different things can still relate to each other. The values must be generalized, i.e., not be too specific to what the people do and who they are, exactly because the people are different.

This sensible schema is at the core of Parsons's theory. As with the work of Edward Shils, which is closely related to Parsons's work,[15] the theory assumes a smooth and nonmanipulative process, whereas many critics rightly underscore that conflict and domination are central or, as I would prefer to put it (leaving room for freedom or contingency), can be as central as consensus. But the basic insight should be acknowledged: some core general values foster the identity of both small groups and complex social orders. No one contests that this is an aspect of simple group life—from children's playgroups to religious sects.

I believe that outside the bounds of narrow academic polemics, this must be recognized as part of complex social orders as well. This is most evident when we think in large-scale comparative terms. There really is a difference between American, French, British, and Russian political cultures. This is demonstrated by the sorts of social and political rhetorics historically common in each of these nations, by the state institutions which shape and have been shaped by the values implicit in these rhetorics, and by the distinct social relations that are shaped and have been shaped by the dynamics of state institutions and the developing rhetorics. Differences between American and British schools,[16] French and American labor relations, and French, Russian, and American bureaucracies, are related to the different political cultures in these nations,[17] let alone the very different state structures. As has been often emphasized by Sovietologists, even the Soviet Union is as much a Russian state as a Marxist state, something that the proponents of perestroika too quickly overlooked.

But value generalization, the common commitment to a general set of values, seems to be going awry, or at least to have reached its limits. This is evident both at home and abroad. In the United States, the general values of liberal democracy have declined in real meaning for American political and social practice. The values of Marxist socialism face a clear crisis not only in Communist-party-dominated and controlled societies,[18] but also among critical Communist activists beyond the sphere of Soviet control. The crisis in values in the political East is well known, and is changing the facts of geopolitics. The crisis in the West has not been adequately examined.

Cynicism is a ubiquitous but a generally unrecognized cultural form. As a substitute for values it has deeply affected a broad variety of social practices, from the family to community life to religion and politics to the arts and sciences, and especially to the relations between these spheres of life. It was Parsons's position that the core values of society regulated society's differentiated institutions and their interrelationships. His critics note that social relationships are not only based on shared values and common ends; between some, in fact, the ends are diametrically opposed. Despite a fear that I present little more than an affectation of choosing the wise middle

ground, I do believe that both conflict and consensus in a nondeter-
minant way are part of the story, as cynicism and democratic
culture, mass and democratic society, are part of our societal life.
The central problem is that cynicism is replacing values.

III

Consider the case of education again, so that we may move beyond
it. In the conflict between the "educationists" and the "taxpayers,"
as we observed, there is substantial interest, if not class conflict. To
put it simply, those who have more disposable income and greater
hopes that their children will be successfully trained for more elite
positions favor higher levels of school taxes. Those who must live
much more tightly, and "know" that their children, like themselves,
are not likely to excel or benefit materially in schools, are much more
likely to oppose high levels of school taxes. To use the language of
Herbert Gans (the prominent sociologist of American social strati-
fication, communications, and community life),[19] high-quality
schools are institutions of the upper-middle-class "taste public,"
while more "lean and mean" no-nonsense schools are institutions
of middle- and lower-middle-class-taste publics. In such a case of
conflicting interest, Gans counsels a working out of benefits for appropriate classes. He is very concerned that cultural policy should
proceed in such a way that the disadvantaged not be forced to subsidize the advantages of the privileged.[20] Since museums, opera
companies, symphony orchestras, public television, and high-quality educational institutions are patronized by the upper middle class
and upper class, general public revenues should be used only spar-
ingly to support these institutions. This view, which Gans does
qualify, focuses on society as a system of social conflicts. It overlooks
common values.

In American education, there are discernible common values that
go beyond specific interest-conflicts. Generally, people share a
sense that schools must help prepare children for the adult world,
that this involves the acquisition of basic social and academic skills,
and these skills are to be applied in economic, political, and cultural
life. Further, more specifically, there is some rudimentary agreement about how preparation for adulthood is to occur, what skills
must be acquired and the hierarchy of their importance, and how
skills are to be applied to the economic, political, and cultural
spheres.

Differences on matters educational, as we have already observed, are substantial, but we should not overlook the shared values which constitute the grounds on which the differences are expressed. People disagree about the techniques of teaching math and reading: whether mathematical reasoning or basic computational skills are of greater importance, whether phonics or appreciation of content-cues more readily lead to reading proficiency. But that math and reading are of the utmost importance, of greater importance than, for example, driver education, is not questioned. Americans also generally agree that education should be linked with both job training and democratic citizenship, though how this is to be done and with what priority are issues of conflict. And of course there are conflicts over the issue of costs and how they are to be balanced between various educational needs, how the needs are to be balanced with the pursuit of private wealth, comfort, and sustenance, and how the needs are to be balanced with other public concerns. That these competing needs and concerns are weighed in fairly conventional ways indicates that common values and competing conflicts together constitute educational practice. Herein lies the real challenge of cynicism, not only to American education, but to many other aspects of American social life.

When the common extraeducational valuative underpinnings of American educational commitment are disbelieved, i.e., the economic ideal of economic opportunity and the political ideal of democracy, or at most are publicly used to rationalize educational practices without critical examination, all that remains is conflict over competing policies and interests. When E. D. Hirsch maintains that the end of learning which best facilitates economic opportunity and democracy is knowledge about the world (bits of information), the critical reflective response should not center on the testing results of a specific learning technique. But in the trenches, i.e., in the local school districts where educational policy is implemented, this is the effective response to his criticism. "Good schools" are those that yield good test results. The schooling, as we have observed, is too intimately integrated into the testing. In everyday practice, especially at the local level, no one critically appraises how the school-testing complex serves our economic or political ideals. To be sure, there is an uproar over our national vulnerability. People note with alarm that we are ranked last among our industrial competitors in the teaching of science and math.[21]

But political discourse and contestation about education is not about education as an end in itself, or about democracy, or even about economic opportunity. It is either technical (about which teaching approach or text yields the best test results or the best college placements), or it is about taxes, or about extraneous exotica and scandals such as prayer or drugs in schools. The high ideals of education, democracy, and economic opportunity are reserved for graduation ceremonies. Talk about education that does not show immediate practical (test) results no longer is a living part of ongoing societal life. Conflict and disorientation then abound. Common values have become "purported" common values, "disbelieved" values (empty pieties), *ideologies*.

IV

This condition is probably less true in education than in other spheres of life. With our care of the young, we are less likely to abandon our ideals. The transformation of value commitments to disbelieved values has deeply penetrated American adult institutional life. The political discourse we have analyzed throughout this inquiry is but the most public, most highly visible articulation of a deep and broad societal malaise. From commercial enterprise to state governance, from popularized entertainment to high academic criticism (i.e., ideological critique), cynicism has replaced common values. The often-observed moral vacuum in American business practice makes the idea of business ethics seem like an oxymoron. This is popularly observed in the mass media, prominently in the Hollywood blockbuster *Wall Street*. It is also a subject of intense academic concern; thus the proliferation of ethics courses in business schools. The widespread market scandals fortify a general sense that the "legitimate" in "legitimate business" is a facade for organized robbery. Even those on the left who are very critical about capitalism as a form of economic organization should note the odd valuative paradox. At a time when alternative forms of economic organization (i.e., socialism) seem ever more remote and far from desirable for a great bulk of the population, the assumption of corruption of existing economic life is common. We expect our capitalists to be corrupt, to stretch the limits of the law. We cynically accept this as inevitable and even reward it.

Such reward has clear political expression. Conflicts of interest, questionable use of influence, and blatant illegality defined the politics of the Reagan era. More officials were forced to resign because of ethical improprieties than in any administration in American history. People confirmed for themselves their cynical wisdom—all politicians are corrupt—but this did not affect their political choice.

Even with their cynicism, they reelected Reagan in 1984, and elected his vice president as president in 1988. Then Bush attempted to distinguish himself when he opened his administration by informing the public that he would insist on high ethical standards, and this was received as little more than an interesting political strategy.

We have reached a cultural crossroads. Corruption is accepted. Proposals for alternatives are cynically interpreted as plausible or implausible strategies. Yet, a solid common sense tells us that utopian solutions in the twentieth century are suspect. Clearly, we must rethink our approach to our present situation. We must develop a different way to think about politics and culture, so that we may criticize mass society and its culture of cynicism and appreciate democratic political and cultural accomplishment and values. We must think about our society critically, but following the insights of Max Weber, with an appreciation of the autonomous aspects of a full variety of human activities. Our cultural life cannot be identified directly with political struggles; politics are not reducible to culture, and neither politics nor culture can be fully explained by economics. These are separate, though related, spheres of human activity.[22]

As we have observed, when experts, political activists, or citizens too quickly conflate the distinctive human realms, cynicism results. Avoiding cynicism requires an understanding of the distinctiveness of separate spheres, while appreciating their relationships. The distinctiveness of culture, as the autonomous arts and sciences, is of central importance not only for culture as an end in itself; it is also crucial for the viability of democratic values in political and social practice.

In the analysis of the separate spheres, we can appreciate and understand enlightenment as it exists in the artifacts and accomplishments of the arts and sciences on their own terms, relate them to other spheres of society, and develop a sound basis for criticizing cynicism. The cultural can then be appreciated as a separate part of a differentiated modern world that strategically shows us how to avoid cynicism. The modern age then would be characterized not only by the rise of capitalism, proletarianism, and the emergence of the modern state, as the "new" comparative historical sociologists from Barrington Moore, Jr., to Charles Tilly to Theda Skocpol tell us,[23] it would be defined as well by science separated from religious dogma, and art that does not simply seek to reveal religious truths. The cultural worlds in this sense are at the center of societal life, a central subject matter, providing the basis for discovering and supporting submerged or besieged critical values.

We need to be certain about how we should understand this subject matter. Too often art and science are said to reflect some social fact. There are fundamentally two things wrong with this position. It takes culture *completely* out of society, and it substitutes vague assertions for investigation. Conventional sociological studies of the production of culture and of art worlds assert a great deal which I find problematic,[24] but one thing they do demonstrate is that the daily life of the creation, production, and distribution of culture is very much within society. One becomes an artist very much as one becomes a marijuana user.[25] Art markets and commodity markets seem to function according to the same laws. The publishing industry and the computer industry are indistinguishable in investment portfolios.

The second, more crucial inadequacy of the notion of reflection is that it not only takes culture out of society, it begs the most interesting sociological and political questions. It does not explain the most complex ways by which culture symbolizes or represents other than cultural practices, hopes, thoughts, etc.—how political, economic, and religious pressure and projects come to shape, support, direct, and repress cultural work and its reception. In the place of analysis is the "simple" assertion of reflection.

The problem with such a position is crucially in evidence in the analysis of mass culture. The prevailing orthodoxy in American sociologies of culture, and in American public opinion, is to dismiss the distinction between mass culture and autonomous culture. Democratic sentiment, as Tocqueville long ago explained, hesitates to make strong qualitative distinctions between cultural works in fear that this would suggest qualitative judgments concerning the worth of their makers and consumers. Yet, we must go beyond such sentiment in order to do justice both to the cultural and the democratic. The primary issue is the necessarily autonomous basis of the arts and sciences, in contrast with the manipulative and highly mediated basis of mass culture.

As we observed in Chapter 3, the primary function of the mass cultural industry is to link cultural product to audience. This is accomplished in one of two ways: by selling the cultural product as a commodity, or by selling a constructed audience as potential consumers of other advertised commodities (the case, e.g., of commercial television and newspapers).

The primary function of autonomous cultural institutions, on the other hand, from universities to loft theaters, is the creation of universes of cultural discourse. The relation between speaker and audience in mass culture is highly asymmetrical, i.e., the degree of cultivation of expression and literacy and of interpretive and judgmental capacity is exponentially greater among the "speakers." In cultural institutions, although of course the "speakers" have a higher degree of cultivation, the distance between them and their audience is not nearly as great. Mass cultural institutions use the distance as opportunities for commodity exchange, packaging culture for the uninformed at a price. Cultural institutions use the distance as opportunities for education and discussion, bringing people into a world of cultural discourse, arising from cultural traditions.

Living cultural traditions and free publics distinguish autonomous cultural worlds from mass culture. The history of cultural forms and creative practices challenges the present generation. Human capacity is summarized by cultural history, as is human failure. A living cultural tradition exists when cultural history is utilized by the present generation as resource and challenge. Poets try to put into words what their predecessors had or had not done, in ways that they could not. Artists attempt to improve upon or reaffirm the value of the work of their predecessors. Scientists hope to answer the questions which theories accepted from the past implied but left unanswered. Such dynamic development of cultural traditions is strikingly missing in institutions of mass culture. In these, traditions may be cynically used to "hook" an audience. But with very rare exceptions, traditions are consumed for extracultural purposes and not worked upon. With the development of traditions in cultural institutions, following an inherent and inherited path, cultural life is set apart from the manipulating powers of society. Though cultural products do become commodities and do have monetary value, as long as cultural institutions function as institutions of culture, evaluations of quality exist. These evaluations are based on the traditions but are sometimes in revolt against them; and these evaluations are at least alongside of and sometimes juxtaposed against monetary values. Embedded values in society persist apart from cynicism.

As has been evident in this inquiry, mass culture promotes mass society. Autonomous culture promotes the development and defense of autonomous publics. In the former, atomized individuals, separated from one another, receive messages—information, entertainments, facts and figures—from a centralized source. In the latter, individuals exchange ideas, experiences, and judgments among themselves. The end of the culture of the public is the free development of culture itself, which is inherently critical of the existing mode of domination, because it operates according to fundamentally different principles. This situation is the sociological condition of cultural freedom.[26]

The problem we face is the determination of cultural activity and artifact as products either of manipulation or cultural freedom; in terms of the earlier critical theory, as positive or critical culture.[27] We should make this determination not only upon our own cultural judgments (which is necessary) but upon the investigation of the life of a cultural work.

An alive critical culture extends a tradition and becomes part of a public. Mass culture and cultural ideology only use tradition as an exploitable resource, adding nothing to it, and such culture is received by a mass. Such delineation between mass and autonomous culture is open to the possibility that a work may be presented as one, but transformed into the other. Given the symbolic density of culture, its overdetermination and resultant ambiguity, a work may be a part of a cultural tradition, both as understood by the work's creator and its audience, but the work can be dislocated from that tradition, through a reinterpretation and appropriation, and become part of mass culture. Products of mass culture, as well, can be used by cultural agents and through creative interpretation can be presented to a public for critical evaluation. This is not as often the case, because the frequent undimensionality of much of mass culture allows little room for interpretation other than satire, and this is a distinctly limited form. But at times explosively expressive and critical forms have been energized and fortified in this fashion. Such is the case, for example, of the reappropriation of pop by jazz musicians (pop, ironically, having emerged as the homogenization of jazz for a mass audience).

Hermeneutic power struggles continue these transformations, with the behemoth of mass culture devouring autonomous culture. This leads toward a one-dimensional society.[28] Those engaged in an autonomous culture must then struggle to maintain the integrity of their work, attempting to insulate it from mass cultural appropriations and attempting to find a public. This is a struggle against cynicism. The value of cultural works belies cynical interpretation.

What has been viewed as autonomous or critical culture should not be confused with agit-prop, or other cultural ideologies of the left or right. Much that is described as critical or even democratic in our times is little more than such ideological culture. In distinguishing autonomous cultural life from the manipulation of the mass-culture industry, we should not simplemindedly confuse the former with any specific ideological political programs. Confusion such as this is the starting point for the oppressive cultural politics of Soviet-type societies.

On the other hand, autonomous culture, even of the most innovative sort, may have quite conservative or even reactionary implications. Sometimes this is the intention of its creators (e.g., Pound and Eliot); at other times this occurs despite its creators' intentions. When an autonomous work appears in a free cultural domain, its interpretation is open to contention. If the existing public life constituted an ideal speech community, as imagined by Germany's most prominent critical theorist, Jürgen Habermas, we could rest assured that the prevailing understanding of a work represented a consensually truthful rendering of it.[29] But of course this is not the case. Cultural works are deformed or, more precisely, re-formed and fitted into established patterns of understanding, which may articulate with mass cultural worldviews, but which as well articulate quite readily with ideologies of the existing modes of domination. Artworks thus become commodities, without the artist intending it; and thus the abstract expressionists, who understood themselves as radicals, may have become, from a certain point of view, ideologists for the "American Century."[30] Even more concretely, in such a fashion avant-garde art movements in New York City have become central agents of the urban gentrification process.[31] Of course, not all autonomous culture is manifestly critical, and all that is overtly critical is not autonomous. But we must recall that the central point of all autonomous culture embodies an undercurrent of critique because it operates according to principles set apart from the steering mechanisms (whether political or economic) of the social order. As such, autonomous culture points to the possible alternatives to our existing way of life, to the distance between our values and our practices.

It should be clear from the preceding that I believe we must make cultural evaluation not idiosyncratically but with respect for the distinction between mass and autonomous culture. To equate autonomous with mass culture is to succumb to cynicism, conflating freedom with its opposite. In the case of a work judged to be autonomous, for example, Philip Roth's *Zuckerman Bound*,[32] the author should be interpreted as creating a universe of reflection, insight, and beauty. The deferential conversation Roth engages in with Malamud and the contentious conversation with Irving Howe, among others, should be analyzed, as should his poetic homage to the novelists of the "other Europe" in "The Prague Orgy." His distinctive voice should be judged within a cultural and social context, especially his call for artistic autonomy.

Should we do the same with the supermarket romances made to the explicit specifications of publishers? I, obviously, don't think so, unless we can demonstrate that some specific pulp novelist in his or her individuality, with a distinctive voice, manages to subvert the restrictions of the manipulated genre, such as Stanislaw Lem has in science fiction.[33] Again, judgment is necessary.

The distinction between autonomous and mass culture is not a clear distinction between high and low or fine and popular culture. The high/low and fine/popular dichotomies are based on class and status distinctions well known to us all. We contrast classical music with jazz, photography in the Museum of Modern Art with newspaper photos, "European films" with "American movies," as we do fine or high art with popular or low art. While such high/low, fine/pop dichotomies assert class privilege and attempts at status display and acquisition, the autonomous vs. mass typology attempts to illuminate the modern (enlightened) accomplishment of cultural freedom. From this point of view, "European" serious music and jazz, museum and popular photography, and films and movies, can all be autonomous or massified. The relationship between such works and other social phenomena, from politics to religion, from socialization to education, from economics to technology, is the proper subject matter of the sociology of culture, as the arts and sciences. It is both a particular scholarly project and practical philosophy for overcoming the problems of a cynical society.

The study of these relationships is an intricate and subtle endeavor. It is both an interpretive enterprise and a study of the social structure of interpretation. The overdetermined nature of the arts and sciences accounts for this. Works in the arts and sciences as symbolic realities are overdetermined in the manner of dreams and daydreams, as Freud has demonstrated.[34] The interpretation of culture, though, in contrast to dreams, is not revealed in the clinical relationship between dreamer and analyst but in social relationships—between and among artists, scientists, critics, producers, universities, political parties, markets, and so forth. This is the social life of culture, not reduced to other social phenomena. Here is a strategic ground for critically separating cynicism from submerged social values and discerning the difference between the functions of a mass society and democratic practices.

V

Before we consider a central American case in point, the sociology of an African-American novel as a means of avoiding cynicism about the "American dilemma," we must ponder a pressing theoretical question: why is autonomous culture, subjected to the strictures of excellence, a key mode of human action for the understanding and supporting of democracy as the alternative to mass society? The answer in one phrase is public freedom. Without public freedom, neither autonomous culture nor democracy can exist.

The constant reassuring refrain in Tocqueville's *Democracy in America* is that America's appreciation and practice of public freedom would control the new tyrants and their tyranny. Here, given the immense problems of mass society and cynicism, Tocqueville's assurance has been called into question, but the import of public freedom for cultural and political life must be underscored. What is involved is not a relationship among behavioral variables, but a political problematic.

Tocqueville was confused on this point. As an aristocrat, he seemed to believe that cultural refinement was a necessary victim of democratization. His reasoning exemplifies what today has become neoconservative common sense. Refinement is seen to be inegalitarian, involving hierarchies of human capacity and judgment. In that democracy requires egalitarianism, it necessarily undermines the reward of such capacity and the outcome of such judgment. But reasoning of this sort lacks fundamental sociological insight and is overly mechanical. Missing is an appreciation of the special position of autonomous public life in mass society.

Both autonomous (critical) culture and democracy (with self-determination as a central principle) require autonomous public freedom. The normative problem, then, is the viability of a public sphere for cultural and political practice.

Tocqueville identified with the normative goal, without perceiving that it could address the problem of fine culture. In his terms, public freedom and voluntary association must be pursued and strengthened in order to avoid the new tyranny, i.e., mass society. Now, clearly, the tyranny is not only of the state, it is, as well, again in Tocqueville's terms, of the aristocracy of manufacturers, i.e., capitalism. A sphere between the market and authoritative command of the state provides the possibility for democracy and for cultural excellence.

This space has often been appropriated through the massification of society, as we have observed. The discourse and action of politics and culture face a common threat. The audience of mass culture and the electorate of mass politics are treated in the same fashion. Formulas for attracting attention to and consumption of cultural and political commodities create audiences and direct atomized action. The action of massified aggregates is directed by the manipulators of the formulas. Through these mediating formulas the action of the aggregates may come to resemble the action of collectivities, but it is the process of the mediation upon which the resemblance depends. The electorate no more determines the grounds of the electoral contest than the mass audience creates the forms of mass culture. In an enervated fashion they support and legitimize each, but, given the manipulative nature of mediation, from political and commercial advertising to computerized political action committees, this support and legitimation should not be confused with self-determination.

The political and cultural actors are not in the presence of one another, as Arendt has shown should be the case in public life;[35] rather, specialized agencies aggregate them and direct their actions. Between them are manipulative formulas, and these have become readily transferable from the realms of commerce and advertising directly to the contests of political campaigns. Ronald Reagan's campaign ads were formulated by those who brought us cola commercials.

Alternatives in politics and culture do exist. Constitutional liberties and traditions of voluntary association, in fact, allow such alternatives to flourish. These are, though, circumscribed, especially in the political realm. The two-party system is firmly, though not formally, institutionalized, even if it has been transformed by media politics. That alternative parties are destined to marginality is well recognized by all but the most naive or utopian political observers and practitioners. Yet, intriguingly, autonomous culture has a much greater critical potential, and this potential can help us perceive the democratic ideals which are alive but embattled in our political practices.

The critical potential of autonomous culture is grounded in the social need to instrumentally use the fruits of cultural traditions. Numerous societal needs are served by autonomous culture. Capital expansion requires basic scientific and technological research.

Corporate and state bureaucracies require computer science. Penal institutions and other control agencies utilize behavioral studies. Most generally, as Talcott Parsons has observed, the social system as a whole utilizes art for the societal subsystem of pattern maintenance, assuring in new and affective ways an attachment to central values; in Habermas's terms, cultural traditions serve a central legitimation function. But all these appropriations of traditions are limited because they require continued functioning of traditions, and such functioning is distinct from the utilization of traditions. For, as Habermas observes, "A cultural tradition loses . . . [its] force as soon as it is objectivistically prepared and strategically employed."[36] Thus the need of tradition must assure some autonomy for culture. Its distance from the steering mechanisms of the social order keeps critique alive. Its utility brings the potentially critical into societal life.

The public that autonomous culture brings into being can and has provided the opportunity for political deliberation that is submerged in mass politics. When efforts are made to keep access open, these publics serve the revitalization of democracy. When open access is pursued without compromising cultural standards, the autonomy of the public is sustainable and its critical potential is at its greatest.

The commitment to culture and democracy obviously involves tensions. These cannot be resolved by specific models, only by action based upon the principle of public freedom for culture and politics. Problems remain. There is much which distinguishes the practice of public freedom for culture and public freedom for politics. In the modern world, it is the imagination of the artist, scholar, and scientist, informed by cultural traditions and extending and rebelling against them, which brings cultural works into being. The works are shared with a public, but it is an affront to cultural freedom if extracultural concerns alter a cultural work; such concerns include not only governmental and market constraints but the demands of a free citizenry. Indeed, a free citizenry can be as threatening to the cultivation of the arts and sciences as are governmental and capitalist institutions. The virtuous republican citizens of the anti-Federalists and Montesquieu can be a threat to free culture if they do not appreciate it as an end in itself, just as an unthinking public can undermine education most profoundly when it is trying to support it. Nonetheless, as we have observed, in mass society the life of democracy and the life of autonomous culture, to the degree in which they are alive, exist in public domains set apart from mass structures. While cultural freedom and excellence do not automatically support democratic deliberation and autonomous political action, they can and have been supportive of them. A sociology of autonomous culture provides a significant theoretical alternative to the cynicism of ideological critique.

T E N

Cynicism and the American Dilemma

There are, of course, good reasons to be cynical. Ordinary people rightly understand that things are not what they appear to be. If we are not part of the successful propertied few, free enterprise does not set us free but confines us to salaried labor. We know that leaders, from the realm of politics to religion, deceive. What they say is not what they do. The promise of education leads not to social mobility for most of us but to social stasis. Ideological critiques and sociologies of knowledge do, then, uncover important correlations: prevailing ideas do generally support the status quo; challenging ideas are often linked to dominated social groups and marginal social movements and institutions. Cynicism, therefore, can be understood as a kind of modern realism, especially given the realistic social conditions of a massified social structure. Manipulation does connect center to periphery, as we have observed, from the nineteenth-century lecture agents to the ideologies of the New Left and New Right to the misuse of testing in education to the all-pervasive manipulations of the aptly named mass media.

To do no more than identify the manipulation and the agent doing the manipulating, as the cynic does (whether as an ordinary citizen or a professional social scientist), is to remain within the limitations of mass structures. Cynicism makes mass society a self-fulfilling prophecy. If we recognize, support, and utilize embedded societal values, criticism of mass society in the name of democracy is possible. Since these values do constitute our lives (along with manipulation), a commonly grounded criticism of manipulation can be understood by the public.

Michael Walzer has shown how the most truly humane social critics are those who are intimately connected with their communities.[1] Here we have observed the sociological grounding and even necessity for community-based social criticism. But is such criticism possible in our mass order? Can we escape cynicism? Are the cultural pessimists such as Jacoby, Hirsch, and Bloom correct? Will the

apparent American decline lead to a cultural fall? The embeddedness of democratic values and the persistent autonomy of the arts
and sciences give reasons to avoid complete pessimism. Given democratic values and cultural autonomy, the social critic can develop a
clear, articulate voice, as Jacoby wishes. She or he would try to reach
Hirsch's culturally literate audience, and would in fact motivate cultural literacy. In the process, Bloom's assertion that only the elite can
be the guardians of cultural values would be disproved. In my judgment, a free democratic culture is not only a possibility; it is a critical
reality.

To this point I have mapped out the cynical terrain and proposed
an intellectual approach, a sociology of culture which can be used to
deconstruct it. But now I attempt to demonstrate that American education has not inevitably failed our youth, that the darkness of
cultural illiteracy is not our predestined future, that generations of
intellectuals will not be lost, that ideology, ideological critique, and
cynicism do have alternatives. I do so by taking on what has been
the central American dilemma since the very founding of the republic—American racism. There are good reasons to be cynical, but
the way the American dilemma has been addressed in our politics of
culture in recent years shows that there are even better reasons not
to be.

Ronald Reagan won his presidential debate with Jimmy Carter in
1980. He asked the American electorate the now-famous question,
Are you better off today than you were four years ago? After four
years of high unemployment and inflation, and after four years of
mounting evidence that American's international power was in relative decline, the citizenry overwhelmingly answered no, and
subsequently voted for Reagan in a landslide. Reagan surely would
have won the election even if he had not won the debate. But the
general sense was that he had won the debate with the question,
and that he went from the question to the White House. It was also
noted that in the Carter-Reagan debates, there were no gross gaffes
such as Gerald Ford's declaration in the 1976 Ford-Carter debate that
Poland was a free country. From the point of view of the American
dilemma, all these theatrics were amazing. For Mr. Reagan, in his
debate, committed more than a gaffe. In answering a question about
race relations in America, he declared that in the 1930s Americans
did not know we had a racial problem. Though Carter criticized this
blatant racist statement, the media commentators did not. The statement and the absence of public reaction to it revealed that Ralph

Ellison's existential statement on the invisibility of African-Americans in his *Invisible Man*,[2] was essentially correct when it came to the 1930s, and that in the post–civil rights era, a process of reinstituting an invisibility of race (and class) problems was becoming evident. Blacks suffered during the Great Depression more than whites, and this and the American caste system were on the agenda of the left and the Popular Front. For Reagan, since the caste system was left relatively undisturbed, there was no race problem. A repressive social order contained the social problem. In memory, then, a racist order is confused with racial peace and justice. The fact that the issue was not raised during the 1980 debate or its aftermath opened up a period of not-so-benign racial neglect.

Reagan himself summarized the period in an interview he gave for the television newsmagazine *Sixty Minutes* during the last weeks of his presidency. He mused about civil-rights leaders: "Sometimes I wonder if they really want what they say they want, because some of those leaders are doing very well leading organizations based on keeping alive the feeling that they're victims of prejudice."[3] Reagan's America of the eighties was an ideologically conceived happy land of increasing diplomatic and military strength, booming prosperity, and receding social problems. Those who pointed to social problems were obviously self-interested. Indeed, in the common discourse, the negative label "special-interest group" was applied not to corporate lobbies or Chambers of Commerce or professional associations but to all groups that sought to speak for the amelioration of unaddressed and growing social problems—urban decay, workers' rights, education, and of course institutionalized racism. There is no satisfying these people (so goes the ideological script), and Reagan cynically understands why—the professional leaders of the special-interest groups, need the appearance of a problem to maintain their status as leaders.

Normal political discourse in its present state cannot explode such reasoning. Statistics can be cooked to show that government programs never solved social problems; that federal spending causes more problems than it solves.[4] The capacity for those inspired by ideology to ignore empirical reality is immense. Reagan has also noted that the homeless are in the street because they want to be. People will argue with his observation, but others will highlight the half-truths it draws upon. Such argumentation ultimately appeals to prejudices and does not seem to change opinions or resolve conflicts. Conflicts are decided either by the most powerful, or by extraordinary political consensus (such as appears during a war).

But there are other ways. The arts and sciences, as autonomous cultural activities, regularly can provide extrapolitical stimulus for addressing the banalities of mass society and its cynicism. Even mass culture can highlight problems, though in the end it may confuse more than it illuminates.

In fact, the television movie has developed as a distinct mass cultural form in highlighting unresolved social or psychological problems. From the homeless to nuclear dangers, from child abuse to the Holocaust, pressing problems have been made real for a huge audience. But melodrama and sentimentality significantly undermine the social message. The definitive brutalities of the modern era, the Holocaust and the slave trade, are turned into sentimental romances and melodrama in the TV movies *Holocaust* and *Roots*. The depth of pain and oppression, and most significantly, its connection with our normal daily lives, is lost by the demands of the genre and the mass media form, with commercial breaks, network identifications, and promotional leads for future TV programs. People come to know that the Holocaust and the slave trade really existed, but their knowledge is both superficial and sentimental. They could pass a test of cultural literacy on the topic, placing cataclysmic events in their proper time and place, identifying the victims and the victimized. But questions of moral and political responsibilities and legacies are blocked by the prevailing TV format.

I realize this need not be the case. Ideally, TV has a great potential as the ground for democratic culture. Dennis Potter, the author of the TV classic *The Singing Detective*, perhaps the single most impressive limited television series in English, explains why he writes for television:

> It probably sounds like political humbug, but I've long had this dream of a common culture, and I know that print would never do it because words of different syllable lengths would be either rejected or received according to what kind of education you had, whereas pictures could do all the things that great literature does.
>
> Dickens, all of [the great writers of the last century] were willing to adapt and use the serial form because it was the most popular means in their day—people would wait anxiously for the serializations to appear. The writers weren't dragged down by that form, they flew with it. And to me, that implies a confidence in a common culture, an assumption that people are very much brighter than the market men say they are—something in them

is capable of responding to things that are very complex.
If Dickens were alive today, I'm not sure he wouldn't
have written television serials.[5]

Potter, who is the author of challenging, critically acclaimed
popular television, can offer this appraisal with significant cultural
authority. He added, though, a telling qualification: "Well, he
wouldn't have if he had moved to America. We take television more
seriously here than in your land, alas. I mean, you've handed it over
to the hucksters."[6] (The qualification should be understood as no
more than a note of caution. After all, I write about Potter after seeing
his works on American television.) Potter has proved that television
is not intrinsically trivial, that one way to reach a broad television
audience is through art. What empirically occurs between author and
public, and between artworks (Potter, using television, keeps alive
popular English serial literature), constitutes autonomous culture,
not the technical media through which it is articulated.

Mass culture does, though, distort in serious ways, and this is
nowhere more evident than in its portrayal of the problems of race.
In the process, cynical ignorance such as that of Reagan's is reproduced. American movies, like American television, have often
been controlled by the "hucksters." As entertainment with no pre-
tensions to art, or significant social criticism, there is perhaps
nothing wrong with this in itself. Of course moral and ethical values
have often been compromised in American movies: the gratuitous
violence and sexism of recent years; the incredible racial stereotyp-
ing of the so-called "golden years." In the thirties, the golden era,
African-Americans appeared as servants, buffoons, or not at all. The
entertainment was, then, not so innocuous. The films of the forties
and fifties followed changes in social mores. Only after the great accomplishments of the civil rights movement have black actors
appeared in a diversity of roles and types of movies. Still, Hollywood has had great difficulty in depicting the richness of the
African-American experience. And when it has tried, it has tragically failed.

The dimensions of the tragedy are revealed in the film *Mississippi
Burning*. The film presents the story of a crucial event of the civil
rights movement, the martyrdom of three civil rights workers on
June 21, 1964—two white New Yorkers, Michael Schwerner and Andrew Goodman, and one black Mississippian, James Chaney. In the
sixties, a moral uproar surrounded the "Mississippi killings," leading to a political transformation. In the eighties, moralism and

cynicism surround the making, distribution, and viewing of *Mississippi Burning*, contributing to political tension, and recriminations.

Chaney, Schwerner, and Goodman were activists in the Mississippi Summer Project.[7] The project sought to expand the civil rights movement in the South by extending voter registrations of African-Americans, by starting Freedom Schools, and by helping to build an alternative political party, the Mississippi Freedom Democrats. White volunteers from the North were enlisted in these tasks in hopes of symbolically representing the goal of the collective action—racial equality and justice—in the integrated form of collective action. The racist murder intervened, ambiguously fostering national concern and resolve for addressing the most blatant forms of legalized racism. Forty-four days after the murders, the bodies were found. The tragedy sparked a national uproar, which in itself was not without a tinge of racism. Of all the racist American brutalities, this event received the attention it did because two whites were murdered along with a black man. The murders of African-Americans struggling for their civil rights or their individual dignity were not that newsworthy. That two whites transgressed this racial barrier was big news.

The Mississippi Summer Project was not an immediate success. Voter registration proceeded slowly, and the Free Democrats lost their challenge to the Dixiecrats at the 1964 Democratic Convention. Yet, without doubt it helped change the ways Americans viewed race relations. The racist white-power structure had proved itself to be based upon murder and brutality. The nation lost tolerance for the peculiar ways of the South, ultimately leading to the passage of the Voting Rights Act of 1965 and the transformation of Southern politics, with an explosion of black participation.

For most Americans today, black and white, the pre–civil rights days, and the accomplishments, heroics, and tragedies of the civil rights movement are remembered vaguely. This is why the movie *Mississippi Burning* is both extremely important and disappointing. The film has incited a critical controversy. The liberties the screenwriter, Chris Gerolmo, and the director, Alan Parker, have taken with the historical record, have deeply offended knowledgeable civil rights veterans and social historians. The collective judgment of the most severe critics was summarized by David Halberstam (who reported on the Freedom Summer Project for *The New York Times*). He declared: "It's a bad movie: *Mississippi False*."[8] Less committed and involved critics, in turn, have noted that the controversy

emanates from the ambiguity of the docu-drama form. Since the division between fact and fiction is blurred, the end result, from the point of view of history, is the appearance of falsification.[9] The movie's defenders, particularly its director, see all this as being beside the point. Alan Parker declared somewhat royally: "Our film isn't about the civil rights movement. It's about why there was a need for the civil rights movement. And because it's a movie, I felt it had to be fictionalized. The two heroes in the story had to be white. That is a reflection of our society as much as of the film industry. At this point, it could not have been any other way."[10]

After the closing credits, the film's makers indicate that it was suggested by facts but is not factual. Indeed, the story line is fundamentally fictive. The central plot device is the FBI investigation of the murders, which it imaginatively presents. Actually, a $30,000 payoff to a Klan informant led to the discovery of the bodies—not a very dramatic business. In the film, the investigation succeeds due to the rough-and-tough police work of the FBI and a developing romance between one of the "G-men" and the wife of one of the murderers; i.e., the film uses a good cop/bad cop buddy-convention and a romance to move the political story line. Clearly, there has been no attempt to be true to the historical record. Condemnations of the film for inaccuracy seem silly. The relationship between even the most realistic (but not real) art and historical and social facts is a matter of both the work of the artist and the interpretation of his or her audience, not one of automatic reflection and historical accuracy. The charge that the film is false to history, then, should not involve the question of accuracy.

The most serious historical critiques do not raise this issue. The concern is not with the historical details but with the broad political and cultural themes that the film seems to miss or fundamentally misrepresent. According to this film, whites were active while blacks were symbolic martyrs, as were their primary community institutions, the black churches. The agents of social change were the FBI and the Kennedy administration. But, in fact, it was the active, contentious involvement of a broad segment of the black community, from the legalistic NAACP to the local ministers and their congregations to radical black (and sometimes white) student activists, that forced the Kennedy administration and the FBI to execute their legal responsibilities.

If the film is so strikingly inaccurate, we must wonder why it has received so much attention. Perhaps it is because white America wants a falsified record, or because the hunger for historical information is so great that even misinformation is eagerly consumed. Or

perhaps it has nothing to do with history. Indeed, in my judgment, each of these propositions is partially true, deriving from the fact that the film is a powerful but ambivalent portrayal of a powerful but ambiguous event, and both the event and its movie portrayal deal with the major contradiction in the American political tradition.

Mississippi Burning is a refined, artistic film, undermined by its mass cultural form and mediation. It presents distinct film images of poetic grace and offers a vivid portrayal of the visual dimensions of the oppression of blacks in America. The work juxtaposes panoramic vistas of racist landscapes with almost still-life portraits of the internalization of oppression: a burning church juxtaposed with a quiet, almost minimalist scene of an electrified water fountain for whites and a makeshift faucet fountain for "coloreds," with a young black boy, when no whites are in sight, drinking according to the segegrationist rules. A car chase of the civil rights workers by the Klansmen (including the sheriff and deputy sheriff), ending with a vividly portrayed murder scene, is juxtaposed with the opening of the investigation by the "G-men" in the local coffee shop, with its orderly segregated white and colored sections, which one of the FBI agents transgresses. The quiet terror on the face of the black man to whom the agent speaks, tells more about an American terrorist state than any scholarly treatise on the Southern caste system. But as the film progresses, even moving images of an angelic black boy falling to his knees in prayer as his church is burned and its congregation brutalized, of a black man fighting back, of a church congregation persisting, and of an integrated civil rights demonstration, are overwhelmed by the fictive story of the investigation and of the developing romance between the FBI agent and the wife of the Klansman deputy sheriff. Yet these later, less successful scenes and the earlier, more powerfully evocative images that open the movie, all contribute to a highly crafted film, revealing the pain of American racism. It is the artistry of the film which tells the historical truth, a truth as profound as the truth the film's critics have to contribute; but the story line undermines the film's veracity.

A sociological interpretation of such a cultural work, then, must not be too hasty. The work is a product of cynicism and ethical integrity, of a developing artistic tradition and of the mass culture industry. Both its critics and defenders do it a disservice, while their points are far from being completely mistaken. The work reveals the power of artistic expression within its mass cultural form, and the limits of such expression. There is a pressing need for a sociological interpretation of the film. Distinctions must be made, so that cynicism may be avoided and collective memory can proceed.

The film must be interpreted as if it were a censored work. The agency of censorship is not that of a political commission, or for that matter of a movie mogul. It is that if the self-censor, probably the most effective censor. It is the censorship of the cynical pseudo-sociologist. Recall that Alan Parker, the director, explained the fact that the film's two major heroes had to be white: "That is a reflection of our society as much as of the film industry." As we have already noted, this sort of explanation is very poor sociology. It begs the interesting sociological questions—how is it that there is this necessary reflection of the overall society and of the movie industry, and what is this reflection? Parker of course does not explain. The implication is that funding for the film would not be forthcoming with black heroes, and that the American filmgoing public would not as readily pay to see a film with black heroes about black oppression, as to see a film about black oppression with white heroes. Some critics have noted that the success of *A Soldier's Story* belies this truism, but even more important than the validity of these generalizations (it seems they are true of the industry, less true of the public), are the ethical and political implications of such generalizations. Quite simply, they are abdications of political and artistic responsibility. Not Parker, in Parker's account, but the industry and the general public are responsible for the shortcomings of his film.

If Parker could show or explain why he undermined his own artistic and political accomplishments, we might wish to interpret the accomplishments as an embedded resistance within an oppressive form, a piece of art resisting its constraining TV-movie formula. As it is, *Mississippi Burning* appears as little more than an effective formula melodrama trivializing its artistic and political expression. It poetically provokes its audience to remember human suffering and the struggle to overcome it, but the formulaic framing turns remembrance into systematic forgetting. The cynicism of the director destroys his own work. Black passivity, white action, the FBI as agent for change, and blacks as recipients of white favors—all this is exactly what did not happen. The movie does not explain why there was a civil rights movement, what was involved in the movement, or the connection linking the pre–civil rights era, the civil rights movement, and our present and future. Ronald Reagan could go to this movie and leave it without confronting his racial cynicism.

A more autonomous art, uncompromised by mass mediation and cynical formulation, can present a direct challenge to racist cynicism. This is most evident in the novels of Toni Morrison, especially in her masterpiece, *Beloved*.[11] The excellence of the writing facilitates a remarkable series of reflections, observations, and depictions of the American dilemma and the American tragedy. The work has received almost universal acclaim. Yet, a highly flawed negative review most clearly, though unintentionally, explains Morrison's accomplishments from our perspective.

According to Stanley Crouch, Morrison's writings suffer from burdens: an overly sentimental depiction of African-American suffering, drawing from a literary tradition established by James Baldwin, and a stereotypical portrayal of "bestial black men," influenced by the feminist writings of black women.[12] He concedes that "Morrison, unlike Alice Walker, has real talent, an ability to organize her novel in a musical structure, deftly using images as motifs," but he condemns the writing for what he calls its "maudlin ideological commercials." He then goes on to review the book as if it were a TV movie and not a finely crafted novel. In order to make his opposing ideological position clear, he tells the story of *Beloved* without its "musical structure":

> Meet Sethe, an ex-slave woman who harbors a deep and terrible secret that has brought terror into her home. (Adolescent sons are shown fleeing.) Meet Paul D, who had a passion for Sethe when they were both slaves, but lost her to another. (Sethe shown walking with first husband Halle, smiling as Paul D looks on longingly.) During slavery they had been treated as human beings at Sweet Home in Kentucky by the Garners. (Garners waving to their slaves, who read books, carry guns into the woods, seem very happy.) That was before the master died, the mistress took sick, and schoolteacher, the cruel overseer, took over. (Master Garner on deathbed, Mrs. Garner enfeebled, schoolteacher being cruel.) No longer treated like human beings, reduced to the condition of work animals, the slaves of Sweet Home plan to escape. (Slaves planning escape around a fire.) Sethe, swollen with child, bravely makes her way to Ohio, determined to see that the child is born free! (Sethe trudging along with great determination.) And there, in Ohio, the terrible deed takes place. (Slave catchers dismounting and Sethe running into a barn with her children.) Sethe's home is ruled by the angry spirit of an innocent child, until Paul D returns to her life. (House shaking, Paul D holding onto table as he shouts.)
> Now they are together, but the weight of the past will

not let them live in the freedom they always dreamed of. Then the mysterious Beloved appears and becomes part of the family, charming Denver, Sethe's only remaining child, and the horrible past begins to come clear. (Scenes of Africans in the holds of ships.) Relive some of America's most painful moments—slavery, the Civil War, the efforts made by ex-slaves to experience freedom in a world that was stacked against them from the moment they were sold as work animals. But, most of all, thrill to a love story about the kinds of Americans who struggled to make this country great. (Sethe, Paul D and Denver walking hand-in-hand.)[13]

This is like summarizing *Romeo and Juliet* as the story of two mixed-up kids from opposite sides of the track who end up killing themselves. Any story, no matter how profound, can be trivialized by such a summary. Take away its artistry, and only banality remains; but with art there is the possibility of confronting the rich texture of human experience and tragedy.

Beloved is not a melodrama; it is, rather, about the will to remember, its impossibility, its necessity and pain. The story unfolds not as a linear narrative but as a painful nightmare, recalled and analyzed. The reader meets the characters with an uncertainty of who and what they are, as they only slowly reveal themselves and their relations. The time and setting of the story are at first uncertain, as are the human motivations behind the narrated action. The cruelties of slavery in both its most benign and most blatant forms, the sweetness and pain of liberty, and the legacies of oppression for the most basic, intimate human relations are illuminated. The illumination both distorts and clarifies. Just when an event or relationship seems to become clear, a new dimension is added or a new point of view is taken to confuse matters. The Czech emigré writer Milan Kundera, another writer who is primarily concerned with memory, maintains that novels are written to ask questions, not answer them.[14] Clearly Morrison concurs.

This is evident both in the overall structure of her storytelling and in specific passages. To tell the plot of *Beloved* without emphasizing the mystery of the story or the poetry of its depiction is to confuse a mass culture formula with autonomous art. In *Mississippi Burning*, the formula not only constrained the work's impact but in significant ways reversed its meaning—remembrance became organized forgetting. *Beloved*'s cultural form, to the contrary, liberates the author and her audience.

Theodor Adorno, the leading critical theorist of the Frankfurt school,[15] asked one of the pressing cultural questions of our century—can there be art after the Holocaust? A generation of Jewish and gentile writers, poets, painters, and dramatists, from Elie Wiesel in the United States to Primo Levi in Italy to Josef Szajna in Poland to Aharon Appelfeld in Israel to Anselm Kiefer in Germany, have affirmatively answered his question. They have shown that art after the Holocaust is a precondition for life after the Holocaust. Memory of the worse than imaginable is not accessible through cultural clichés. Art facilitates memory, which makes possible the constitution of human dignity despite the most horrific human experiences. *Beloved* re-remembers (as Morrison puts it in her text) the pains and consequences of slavery, artistically giving them life.

We come to understand the pained relationship between black men and women. On her escape from slavery, Sethe, the heroine of sorts, was brutalized when waiting to meet her husband, as had been prearranged. Seventeen years later she finds out what happened in an interchange with an old friend:

> "The day I came in here. You said they stole your milk. I never knew what it was that messed him up. That was it, I guess. All I knew was that something broke him. Not a one of them years of Saturdays, Sundays, and nighttime extra never touched him. But whatever he saw go on in that barn that day broke him like a twig."
>
> "He saw?" Sethe was gripping her elbows as though to keep them from flying away.
>
> "He saw. Must have."
>
> "He saw them boys do that to me and let them keep on breathing air? He saw? He saw? He saw?"
>
> "Hey! Hey! Listen up. Let me tell you something. A man ain't a goddamn ax. Chopping, hacking, busting every goddamn minute of the day. Things get to him. Things he can't chop down because they're inside."
>
> Sethe was pacing up and down, up and down in the lamplight. "The underground agent said, By Sunday. They took my milk and he saw it and didn't come down? Sunday came and he didn't. Monday came and no Halle. I thought he was dead, that's why; then I thought they caught him, that's why. Then I thought, No, he's not dead because if he was I'd know it, and then you come here after all this time and you didn't say he was dead, because you didn't know either, so I thought, Well, he just found him another better way to live. Because if he

was anywhere near here, he'd come to Baby Suggs, if not
to me. But I never knew he saw."

"What does that matter now?"

"If he is alive, and saw that, he won't step foot in my
door. Not Halle."

"It broke him, Sethe." Paul D looked up at her and
sighed. "You may as well know it all. Last time I saw him
he was sitting by the churn. He had butter all over his
face."

Nothing happened, and she was grateful for that.
Usually she could see the picture right away of what she
heard. But she could not picture what Paul D said. Nothing came to mind. Carefully, carefully, she passed on to a
reasonable question.

"What did he say?"

"Nothing."

"Not a word?"

"Not a word."

"Did you speak to him? Didn't you say anything to
him? Something!"

"I couldn't, Sethe. I just . . . couldn't."

"Why!"

"I had a bit in my mouth."[16]

This event is told and retold. New details are revealed. Brutaliza-
tion, powerlessness, and the distortion of normal human relations
are given artistic shape. The story of a pregnant slave woman seeking her freedom attacked by a gang of white boys while her husband
helplessly watched, told directly, is but a sentimental example of
what we now know to be a reprehensible "peculiar institution." But
telling the story as it is subjectively remembered in bits and pieces
gives both the reprehensible actions and their legacies life. We observe how under the strain of racism the understanding between
black men and women becomes next to impossible. This is revealed
not polemically but poetically.

The distorted relations examined in *Beloved* include not only
those between men and women, but between mothers and their
children. *Beloved* is the ghost of the child Sethe murdered, when
Sethe and her children were about to be reclaimed in their Ohio refuge by their Kentucky (schoolteaching) slavemaster. For Sethe the
murder was an act of deliverance:

she was squatting in the garden and when she saw them
coming and recognized schoolteacher's hat, she heard

wings. Little hummingbirds stuck their needle beaks right through her headcloth into her hair and beat their wings. And if she thought anything, it was No. No. Nono. Nonono.[17]

More graphically, towards the book's end Denver, Sethe's remaining child, reflects on Sethe's relations with Beloved, the ghost of the murdered child:

> she knew Sethe's greatest fear was the same one Denver had in the beginning—that Beloved might leave. That before Sethe could make her understand what it meant— what it took to drag the teeth of that saw under the little chin; to feel the baby blood pump like oil in her hands; to hold her face so her head would stay on; to squeeze her so she could absorb, still the death spasms that shot through that adored body, plump and sweet with life— Beloved might leave. Leave before Sethe could make her realize that worse than that—far worse—was what Baby Suggs died of, what Ella knew, what Stamp saw and what made Paul D tremble. That anybody white could take your whole self for anything that came to mind. Not just work, kill or maim you, but dirty you. Dirty you so bad you couldn't like yourself anymore. Dirty you so bad you forgot who you were and couldn't think it up. And though she and others lived through and got over it, she could never let it happen to her own. The best thing she was, was her children. Whites might dirty *her* all right, but not her best thing, her beautiful, magical best thing— the part of her that was clean. No undreamable dreams about the headless, feetless torso hanging in the tree with a sign on it was her husband or Paul D; whether the bubbling-hot girls in the colored-school fire set by patriots included her daughter; whether a gang of whites invaded her daughter's private parts, soiled her daughter's thighs and threw her daughter out of the wagon. *She* might have to work the slaughterhouse yard, but not her daughter.[18]

Of this emotion, Paul D, Sethe's old friend and lover, says, "Your love is too thick," and she responds, "Love is or it ain't. Thin love ain't love at all." But most significantly, her love is not understood by the children. Of Sethe's three other children, the two sons run away, and the surviving daughter, Denver, apparently stays very devoted to her mother, but only outwardly. Earlier she revealed, "I love my mother but I know she killed one of her own daughters, and tender as she is with me, I'm scared of her because of it. She missed killing my brothers and they knew it. . . .

"Maybe it was getting that close to dying made them want to fight the War. That's what they told me they were going to do. I guess they rather be around killing men than killing women, and there sure is something in her that makes it all right to kill her own."[19] The daughter's devotion was but an act of self-protection.

Surely the scenes in *Mississippi Burning* are as strong as the scenes in Morrison's novel, but the novel's are formed by cultural freedom rather than mass culture. In the constituted work, Morrison engaged in ongoing cultural "conversations" about the novel as a form, and about the black experience. The conversations are with both her contemporaries and predecessors. As a black feminist writer, she holds a most subtle position. She portrays the rage of black men, understanding the distance between expectations of what it means to be a man and the minimal possibilities of fulfilling the expectations. The resulting rage, exemplified sometimes outrageously by authors such as Eldridge Cleaver in his *Soul on Ice*,[20] is not justified, but is understood. That black women suffer from the inability and the rage is beautifully depicted. Their responses, also, are not romantically glorified. As a solution to racist oppression at the hands of white men, the murder of children seems unconscionable. But of course, a solution is not being posed, rather a world of moral outrage and dilemmas is being depicted. There are no clear heroes, only victims. An anomic love, a distrust between the sexes, male wanderlust, children who either misunderstand or understand too well their parents' condition, all are legacies of slavery that Morrison deftly finds in the past but links to the present and future.

By making memory and its inadequacies the form of the novel, using a magical realistic technique, Morrison covers familiar ground of moral outrage, as did James Baldwin, but makes problematic the interpretation of outrage. Morrison does not simply condemn; she explores. She does not too quickly answer; she questions. She has not written a commentary (in novelistic form) on the African-American experience, she has written a fine novel. It is as a novel independent of its social conditioning that the work helps its readership address our social condition.

The forcefulness and mystery of Morrison's writing, its refined character, makes it possible for the reader to confront the American dilemma. The novel is embedded within literary traditions—

African-American, American feminist, and modern—and addresses vibrant cultural publics, from the specifically African-
American to the ephemeral general reading public. The demands of
art and cultural integrity inform the writing, not preconceived notions of how a mass audience is best attracted to a controversial
topic, as clearly was the case in *Mississippi Burning*. By recognizing
Beloved as a work of autonomous art and *Mississippi Burning* as a
work of mass culture, we can observe how American racism can and
cannot be addressed in our culture, and how we can hope to avoid
cynicism.

VI

Comparing *Mississippi Burning* with *Beloved* may seem unfair. Even
the film's strongest supporters are likely to admit that it should not
be judged against a literary masterpiece. If I were making a simple
aesthetic comparison such reservations would be well taken. Yet our
inquiry here is sociological; our concern is with how art and mass
culture address the American dilemma and cynicism. Mass culture
obviously has its strengths. Many more millions will see *Mississippi
Burning* than read *Beloved*, at least in the immediate future. As a
work of art, *Beloved* likely will endure and be read for generations,
along with other novels of the past, from *The Scarlet Letter* to
Huckleberry Finn to *Invisible Man*. *Beloved* may have a long-term impact on American literature, American culture and politics, even on
the referent for the word "American." It could open up a series of
accessible public reflections on the human legacies of slavery, even
though "It was not a story to pass on." "Remembering seemed un-
wise," as Morrison put it in the closing pages of her text. Literature
and not cliché makes memory and informed action possible. Yet
cultures do change slowly, and practical transformations are evident only after a significant passage of time. Mass culture provides
results more quickly. For those who matured after the civil rights
movement, *Mississippi Burning* brings to life the reasons for the
movement. The renewed public consciousness, even though it is
fundamentally misinformed, can be politically consequential. A
more heightened, more sympathetic sensibility regarding the tense
condition of black-white relations is the likely result of both *Beloved*
and *Mississippi Burning*. While the novel reaches a more restricted,
relatively informed audience, and the movie a highly mediated
mass audience, both of these works and the debates surrounding

them provide Americans with the possibility of public deliberation about important matters, something too often missing in our mass politics.

Nonetheless, we must be cognizant, reflective, and critical about the cynicism that permeates mass culture. The half-truths and untruths of *Mississippi Burning* makes reasoned discourse difficult. The compromises made in the film do not serve art but cynicism. Shakespeare, too, distorted history in his dramatic works, it has been pointed out by the film's supporters. Yet, Parker distorts history to serve mass clichés, the stories of a romantic duo and "two buddies," while Shakespeare serves high comedy and tragedy. The cynicism of Parker's movie-making, especially evident in his justification for using white heroes, feeds the cynicism of people like Ronald Reagan. After all, if they are shown that the FBI, not African-Americans, were central at the height of the civil rights movement, certainly now that we have overcome past brutalities civil rights advocates naturally appear as little more than another special-interest group. J. Edgar Hoover, the perennial FBI director, during the course of the civil rights movement, was more concerned with Communist infiltration than civil rights enforcement.[21] For him, Martin Luther King was a Communist agent. Twenty years later, black leaders are portrayed as political entrepreneurs (who in fact were well known in the Reagan regime). One form of cynicism replaces another in explaining away the American dilemma.

Before turning to the conclusion and the issue of fundamentalism and democratic culture, I want to emphasize that the analyzed differences between *Beloved* and *Mississippi Burning* have little, if anything, to do with the cultural forms of literature versus film. Some, if not most, literary works sold in American society are pitched to the mass audience. Through mass structures (with, e.g., supermarkets serving as booksellers), these works are limited by the process. There is no more intrinsic cultural value to most Gothic romances and crime novels than there is to TV soap operas and sci-fi flicks. Even literature with serious intent, when it is packaged for mass marketing, can be compromised by the packaging. *The Bonfire of the Vanities* is not only a satire of cynical practices. In my judgment, it is a cynical creation, cynically marketed. Everything and everyone is mocked. Sympathy is elicited only for the highly stylized creation. The only sympathetic character is in a coma. All else is crude, the social drama of conflicting brute interests, of racial and ethnic conflict and sexism. Such a product is readily consumed, and has been celebrated in the popular press. Critics point out that the novel is a good read, even while they note it is not great literature. Wolfe has articulated popular prejudice and it has gone down easily.

It can be argued, to the contrary, that I have overlooked the Swiftean elements of satire in *The Bonfire of the Vanities* and in Wolfe's other writings; that Wolfe, in fact, distances himself from all expressed values as a way of presenting a satire, as in the cynicism of Diogenes. I both respect such judgments and want to emphasize that there ought to be room for such conflicting judgments in a democratic society. Yet, and this is crucial, we also should not overlook that such room is severely limited by key mass structures, making cynicism (especially about race) likely.

When artists reflect on important issues, both the works themselves can be compromised by the logic of mass structures and the reception can be compromised. Thus, for example, the film based on Milan Kundera's novel *The Unbearable Lightness of Being* clearly compromised the philosophic thrust of the novel. All that remained was Central European cultural exoticism, anti-communist kitsch, and sex farce. On the other hand, when Spike Lee made a film about American racism, he overcame all the institutionalized practices in the American movie industry that work against making a highly individual and critical film about race. Yet, while he clearly, even if with purposeful ambiguity, reflected upon the immediate political problems of New York City, the film was reduced to a TV sound bite by the mass media. On a network television nightly program, "Nightline," and in *The New York Times*, *The Village Voice* and elsewhere, a great pseudo-debate went on—would *Do the Right Thing* instigate a race riot in New York City? Among serious film critics, there is wide agreement that Lee is a filmmaker of remarkable talent and accomplishment, but in the mass-mediated discourse he was vilified. A complex cultural work was simplified and then its simplification was attacked. Mass culture works on such simple information and analyses. It obliterates complication and subtlety while creating mass audiences. It thus fosters cynicism, as it is constituted by cynicism.

As we have observed throughout this inquiry, whether in film or literature, in politics or education, mass society with its cynical culture works against cultural and political autonomy. But, cultural and political autonomy can and do work against cynicism and the building of mass structures. This, then, is the central problematic of a democratic culture.

Cynicism, Fundamentalism, and the Prospects for Democratic Culture

I have attempted to show how cynicism is a response to relativism and the structural problems posed by mass society, and how cynicism, further, fosters the development of mass structures in the politics of the left, right, and center in the practice of education and the productions of the culture industry. The politics of cynicism goes beyond the formal political realm, and, indeed, a primary alternative is lodged in the relatively autonomous arts and sciences. We have seen that the net of a cynical culture goes broad and deep. Yet, much if not most of the implications of a cynical culture have not been analyzed directly. I have confined myself to politics, education, the arts and sciences, and mass culture, seeking to demonstrate cultural alternatives. The psychology of cynicism, cynical interpersonal relations, and cynical economic practices have only been alluded to. Of course these are all part of our cynical society, as are alternatives which have gone unexamined in this study—most predominantly that of religious belief—which take into account the complexities of modernity.[1]

I did not "complete" the analysis, not only because of an awareness of my limited competence. (I am neither a psychologist nor an economist nor an expert on religion.) More crucially, I turned away from total explanations of individual and social existence and experience as a matter of principle. Complete explanations are, in my judgment, politically and morally suspect. Such explanations tie together the diversity and ambiguities of human life in too neat a package. The extreme cases in point are the class theory of Marxism and the race theory of Nazism. When these theories become official truths, a distinctively modern tyranny developed. The appearance of scientific validation justified a modern barbarism. Closer to home, conventional psychological and political theories of behaviorism have been put to barbaric use in Uruguay.[2] Unified theories may be appropriate for the world of particle physics, but they do not work for the world of human affairs. They are tools of totalitarian states and in important ways contribute to a totalitarian mentality which promotes the development of totalitarian orders.[3]

Though cynicism permeates our society, it does not completely explain our world. Significant alternatives and resistances exist. To attempt a complete and critical explanation of our life around the theme of cynicism leads, ironically, to a very different alternative to cynicism—not democracy and democratic culture, which motivate this inquiry, but fundamentalism. A complete rejection of modernity, of democracy's underside as well as its promise, leads to a variety of old-time religions. At the end of the twentieth century this is most striking in the radical Islamic orders. Their rejection of Western ideas, of the immorality and materialism of both the socialist and capitalist blocs, is more than a new demonology. As we have observed, a cynical amoralism does permeate modern life. But the fundamentalists take this very far. They view cynical amorality and immorality as completely defining modern existence. Present-day Islamic fundamentalists, along with Christian and Jewish fundamentalists, not only turn away from, but also against, modernity and its relativism and cynicism. In the old revival song, fundamentalist preachers and congregations sang, "Give me that old-time religion, it's good enough for me." The new fundamentalists add, "and you." Khomeini cannot tolerate a Rushdie on the other side of the globe. For the fundamentalist, any deviation from the truth must be condemned and eradicated.

On these grounds, even American fundamentalists agree. Pat Buchanan, a right-wing ideologue, does question Khomeini on tactical and aesthetic grounds (a death sentence seems extreme), but Buchanan concurs that the blasphemy of secularists must be condemned. Amorality or even a principled secular morality is the enemy. That any American commentator or political figure should hold such a position seems odd to the extreme, but with the ascendance of right-wing ideology, such a position proved to be not at all uncommon. Cardinal O'Connor of New York condemned not only the Rushdie death sentence but also the Rushdie book, *The Satanic Verses*, and the rather slow and tepid attack on the death sentence by the Bush administration seemed to suggest more than a careful (even cynical) game of geopolitics (hoping to keep options open for future ties with Iran). It also seemed to involve a concern that blasphemy such as Rushdie's not be endorsed. The blasphemers, those who write books such as *The Satanic Verses* and make films like Martin Scorsese's *The Last Temptation of Christ*, and the liberals of the press and universities who have a special interest in the freedom to say and write heresies, were the enemies in Bush's political campaign, and he dared not turn about and support them.

In a political culture with a long tradition of democracy, while cynicism is a cancer, fundamentalist defenses against it threaten to overwhelm democratic commitment. Supreme Court Justice Sandra Day O'Connor improperly lent support to a political campaign in Arizona explicitly propagating the idea that the United States is a Christian and not a democratic nation. She later defended herself on the grounds that she thought her correspondence was private.[4] Nonetheless, the propriety of her letter is less important than the judgments behind it—support of an opposition between Christianity and democracy on constitutional grounds. Some, including the Supreme Court justice, seem to think that the only answers to the problems of political and cultural enlightenment are absolutist beliefs. Important elements of the American political tradition suggest much more promising answers from the point of view of democracy. While a negative cultural logic leads from democracy to relativism, mass structures, cynicism, and then fundamentalism, a more promising logic of enlightenment links democracy with reason. It is the means for avoiding cynicism and fundamentalism, and keeping our political experiment vital.

I

Democracy, when viewed as an ongoing process demanding enlightened commitment and justification, requires an excellent culture for the many. In aristocracy and monarchy, the special qualities of the few or of the one justify leadership over the populace. In democracy, there is an understanding that the people can know best their interest and the common good. But in order for the people to know the common good and their interest, they must have access to knowledge and be capable of reason. Thus, though culture as the cultivation of the arts and sciences is by necessity hierarchical (there are good and bad judgments, fine and not so fine works), and democracy is in principle egalitarian, a central cultural problem for democracies is to make democracy and culture compatible, with neither being compromised. This is no small task.

In our discussion of cynicism and the American dilemma, we found that a refined literary expression, Toni Morrison's *Beloved*, richly revealed the texture of American racism, while the movie *Mississippi Burning* simplified complexities to the point that it concealed more than it revealed about some sad facts of the American experience. This comparison suggests a political dilemma. Without the fundamentalist authority of a religious leader or a revered text, can the culturally excellent be made compatible with popular tastes and capacities? Or is support of refined culture necessarily elitist? Is there a possibility of a (truly) democratic (refined) culture?

II

The normative problem of democratic culture is central in American history, shaping the development of major American political institutions. At the formative stage of the constitution of the republic, a key element of the debate between the Federalists and the anti-Federalists concerned the relationship between excellence and egalitarianism. There was a debate over the role of the so-called "natural aristocracy" in a republican order. The pro-Constitution Federalists, led by Hamilton, Jay, and Madison, maintained the need for an open meritocratic elite for good governance. Though they denounced the absolutely despotic nature of monarchy and aristocracy with ever greater intensity from the early 1770s through the 1780s, these American revolutionists, led by Hamilton, still recognized that in order to avoid the "rule of the rabble," they must ensure that society be governed by its "betters," cultivated in the science of governance and the nature of man. For the Federalists, the relationship between cultural excellence and democracy involved the protection of the former from the latter. A definitely minor chord was sounded by the anti-Federalists, who questioned the need for a governing elite and judged the Constitution wanting because it would lead to elitism. For them, popular participation was not only a key to good republican governance, but an educational enterprise necessary for the creation of a general republican virtue. A distinctive sort of democratic excellence was sought. Luxury, not the rabble, was seen as the enemy of the republic. One observed, "As people become more luxurious, they become more incapacitated of governing themselves." Republican education was a primary defense against luxury. "The small republic was seen as a school of citizenship as much as a scheme of government." For the anti-Federalist, the proper relationship between excellence and democracy was achieved by defending the virtuous polity from the decadent "excellence" of aristocracy.

The anti-Federalist position draws upon the wisdom of earlier political theory, and it imagines a more thoroughly democratic future than proved to be the case. That it was formulated by people very different from present-day democrats—some of whom were committed to slavery, most of whom believed that shared religious belief was a necessary foundation for a republic, and almost all of whom assumed that ethnic homogeneity was required for republican life—has, unfortunately, discouraged the cynical from considering the challenge these early democrats pose. Indeed, both the Federalists and the anti-Federalists were embarking upon an extraordinary political revolution which is far from complete. They questioned the prevailing contemporary opinion concerning the wisdom of monarchy, and they took seriously the ideal of self-rule. Their monumental achievement was to initiate the end of monarchy. The task they set for themselves and for us is the realization of self-rule. The set task involved for each a distinctive approach to the problem of democratic culture. For the Federalists, self-rule fundamentally had to include the utilization of the European and largely aristocratic cultural inheritance; for the anti-Federalists the inheritance was viewed with suspicion. They preferred instead, in the language of our day, "the school of hard knocks." A Maryland anti-Federalist farmer proposed the establishment of "seminaries of useful learning" where citizens would be educated not in "the philosophy of the moon and skies but in what is useful in this world. . . . The sciences of morality, agriculture, commerce, the management of farms and household affairs."[5]

An egalitarian suspicion of cultural refinements motivates such a proposal. In the 1780s it led some to denounce the development of theater and the arts in the republic.[6] In the nineteenth century, such an egalitarian sensibility was the cultural foundation for the establishment of land-grant colleges, which, at least to begin with, were antagonistic to the theoretical and the not immediately practical "elitist" curriculum of liberal studies.[7] Theater, the arts, philosophy, and the sciences were viewed as kinds of aristocratic finery inimical to the needs of republican virtue.

The latter was viewed as it had been understood in the tradition of political theory. Montesquieu, for example, observed:

> Virtue in a republic is a most simple thing; it is a love of the republic. . . . A love of the republic in a democracy is the love of democracy; as the latter is that of equality. . . . A love of democracy is likewise that of frugality. Since every individual ought here to enjoy the same happiness and the same advantages, they should consequently taste the same pleasures and form the same hopes, which can not be expected but from a general frugality. . . . The

> love of equality in a democracy limits ambition to the sole
> desire, the sole happiness, of doing greater service to our
> country.[8]

In contemporary mass society, the problems involved in such
thinking are evident. We know that in societies where mass structures are well crystallized and a mass-culture industry is well
developed, the enjoyment of the same happiness, advantages, plea-
sures, and hopes are most likely products of a homogenizing
production. These do not lead to self-reliant citizens devoted to the
public good but to atomized consumers of political, economic, and
cultural goods. But before we complete our analysis of our contemporary predicaments, we should pause a bit longer and note how
our contemporary dilemma is very much rooted in our political and
cultural history.

The Federalists' fear of the rabble had a positive dimension. They
judged that the primary challenge facing the republic was its potential degeneration into tyranny, coming about as a result of public
disenchantment with the salience of popular government. The best
defense against this was seen to be good government. "Effective
government, in addition to being intrinsically desirable, is also a key
to the attachment of the people and to civic virtue itself."[9] The quality of political culture and the cultural excellence of the government
would yield the freely chosen attachment of the governed, forming
a commonwealth.

The debate was immediately won by the Federalists. But it raged
on in the nineteenth century and rages on in the twentieth. To be
sure, what is at stake has changed, but a similar challenge persists.
During the revolutionary period the stakes concerned the development of democracy as a positive political value. At the time of the
Declaration of Independence, the referent of the term "democracy"
was ambiguous. It was understood as a synonym for the disorder
which necessarily precedes tyranny. On the other hand, it was beginning to be understood as the fundamental social condition
requisite for the rule of the public. Democracy was an ascendant value, and the ambivalence towards the term and the ambiguity
lessened to the point that during the Jacksonian period democracy
came to be understood as the definitive first principle of the new nation. But this was not the case in the eighteenth century. Thus James
Madison at the Constitutional Convention could argue for the need
to control "the inconveniences of democracy" in order to resolve the
principles of "the democratic form of government,"[10] and he was
understood by his colleagues. The Federalists were especially con-

cerned that democracy not lead to a dilution of talent and a lessening of collective capacity for self-rule. Following this sort of argument, a rationalization for elite public service developed. Social hierarchy and privilege were seen as being compatible with the ideals of democracy.

Excellence not only enlightens leadership, but in the process it justifies privilege. For this reason we may look askance at the "Federalist" solution, as the ideological critics dismiss the notion of culture today. But caution is in order; not because privilege is desirable, but because an enlightening (and potentially critical) culture might otherwise be lost. The anti-Federalist attack upon "impractical" culture suggests this, as do the contemporary ideological critics and sociologists of knowledge.

The challenge for us as part of a live political tradition is not necessarily to endorse the Federalist or the anti-Federalist positions, but to keep their debate ongoing. This is the practical answer to cynicism and fundamentalism. It involves making problematic the issues of democracy and culture in our everyday social and political life, in our political parties and newspapers, our universities and public schools, in social movements and cultural institutions. Most crucially, as we have observed throughout this inquiry, it involves contrasting the appearance of mass structures with democratic norms.

III

I have argued that democracy distinguishes American political practices from that of the Soviet tradition, even though not all aspects of our politics are democratic. Yet viewed from a certain critical objective distance, American and Soviet practices seem to function according to identical laws. Both we and they have operated within relatively narrow political values, norms, and practices. In the Soviet Union, an openly pro-American, capitalist liberal political movement has had no chance to change the nature of the political order, even in the age of glasnost and perestroika. But in the United States, an openly pro-Soviet communist or even socialist movement has had no greater chance of success, perhaps even less. In both societies, a power elite seems to rule. A significant overthrow of American corporate capital is even less likely than the overthrow of the Soviet Communist party. Privilege reproduces itself, and all sorts of subtle and not so subtle techniques are used to ensure that it is not challenged. The mass media in both societies have been used to manipulate public opinion; there, through propaganda and censorship, here through consumer, corporate, and political advertising. In both societies, the educational system has not only bestowed advantages upon the children of the powerful and disadvantages upon the children of the less privileged, but it has socialized all children to view the way things are as the way they must be. A broad variety of institutions of discipline have effectively served the powers in both the political East and West, suggesting, at least to such extreme objectivists as Michel Foucault, that the proclaimed ideals of the Enlightenment, including culture (as the refined arts and sciences) and democracy are at best a sham and, more significantly, mechanisms of social control.[11]

Such objective views, though, miss a great deal. Distance does not necessarily improve social knowledge or criticism.[12] An important part of politics is politics as experienced. Democracy as an ideal is experienced as alive when opposition is articulated in thought and action. Success of the opposition is not required. Its persistent appearance is. Democracy as self-rule requires that people experience politics as involving choice and decisions. Cynical observers note that the subjectively engaged experience of being able to make a difference does not conform to their more distanced objective view. They know that all choices are between Tweedledum and Tweedledee. Such observers overlook the fact that the experience of democracy, its mere appearance to the citizenry, is an important social reality.

When a citizenry does not experience democracy as a reality, it cannot be one. This has been the case with the nations of the Soviet Union. Even with very significant democratic reforms, and a sense that they are beginning to make a difference, the subjects of the Soviet republics still persist in trying to figure out what "they" are up to, and the Soviet subjects engage in machinations to use the party position for their own purposes, both in opposition and in support. They define their situation as undemocratic, and even if it is objectively more democratic, it cannot become democratic without a complete political revolution. They cannot achieve democracy unless they perceive it as a real possibility, develop a democratic culture, and commit themselves to its principles.

But with the perception of democracy, it is a possibility. Thus the Polish people, led by such brilliant political theorists as Adam Michnik, acted over a long repressive decade as if they were free and democratic. They perceived democratic possibilities and created a democratic culture in a decidedly undemocratic environment. But when the environment changed, a robust democratization developed.

A democracy is truly vibrant when the democratic perception and culture are based upon an ongoing appraisal and refinement by the citizenry, such as the developing American debate about democracy and culture. A contentious discourse through time about fundamental ideals constitutes a normative democratic reality, even when contemporary political practices are far from ideal. Objectively speaking, the politics of America may be characterized as being a corporate-military oligarchy. But such objective facts as reported by C. Wright Mills are not the only kind of facts.[13] People define their situation as democratic, so they act accordingly. Even if oligarchy persists, so does democratic opposition. Further, both the oligarchs and the democrats know that a sustained democratic challenge can change the rules of the political-economic game, as it did with the development of the various types of welfare states of Western Europe and North America. Corporations may manipulate public opinion to sustain popular support, but from our point of view the significant fact is that they find this necessary. The American "power elite" knows, as does its opposition, that a sustained democratic movement can make and has made a political, cultural, and social difference in America. Viewed with pseudo-objectivity, rules of formal democratic practice, the rules of law and explicit civil and political rights, may appear as facades of control, functioning to make tolerance repressive,[14] but that people act upon these so-called illusions make them very real political realities. This is why the emergence of ideology in America is so tragic, both the leftist defeats and the rightist successes.

I have argued that America has to be considered both as a democracy and as a mass society. While the inclusion of the populous in the central political, economic, and cultural life has been manipulated through mass structures, democratic norms persist. These norms have a significant life only when they are openly identified and critically appraised. This is the significance of the debates stimulated by the books of Bloom, Hirsch, and Jacoby. They point to problems of democratic culture today, thus keeping alive the problematic of democratic culture. In different ways they claim that American culture is in decline. Bloom asserts that this is because of democracy, while Hirsch and Jacoby see it as a problem for democracy. The works of the authors are flawed, yet they remind us of important issues. Bloom, like an old Tory, opts for the aristocracy of old over democracy. Hirsch is a neo-anti-Federalist of sorts. Though his items of cultural literacy include refined culture, he seeks practical education with the necessary information for our age. Jacoby longs for the role of an old Federalist Enlightenment thinker. He believes that America needs literate critics to sustain its culture but regrets that, at least on the left, clear literate voices are not to be heard among the younger generation. Whether or not Jacoby is accurate in his appraisal, the significance of his book, along with the works of Bloom and Hirsch, is that both culture and democracy are taken seriously, as is their problematic relationship.

This is missing in the tragic ideologies of the left and the happy ideologies of the right. They both addressed the problems posed by mass society by succumbing to it. On the left, this has taken different guises, from vanguardist Marxist-Leninism to media politics and ideologies of despair. On the right, fundamentalism and anti-communism plus media performance and computer mailing lists equalled political ascendance. Yet both the failed ideologies of the left and the successful ideology of the right turned away from the problems of democracy and culture. Absolute beliefs or claims substituted for the pursuit of culture; and reaching the masses substituted for democratic inclusion of the populace into political deliberations. That the left based its absolute beliefs on a secular certainty (a scientific socialism) and the right on religious revelation, from the viewpoint of democratic cultural ideals, only made for instrumental differences. The fundamentalism of the right has much more resonance with the population, but like the Marxism of the left, it opposes democratic Enlightenment ideals.

The Federalists and the anti-Federalists argued for and against the Constitution on reasonable grounds. They hoped to convince their fellow citizens by rational persuasion. The modern ideologues have and disseminate the truth. For those committed to democracy, an informed citizenry, capable of reason, is a necessity if governance is to be wise and effective. For ideologues, propagation of the revealed truth is all that is necessary. This is why the history of the New Left is a history of decline. It started with a clear appreciation of participatory democracy and ended with mass theatrics and ideology. Democracy was confused with mass society, and cynicism resulted. In a parallel fashion, the conservative commitment to education was lost when the right wing took up the ideological gauntlet. Preservation of our cultural inheritance and concern for cultural excellence, both necessary for a democratic culture and key to the political commitment of the Constitution's conservative supporters, have been lost to ideological campaigns for prayer in schools and tax vouchers.

I believe our democratic ideals need not be overwhelmed by ideology, mass structures, and cynical interpretation. Mass society, as we have observed, emerges from democracy, but democratic ideals are not completely absent from mass structures. The American nominating conventions, no matter how manipulated, technocratic, or ideological they may be, still operationalize central democratic ideals. Even television, the quintessential platform of mass culture, can become a powerful medium for the expression of democratic cultural ideals (recall the viewpoint of David Potter). But if the embedded and embattled alternatives to mass society are to be activated, cynical interpretation must be avoided. This is why public cynicism is the single most pressing challenge facing American democracy. Interpretation that judges the quality of an argument by its source takes manipulation and ideology to be the sum and substance of democratic practice. When democracy is understood as being linked with reasoned persuasion, a sociological reductionism must be avoided. This suggests to us that the "insights" of the sociology of knowledge and ideological critique lead in the wrong direction, and that they have an especially pernicious effect as they inform journalistic interpretation and public opinion.

It does not, for example, improve our educational systems to know that the upper middle class generally supports more taxes for better schools and the lower middle class does not, or that, oddly, in the city of Chicago, support for the public schools has a racial component; blacks want more money spent on the schools and whites, because so many of them send their children to parochial schools, generally oppose more funding. Knowing and judging the arguments for school improvement is a much more likely avenue for democratic reform. A public discourse about the ends and means of education, with a consideration of progressive and conservative positions, can and should keep alive the problematic of democratic culture in everyday political life. If a community concerned itself with the relative merits of liberal versus vocational education, the importance of information versus learning skills, and the civic versus the individual orientation of schooling, not only would issues be resolved through popular wisdom but, more importantly, popular wisdom would be constituted. Concern for civic ideals should not always be interpreted as empty pieties; they are central political principles which conflict and must be resolved. The ways a community attempts to resolve the dilemmas, while not explaining them away or ignoring them, is the real news on the educational front. Such an attempt is a precondition for resolving the educational crisis, as we have observed. That people are sensitive to the issues involved is indicated by the popularity of and debates around the books of Bloom, Hirsch, and Jacoby.

I have tried to demonstrate how excellent cultural works, viewed in terms of their excellence, can best sensitize us to the pressing normative problems of our times. My argument should be understood within the context of the debate about democratic culture, as should any critique of mass culture. Mine is a neo-Federalist sort of argument. I believe that the full reach of human imagination can illuminate (enlighten) our understanding of our human condition, and that this forms the soundest basis for collective action. Though mass culture has the appearance of democracy (it is readily consumed by a large, constructed audience), its systematic distortion of human intelligence and creativity enervates democratic capacity. Though autonomous culture, especially when it is most imaginative and distinctive, may appear to be elitist, it is only when those with the capacity stretch themselves to understand and communicate their understanding to their fellow citizens that democracy has a chance to be reasonable. And the capacity to understand the challenging need not be as limited as conservative elitists and mass-culture populists often claim. Autonomous culture ought to be open; cultural literacy needs to be expanded, and an excellent autonomous cultural work such as Toni Morrison's *Beloved* can and does contribute to excellence and the expansion. It was, after all, a best-seller. It will no doubt inform popular understanding of slavery and its legacies in a profound way.

Alexander Hamilton, the quintessential Federalist, argued that the government ought to be effective both as an end in itself and as a means of assuring popular support. I am making a parallel argument and drawing out its implications. Open, pluralist, and excellent cultural work can teach citizens to think for themselves about their society, so that they can act democratically. Populists, both of the left and the right, will argue that my position, like that of Hamilton's, is elitist. To this I have a closing measured response, based on remembrance and critical reflection. I recall the work of intellectual and political elites, especially those who made, supported, and opposed the American Constitution; artistic elites, both those who made up the so-called American literary renaissance of the nineteenth century (when Tocqueville claimed fine culture was an impossibility in a democracy) and the present-day African-American literary elite circle of women writers; and scientific elites, from the Athenian Academy to the modern universities. I also recall that totalitarianism in its classical phase was popular, based on earlier forms of the mass populism of central Europe, and that it had a family resemblance to some forms of populism in America. But this leads me to critically reflect on the very meaning of elitism and populism within a democratic tradition. Is it more democratic cynically to compromise cultural and political expression so that a mass market can be served? Or does democracy require that we all speak our minds as clearly, openly, and imaginatively as we can? In my judgment, autonomous authentic voices constitute a pluralistic democracy; manipulated mass culture produces a cynical society.

NOTES

Chapter One

1. For an interesting sample, see *The New Republic*, December 5, 1988, "The Quadrennial Recriminations Issue."

2. The most striking and tragic instance of this sort of media complicity in service of a reprehensible partisan purpose was the way the mainstream press dutifully reported all the wild accusations of Senator Joseph McCarthy in the early fifties. The Senator said it, so the press automatically reported it, no matter how wild and how damaging to specific individuals and to the common good.

3. See, for example, Edmund Burke, *Reflections on the Revolution in France, and on the proceedings in certain societies in London relative to that event* (Middlesex, Eng.: Pelican Books, 1968; first published in 1790); and Michael Oakeshott, *On Human Conduct* (Oxford: Clarendon Press, 1975).

4. See, e.g., Kathleen Hall Jamieson, *Packaging the Presidency: A History and Criticism of Presidential Campaign Advertising* (New York: Oxford University Press, 1984).

5. Mancur Olson, Jr., *The Logic of Collective Action: Public Goods and the Theory of Groups* (New York: Schocken, 1968).

6. This is the position of Allan Bloom. For an extensive analysis, see Chapter 5.

7. See Jeffrey C. Goldfarb, *Beyond Glasnost: The Post-Totalitarian Mind* (Chicago: University of Chicago Press, 1989).

8. See Hannah Arendt, *The Origins of Totalitarianism* (New York: Harcourt Brace Jovanovich, 1951), pp. 250–55; and *On Revolution* (New York: Viking, 1963).

9. See Chapters 6 and 7.

Chapter Two

1. Max Weber, *The Protestant Ethic and the Spirit of Capitalism* (New York: Scribner's, 1958).

2. Peter Slotendijk has presented an effective historical and philosophic critique of cynicism. See his *Critique of Cynical Reason*, trans. Michael Eldred (Minneapolis: University of Minnesota Press, 1987). He works primarily with a cynical duality: as critique and resignation. The present inquiry used the dualism as it historically emerged but seeks to find alternatives to cynicism in both of its senses in a democratic culture.

3. Ibid., p. 160.

4. See, for example, D. R. Dudley, *A History of Cynicism* (London: Methuen, 1937).

5. See Arendt, *The Origins of Totalitarianism*, pp. 305–88.

6. For an analysis of the rational-choice paradigm and its problems, see Alan Wolfe, *Whose Keeper? Social Science and Moral Obligation* (Berkeley: University of California Press, 1989), pp. 27–104.

7. See, for example, Samuel Huntington, "The Democratic Distemper," in *The American Commonwealth—1976*, ed. Nathan Glazer and Irving Kristol (New York: Basic Books, 1976), pp. 5–38.

8. See Benjamin Barber, *The Conquest of Politics: Liberal Philosophy in Democratic Times* (Princeton: Princeton University Press, 1988), especially pp. 3–21.

9. William F. Buckley, Jr., *God and Man at Yale: The Superstitions of "Academic Freedom"* (Chicago: Henry Regnery, 1951).

10. Abbie Hoffman, *Steal This Book* (New York: Grove Press, 1971).

11. For an analysis of examples, see Michael Walzer, *The Company of Critics: Social Criticism and Political Commitment in the Twentieth Century* (New York: Basic Books, 1988).

12. Michel Foucault, *Madness and Civilization: A History of Insanity in the Age of Reason* (New York: Pantheon, 1965); *History of Sexuality* (New York: Pantheon, 1980); *Power/Knowledge: Selected Interviews and Other Writings, 1972–1977* (New York: Pantheon, 1980).

13. Tom Wolfe, *The Bonfire of the Vanities* (New York: Farrar, Straus and Giroux, 1987).

14. See, e.g., Tom Wolfe, *The Kandy-Kolored Tangerine-Flake Streamline Baby* (New York: Farrar, Straus and Giroux, 1965); *Electric Kool-aid Acid Test* (New York: Farrar, Straus and Giroux, 1968): *Mauve Gloves & Madmen, Clutter and Vine* (New York: Farrar, Straus and Giroux, 1976); *In Our Time* (New York: Farrar, Straus and Giroux, 1980).

Chapter Three

1. See Goldfarb, *Beyond Glasnost*.

2. José Ortega y Gasset, *The Revolt of the Masses*, trans. Anthony Kerrigan; ed. Kenneth Moore (Notre Dame, Ind.: University of Notre Dame Press, 1985).

3. Elias Canetti, *Crowds and Power*, trans. Carol Stewart (New York: Farrar, Straus and Giroux, 1962).

4. Daniel Bell, *The Coming of Post-Industrial Society: A Venture in Social Forecasting* (New York: Basic Books, 1973).

5. Edward Shils, *The Constitution of Society* (Chicago: University of Chicago Press, 1982).

6. Quoted in Serge Guilbaut, *How New York Stole the Idea of Modern Art: Abstract Expressionism, Freedom, and the Cold War*, trans. Arthur Goldhammer (Chicago: University of Chicago Press, 1983), p. 63.

7. Arendt, *The Origins of Totalitarianism*, pp. 250–66.

8. Max Horkheimer and Theodor Adorno, *The Dialectic of Enlightenment*, trans. John Cumming (New York: Herder and Herder, 1972).

9. Shils, "The Theory of Mass Society," in *The Constitution of Societies*, pp. 69–89.

10. Ferenc Fehér, "Redemptive and Democratic Paradigms in Radical Politics," in Ferenc Fehér and Agnes Heller, *Eastern Left, Western Left: Totalitarianism, Freedom and Democracy* (Atlantic Highlands, N.J.: Humanities Press International, 1987), pp. 61–76.

11. Stanislaw Witkiewiciz, *The Shoemakers*, in *The Madman and the Nun and Other Plays*, trans. and ed. Daniel C. Gerould and C. S. Durer (Seattle: University of Washington Press, 1968).

12. Talcott Parsons, *The System of Modern Societies* (Englewood Cliffs, N.J.: Prentice-Hall, 1971).

13. Herbert J. Gans, *Popular Culture and High Culture; An Analysis and Evaluation of Taste* (New York: Basic Books, 1974), pp. 4–9.

14. See, for example, Norman Podhoretz, *The Bloody Crossroads: Where Literature and Politics Meet* (New York: Simon and Schuster, 1986).

15. Paul Hollander, *Political Pilgrims: Travels of Western Intellectuals to the Soviet Union* (New York: Oxford University Press, 1981).

16. Alexis de Tocqueville, *Democracy in America*, ed. Phillips Bradley (New York: Alfred A. Knopf, 1980).

17. See Robert Bellah, Richard Marsden, William M. Sullivan, Ann Swidler, and Steven M. Tipton, *Habits of the Heart: Individualism and Commitment in American Life* (Berkeley: University of California Press, 1985).

18. Tocqueville, *Democracy in America*, 2: 318–19.

19. In the next section this will be analyzed extensively.

20. Robert Dahl, *Democracy in the United States: Promise and Performance* (Chicago: Rand NcNally, 1976).

21. Phillipe Schmitter, "Democratic Theory and Neocorporatist Practice," *Social Research* 50, (Winter 1983): 885–928.

22. Robert Michels, *Political Parties* (Glencoe: The Free Press, 1949, first published in Germany in 1911).

23. Seymour Martin Lipset, Martin A. Trow, and James S. Coleman, *Union Democracy: The Internal Politics of the International Typographical Union* (Glencoe: The Free Press, 1956).

24. Edward Shils, "The Theory of Mass Society," p. 69.

25. Ibid, p. 70.

26. Ibid.

27. Ibid, p. 71.

28. Burke, *Reflections on the Revolution in France*, and Joseph Marie de-Maistre, 1753–1821, *Works*, selected and trans. by Jack Lively (New York: Macmillan, 1965).

29. Isaiah Berlin, "Two Concepts of Liberty," in his *Four Essays on Liberty* (New York: Oxford University Press, 1969), pp. 118–72.

30. For a recent critique and a revisionist radical position, see Agnes Heller, *Beyond Justice* (Oxford: Blackwell, 1987).

31. See especially, Emile Durkheim, *The Division of Labor in Society* (New

York: The Free Press, 1933); Max Weber, *Economy and Society: An Outline of Interpretive Sociology,* ed. Guenther Roth and Claus Wittich, trans. Ephraim Fischoff et al. (Berkeley: University of California Press, 1978); C. Wright Mills, *The Power Elite* (New York: Oxford University Press, 1956), and *The Sociological Imagination* (New York: Oxford University Press, 1959); Talcott Parsons, *The Social System,* (Glencoe: The Free Press, 1951); and Alvin Ward Gouldner, *The Coming Crisis of Western Sociology* (New York: Basic Books, 1970).

32. This is especially the case in his later works. See Alvin Gouldner, *The Two Marxisms: Contradictions and Anomalies in the Development of Theory* (New York: Oxford University Press, 1980); and *Against Fragmentation: The Origins of Marxism and the Sociology of Intellectuals* (New York: Oxford University Press, 1985).

33. See Mills, *The Power Elite,* esp. pp. 298–324.

34. See L. William Dohmhoff and Hoyt B. Ballard, eds. *C. Wright Mills and the Power Elite* (Boston: Beacon Press, 1968).

35. See Mills, *The Power Elite,* pp. 323–24.

36. James Miller, *"Democracy Is in the Streets": From Port Huron to the Siege of Chicago* (New York: Simon and Schuster, 1987), p. 307.

37. See Parsons, *The Social System,* and Jürgen Habermas, *The Legitimation Crisis,* trans. Thomas McCarthy (Boston: Beacon Press, 1975).

38. Shils, "The Theory of Mass Society," p. 77.

39. Shils, "The Center and Periphery," in *The Constitution of Mass Society.*

40. See Edward Shils, *The Calling of Sociology and Other Essays on the Pursuit of Learning* (Chicago: University of Chicago Press, 1980); *Center and Periphery: Essays in Macrosociology* (Chicago: University of Chicago Press, 1975); and *The Intellectuals and the Power, and Other Essays* (Chicago: University of Chicago Press, 1972).

41. Shils, "The Theory of Mass Society," pp. 95–96.

42. Ibid, pp. 96–97.

Chapter Four

1. Charles A. Beard, *An Economic Interpretation of the Constitution of the United States* (New York: The Free Press, 1941).

2. Garry Wills, *Explaining America: The Federalist* (New York: Penguin Books, 1981), pp. 3–12.

3. Ibid, p. 9. Italics in original.

4. Jackson Turner Main, *The Anti-Federalists: Critics of the Constitution, 1781–1788* (Chapel Hill: University of North Carolina Press, 1961).

5. Wills, *Explaining America,* p. 7.

6. See, e.g., James MacGregor Burns, *The Vineyard of Liberty* (New York: Alfred A. Knopf, 1982), pp. 3–63.

7. See Gordon Wood, *The Creation of the American Republic, 1776–1787* (Chapel Hill: University of North Carolina Press, 1969).

8. See Richard Hofstadter, *The Idea of the Party System: The Rise of a Legiti-*

mate Opposition in the United States, 1780–1840 (Berkeley: University of California Press, 1969), pp. 212–71.

9. Main, *The Anti-Federalists,*

10. Russell Baker, "Rewriting the Book," *New York Times,* August 22, 1984, p. A23.

11. See Chaim Isaac Waxman, ed., *The End of Ideology Debate* (New York: Fund and Wagnalls, 1968); and Arthur Vidich, unpublished review essay of *Talcott Parsons and the Capitalist Nation-State: Political Sociology as a Strategic Vocation,* by William Buxton (Toronto: University of Toronto Press, 1985).

12. Alexander Hamilton, James Madison, and John Jay, *The Federalist Papers* (New York: New American Library, 1961; first published in 1787 and 1788).

13. See Robert H. Wiebe, *The Opening of American Society* (New York: Vintage Books, 1985), pp. 1–67.

14. See, e.g., Daniel J. Boorstin, *The Americans: The Democratic Experience* (New York: Random House, 1973), pp. 449–522; Donald Scott, *Democracy and Knowledge in Nineteenth-Century America* (forthcoming, University of Chicago Press); and Thomas Bender, *New York Intellect* (Baltimore: Johns Hopkins University Press, 1987).

15. See Bernard Bailyn, *The Ideological Origins of the American Revolution* (Cambridge: Harvard University Press, 1967), esp. pp. 1–54.

16. Pierre Bourdieu, *Distinction: A Social Critique of the Judgment of Taste* (Cambridge: Harvard University Press, 1984).

17. The analysis of the lecture-hall circuit is drawn from the historical research of Donald Scott and intensive discussion with Scott. See his *Democracy and Knowledge.*

18. Mills, *The Power Elite,* p. 304.

19. For an account of the early life of the *New Yorker,* see James Thurber, *The Years with Ross* (Boston: Little Brown, 1957).

20. I analyze the *New Yorker* and other American cultural institutions, focusing on cultural freedom, in my *On Cultural Freedom: An Exploration of Public Life in Poland and America* (Chicago: University of Chicago Press, 1983).

21. This is the pressing concern of Russell Jacoby in *The Last Intellectuals: American Culture in the Age of Academe* (New York: Basic Books, 1987). See my critique below.

22. For my analysis of the politics of culture in totalitarian orders, see Goldfarb, *Beyond Glasnost.*

23. This is one of the major points in Goldfarb, *On Cultural Freedom.*

24. As reported in the *New York Times* September 18, 1988, "Issues or Their Lack Reflect Voter Concern, or Its Lack," by E. J. Dionne, Jr., pp. 1, 30.

Chapter Five

1. Jacoby, *The Last Intellectuals.*

2. E. D. Hirsch, Jr., *Cultural Literacy: What Every American Needs to Know* (Boston: Houghton, Mifflin, 1987).

3. Allan Bloom, *The Closing of the American Mind, How Higher Education Has Failed Democracy and Impoverished the Souls of Today's Students* (New York: Simon and Schuster, 1987).

4. Robert Paul Wolff, *"The Closing of the American Mind* by Allan Bloom," *Academe* (September—October, 1987).

5. Bloom, *American Mind*, pp. 79–80.

6. Ibid, p. 79.

7. Ibid, pp. 79–80.

8. For an overview of the Straussian school's recent works on America, see Gordon Wood, "The Fundamentalists and the Constitution," *New York Review of Books* 35, no. 2, February 18, 1988, pp. 33–40.

9. Saul Bellow, *The Dean's December* (New York: Harper and Row, 1982).

10. Bloom, *American Mind*, p. 313.

11. Ibid, p. 63.

12. Hirsch, *Cultural Literacy*, p. viii.

13. See George Herbert Mead, *Mind, Self, and Society* (Chicago: University of Chicago Press, 1934).

14. Hirsch, *Cultural Literacy*, p. 12.

15. Ibid, pp. 12–13.

16. Ibid, p. 74.

17. Ibid, p. 83.

18. Ibid, p. 107.

19. Ibid, pp. 10–11.

20. See Orlando Patterson, *Slavery and Social Death: A Comparative Study.* Cambridge: Harvard University Press, 1982.

21. Hirsch, *Cultural Literacy*, p. 23.

22. Ibid, pp. 20–21.

23. Jacoby, *Last Intellectuals*, p. 3.

24. Ibid, p. 17.

25. Ibid, p. 19.

26. Ibid, p. 19.

27. Ibid, pp. 185–86.

28. Ibid, p. 174–75.

29. Ibid, pp. 166–74.

30. *New York Times Magazine*, January 3, 1988, p. 13.

Chapter Six

1. See Daniel Bell, *The End of Ideology: On the Exhaustion of Political Ideas in the Fifties* (New York: The Free Press), 1960.

2. Werner Sombart, *Why Is There No Socialism in the United States?* (White Plains, N.Y.: International Arts and Sciences Press, 1976).

3. Quoted in William L. O'Neill, *A Better World: The Great Schism: Stalinism and the American Intellectuals* (New York: Simon and Schuster, 1982), p. 67.

4. Ibid, p. 37.

5. Ibid, p. 78.

6. Ibid, pp. 75–78.

7. See especially David Caute, *The Great Fear: The Anti-Communist Purge Under Truman and Eisenhower* (New York: Simon and Schuster, 1979).

8. See, e.g., Sidney Hook, *Heresy Yes—Conspiracy No!* (New York: T. Day, 1985), and *The Paradoxes of Freedom* (Berkeley: University of California Press, 1962).

9. David Reisman, "Interviewers, Elites and Academic Freedom," in *Abundance for What?* (Garden City: Doubleday, 1964), pp. 581–83.

10. Peter M. Rutkoff and William B. Scott, *The New School: A History of the New School for Social Research* (New York: The Free Press, 1986), pp. 225–28.

11. See Victor Navasky, *Naming Names* (New York: Penguin Books, 1980).

12. See, e.g., William Barrett, *The Truants: Adventures Among the Intellectuals* (Garden City: Anchor Press/Doubleday, 1982); and Norman Podhoretz, *Breaking Ranks: A Political Memoir* (New York: Harper and Row, 1979).

13. Edward Shils, *Torment of Secrecy, the Background and Consequences of American Security Policies* (Glencoe: The Free Press, 1956).

14. For a careful, historical, but sometimes ideologized analysis of the transition from Old to New Left, see Maurice Isserman, *If I Had a Hammer. . .The Death of the Old Left and the Birth of the New Left* (New York: Basic Books, 1987).

15. See Taylor Branch, *Parting the Waters: American in the King Years, 1954–63* (New York: Simon and Schuster, 1988).

16. See James Miller, *"Democracy in the Streets": From Port Huron to the Siege of Chicago*, pp. 78–91, on the importance of C. Wright Mills to the American New Left.

17. In ibid., p. 112

18. From the Port Huron Statement, reprinted in ibid., p. 329.

19. Michael Harrington, *The Other America* (New York: Penguin Books, 1971).

20. Miller, *"Democracy"*, p. 113.

21. Ibid, p. 114.

22. Tom Hayden, *Reunion* (New York: Random House, 1988), p. 87.

23. Miller, *"Democracy"*, p. 333.

24. Todd Gitlin, *The Whole World Is Watching: Mass Media in the Making and Unmaking of the New Left* (Berkeley: University of California Press, 1981).

25. The debates between the conservative or moderate wings of the party and the progressive wing of the party can be viewed as debates between those against and those for the SDS program.

26. Robert Michels, *Political Parties*.

27. David Faber, *Chicago '68*, (Chicago: University of Chicago Press, 1988), p. 216.

28. Ibid, p. 220.

29. Quoted in ibid., p. 217.

30. See their recent work: Todd Gitlin, *The Sixties: Years of Hope, Days of Rage* (New York: Bantam, 1989); and Richard Flacks, *The Making of History:*

The American Left and the American Mind (New York: Columbia University Press, 1988).

31. See Clifford Geertz, "Ideology as a Cultural System," in *The Interpretation of Culture* (New York: Basic Books, 1973); and Paul Ricoeur, *Lectures on Ideology and Utopia*, ed. George H. Taylor (New York: Columbia University Press, 1986).

32. See Georg Lukács, *History and Class Consciousness: Studies in Marxist Dialectics* (Cambridge: MIT Press, 1971).

33. Such was the case of Tadeusz Borowski, author of *This Way to the Gas Chambers, Ladies and Gentlemen*, trans. Barbara Vedder (New York: Penguin Books, 1976).

34. Indirectly, radical excesses in the West have had profoundly tragic effects upon the politics of the Third World. There is a direct connection between fashionable French radicalism and the holocaust of Pol Pot.

35. See particularly Herbert Marcuse, *One-Dimensional Man: Studies in the Ideology of Advanced Industrial Society* (Boston: Beacon Press, 1964).

36. See description in Miller, *"Democracy,"* op. cit., pp. 174–217.

Chapter Seven

1. For an analysis of the escalation of repressive attacks upon the press, see Anthony Lewis, "The Intimidated Press," *New York Review of Books* 35, January 19, 1989, pp. 26–28, nn. 21, 22.

2. Louis Hartz, *The Liberal Tradition in America* (New York: Harcourt Brace, 1955).

3. See Bernard Bailyn, *The Ideological Origins of the American Revolution* (Cambridge, MA: Harvard University Press, 1967).

4. See Bellah et al., *Habits of the Heart*.

5. See Margaret Weir and Ira Katznelson, *Schooling for All: Class, Race and the Decline of the Democratic Ideal* (New York: Basic Books, 1985).

6. Barry Goldwater, *The Conscience of a Conservative* (New York: MacFadden 1960), p. 3, quoted in Richard Hofstadter, "Goldwater and Pseudo-Conservative Politics," in Hofstadter, *The Paranoid Style of Politics and Other Essays* (New York: Alfred A. Knopf, 1966), pp. 94–95.

7. Hofstadter, *The Paranoid Style*, pp. 94–95.

8. It continued to play itself out in the various nativist movements of the nineteenth century. If people unprepared for democracy and the American experiment took part in American political life—as they did—it was not at all clear that the republican political system or the American social order could withstand their lack of preparation. Even now, the resilience of the polity and society is remarkable. Fears that it would not be so surely emanate from some reasonable grounds.

9. For a telling portrait of this, see Garry Wills, *Reagan's America: Innocents at Home* (Garden City: Doubleday, 1987).

10. See Jeffrey Hart, *The American Dissent: A Decade of Modern Conservatism* (Garden City: Doubleday, 1966), for a sympathetic account of the role played

by Buckley and the *National Review* in supporting a sustained and coherent conservative movement in America.

11. Buckley, *God and Man at Yale*, p. xiii.

12. Richard Viguerie, "Ends and Means," in *The New Right Papers*, ed. Robert W. Whitaker (New York: St. Martins Press, 1982), p. 30.

13. Ibid, p. 31.

14. Max Horkheimer and Theodor Adorno, *The Dialectic of Enlightenment* (New York: Herder and Herder, 1972).

15. See William J. Wilson, *The Truly Disadvantaged: The Inner City, the Underclass and Public Policy* (Chicago: University of Chicago Press, 1987).

Chapter Eight

1. See Richard Hofstadter, *Anti-Intellectualism in American Life* (New York: Knopf, 1963).

2. See, e.g., Hannah Arendt, "The Crisis in Education," in *Between Past and Future* (New York: Penguin Books, 1980), pp. 173–96; and Michael Oakeshott, "Rationalism in Politics and Other Essays" (Totowa, N.J.: Rowman and Littlefield, 1977), esp. pp. 111–36 and 168–96.

3. Hannah Arendt is especially eloquent on this point in her "Crisis in Education".

4. See Garry Wills, *Reagan's America*.

5. Reagan's first secretary of education has written a detailed account of his struggle as a conservative educator against a right-wing ideological approach to education. See Terrell Bell, *The Thirteenth Man* (New York: The Free Press, 1988). For a cogent overview of Bell's book, along with other insider accounts of Reagan's White House, see Frances FitzGerald, "A Critic at Large (Memoirs of the Reagan Era)," *New Yorker*, January 16, 1989, pp. 71–94.

6. Quoted in FitzGerald, "A Critic at Large," p. 76.

7. See Lawrence Cremin, *Traditions of American Education* (New York: Basic Books, 1977).

8. Hannah Arendt, "The Crisis in Education."

Chapter Nine

1. For a graphic account of this in nuclear-weapons policy, see John Newhouse, *War and Peace in the Nuclear Age* (New York: Knopf, 1989).

2. Karl Marx and Frederich Engels, "The German Ideology," in Robert C. Tucker, ed., *The Marx-Engels Reader* (New York: W. W. Norton, 1972), pp. 136–37.

3. For an analysis, see Leszek Kolakowski, *Main Currents of Marxism*, vol. 2 (Oxford: Oxford University Press, 1978).

4. For a cogent analysis of Lukács's theory and politics, see Andrew Arato and Paul Breines, *The Young Lukács and The Origins of Western Marxism* (New York: The Seabury Press, 1979).

5. Walzer, *The Company of Critics*.

6. See Karl Mannheim, *Man and Society in an Age of Reconstruction* (New York: Harcourt, Brace and World, 1940).

7. For a description of the Marxist and non-Marxist academic debate, see Gouldner, *The Coming Crisis*.

8. See Terry Eagleton, *Marxism and Literary Criticism* (Berkeley: University of California Press, 1976).

9. See Herbert Gans, *Popular Culture and High Culture: An Evaluation of Tastes* (New York: Basic Books, 1974).

10. Thus the major American sociologist of art, Howard S. Becker, takes the "democratic" starting point of not evaluating art. See his study *Art Worlds* (Berkeley: University of California Press, 1982).

11. See Gouldner, *The Coming Crisis*, and C. Wright Mills, *The Sociological Imagination*.

12. Lewis Coser, *The Functions of Social Conflict* (Glencoe: The Free Press, 1956).

13. Mills, *The Power Elite*.

14. Charles Tilly, *Big Structures, Large Processes, Huge Comparisons* (New York: Russell Sage, 1985).

15. In fact, they have worked together. See Robert F. Bales, Talcott Parsons and Edward Shils, *Working Papers on the Theory of Action* (New York: The Free Press of Glencoe, 1953).

16. Ralph Turner, "Sponsored and Contest Mobility and the School System," *American Sociological Review* 25, no. 6 (December 1960).

17. Michel Crozier, *The Bureaucratic Phenomenon* (Chicago: University of Chicago Press, 1964).

18. See Goldfarb, *Beyond Glasnost*.

19. See Herbert Gans, *Middle American Individualism: The Future of Liberal Democracy* (New York: The Free Press, 1988).

20. See Herbert Gans, *Popular Culture and High Culture*, pp. 132–59.

21. See E. D. Hirsch, Jr., "The Primal Scene of Education," *New York Review of Books* 36, no. 3, March 2, 1989, pp. 29–35.

22. For a cogent Weberian analysis of these points, see Daniel Bell, *The Cultural Contradictions of Capitalism*.

23. See Barrington Moore, Jr., *Social Origins of Dictatorship and Democracy* (Boston: Beacon Press, 1966); Charles Tilly, *From Mobilization to Revolution* (Reading, Mass.: Addison-Wesley, 1978); and Theda Skocpol, *States and Social Revolutions* (New York: Cambridge University Press, 1979).

24. For an overview of these perspectives, see Becker, *Art Worlds;* and a special issue of *Social Research*, "The Production of Culture," Lewis Coser, ed., Summer 1978.

25. Howard Becker, "Becoming a Marijuana User," *American Journal of Sociology* 59 (November 1953): 235–42.

26. Jeffrey C. Goldfarb, *On Cultural Freedom, an Exploration of Public Life in Poland and America*.

27. See Max Horkheimer and Theodor Adorno, *The Dialectic of Enlighten-ment.*

28. Marcuse, *One Dimensional Man.*

29. See Jürgen Habermas, *Knowledge and Human Interest.*

30. See Serge Guilaut, *How New York Stole the Idea of Modern Art.*

31. See Anne Bowler and Blaine McBurney, "Gentrification and the Ava-nt-Garde in New York's East Village," paper presented at the annual meeting of the American Sociological Association, August 1989.

32. Philip Roth, *Zuckerman Bound: A Trilogy and Epilogue* (New York: Farrar, Straus, and Giroux, 1985).

33. See, e.g., Stanislaw Lem, *Hospital of the Transfiguration,* trans. William Brand (New York: Harcourt, Brace, Jovanovich, 1988).

34. See Sigmund Freud, *Interpretation of Dreams* (New York: Random House, 1950).

35. Hannah Arendt, *The Human Condition* (Chicago: University of Chicago Press, 1968), pp. 50–58.

36. Jürgen Habermas, *The Legitimation Crisis* (Boston: Beacon Press, 1975), p. 47.

Chapter Ten

1. Walzer has demonstrated this philosophically in his *Interpretation and Social Criticism* (Cambridge: Harvard University Press, 1987); and through intellectual biographies of some of the twentieth-century's leading social critics in *The Company of Critics.*

2. See the *New York Times* transcript of the debate, October 29, 1980, pp. 26–7; and Ralph Ellison, *Invisible Man* (New York: Random House, 1952).

3. Quoted in Elizabeth Drew, "Letter from Washington," *New Yorker,* February 27, 1989, p. 78.

4. Charles A. Murray, *Losing Ground: American Social Policy, 1950–1980* (New York: Basic Books, 1984).

5. Alex Ward, "TV's Tormented Master," *New York Times Magazine,* November 13, 1988, p. 88.

6. Ibid.

7. For a complete account, see Seth Cagin and Philip Dray, *We Are Not Afraid: The Story of Goodman, Schwerner and Chaney and the Civil Rights Cam-paign for Mississippi* (Macmillan, 1988).

8. Quoted in Richard Corliss, "Fire This Time," *Time,* 1–9, January 9, 1989, p. 58.

9. See, e.g., Stanley Kauffmann, "Matters of Fact," *New Republic,* January 9 and 16, 1989, p. 24.

10. Corliss, "Fire This Time," p. 58.

11. Toni Morrison, *Beloved* (New York: New American Library, 1987).

12. Stanley Crouch, "Aunt Medea," review of *Beloved* by Toni Morrison, *New Republic,* October 19, 1987, pp. 38–43.

13. Ibid, pp. 41–42.

14. Milan Kundera, *The Art of the Novel* (New York: Grove Press, 1988).

15. Theodor Adorno, *Aesthetic Theory* (London: Routledge and Kegan Paul, 1983).

16. Morrison, *Beloved*, pp. 68–69.

17. Ibid, p. 163.

18. Ibid, p. 251.

19. Ibid, p. 251.

20. Eldridge Cleaver, *Soul on Ice* (New York: Dell Publishing, 1968).

21. See Taylor Branch, *Parting the Waters: America in the King Years, 1954–63.* (New York: Simon and Schuster, 1988).

Chapter Eleven

1. For an analysis of the religious confrontation with modernity, see Lester R. Kurtz, *The Politics of Heresy* (Berkeley: University of California Press, 1986). For an analysis of the role of religious belief in countering cynicism, see Robert Bellah et al., *Habits of the Heart.*

2. See Lawrence Wechsler, "A Reporter at Large: Uruguay," *New Yorker,* April 3, 1989, pp. 43–85.

3. This is a major theme of Goldfarb, *Beyond Glasnost.*

4. *New York Times,* April 2, 1988, Op Ed page.

5. See Herbert Storing, *What the Anti-Federalists Were For: The Political Thought of the Opponents of the Constitution* (Chicago: University of Chicago Press, 1981), p. 21.

6. See Gordon S. Wood, *The Creation of the American Republic, 1776–1787* (Chapel Hill: University of North Carolina Press, 1969), p. 418.

7. See Daniel Boorstin, *The Americans: The Democratic Experience* (New York: Random House, 1973), pp. 478–90.

8. Baron de Montesquieu, *The Spirit of the Laws* (New York: D. Appleton, 1912), pp. 49–50.

9. Storing, *The Anti-Federalists*, p. 43.

10. Ibid, p. 90.

11. See Michel Foucault, *Power/Knowledge: Selected Interviews and Other Writings, 1972–1977* (New York: Pantheon Books, 1980).

12. Walzer, *Interpretation and Social Criticism.*

13. See Mills, *The Power Elite.*

14. See Herbert Marcuse, "Repressive Tolerance," in Robert Paul Wolff, Barrington Moore and Herbert Marcuse, eds., *A Critique of Pure Tolerance* (Boston: Beacon Press, 1969), pp. 81–123.

Index